BART EHRMAN INTERPRETED

BART EHRMAN INTERPRETED

*How One Radical
New Testament Scholar
Understands Another*

ROBERT M. PRICE

PITCHSTONE PUBLISHING
DURHAM, NORTH CAROLINA

Pitchstone Publishing
Durham, North Carolina
www.pitchstonepublishing.com

10 9 8 7 6 5 4 3 2 1

Library of Congress Cataloging-in-Publication Data

Names: Price, Robert M., 1954- author.
Title: Bart Ehrman interpreted : how one radical New Testament scholar
   understands another / Robert M. Price.
Description: Durham, North Carolina : Pitchstone Publishing, 2018. | Includes
   bibliographical references.
Identifiers: LCCN 2017058143 (print) | LCCN 2018002214 (ebook) | ISBN
   9781634311595 (epub) | ISBN 9781634311601 (ePDF) | ISBN 9781634311618 (
   mobi) | ISBN 9781634311588 (pbk. : alk. paper)
Subjects: LCSH: Ehrman, Bart D. | New Testament scholars.
Classification: LCC BS2351.E47 (ebook) | LCC BS2351.E47 P75 2018 (print) |
   DDC 220.6092—dc23
LC record available at https://lccn.loc.gov/2017058143

Cover photo by Dan Sears

Dedicated to Lori and Kevin Carlisle,
A Pair of Beloved Friends, Spiritual Family, and Savvy Theologians

CONTENTS

INTRODUCTION

HOPEFULLY NOT MISQUOTING BART

Bart D. Ehrman has performed a great service by introducing many new readers to crucial questions of biblical criticism in a series of books both scholarly and popular. In this his work recalls that of Edgar J. Goodspeed and Robert W. Funk, both of whom were great scholars but refused to barricade themselves in the academic ivory tower. Concerned neither to protect the faithful from the discomfort of critical challenges nor to protect themselves from the ire of the faithful, these scholars insisted on "taking it to the streets." Unafraid of controversy, they knew their work would offer relief and new hope to many who loved scripture but could no longer suppress their questions ("doubts") about it. Professor Ehrman has not avoided controversy but has even invited it by his refusal to hide behind diplomatic and equivocal language. My goal in the present book, *Bart Ehrman Interpreted*, is to expound on and to evaluate his work under six headings: the apocalyptic Jesus, the Christ Myth theory, textual criticism, oral tradition, the evolution of New Testament Christology, and scriptural forgery ("pseudepigraphy").

Throughout, my approach will be irenic and collegial, rejecting polemics. I will defend Dr. Ehrman's work against conservative/apologetical attacks upon it. I will also suggest a number of points at which he seems to me insufficiently or inconsistently critical in his judgments. I believe and hope this book will prompt much fruitful and positive discussion of Professor Ehrman's important work and of the issues he treats.

I will examine the case Ehrman makes for the historical Jesus as an eschatological preacher in his *Jesus: Apocalyptic Prophet of the New Millennium*. How close to the conclusions of Johannes Weiss (*Jesus' Proclamation of the Kingdom of God*) and Albert Schweitzer (*The Mystery of the Kingdom of God* and *The Quest of the Historical Jesus*) does Bart come? Where does he differ, and has he rehabilitated their case? And is Ehrman perhaps overly *optimistic* as to the authenticity of the gospel materials on which he builds his case?

How credible are the gospels as historical sources? Professor Ehrman casts very serious doubts on the reliability of the gospel narratives in his books *Misquoting Jesus* and *Jesus Interrupted*. An apparently very different evaluation of gospel reliability appears in Ehrman's *Did Jesus Exist?* Can the two estimates be reconciled? Are they really contradictory?

The first of Bart's books that I read, and still my favorite, is his pioneering *The Orthodox Corruption of Scripture*. In it he shows how numerous "errors" in the manuscripts are actually theological "corrections" intended to render scripture useless as a source for "heretical" proof-texts. But how seriously has the textual integrity of the New Testament been affected? And is there a contradiction between Bart's pessimistic estimate of textual authenticity on the one hand and his unwillingness to accept interpolation hypotheses without manuscript evidence on the other?

Bart's book *Jesus Before the Gospels* offers a devastating critique of apologists' misunderstanding and misuse of recent studies of oral tradition and communal memory, but it also appears to undermine what credence he still places in the gospel tradition and his confidence in having delineated the true historical Jesus. In my discussion of this fascinating book I question whether the gospel materials are even *supposed* to stem from oral transmission of eyewitness memory, and if there is a better, purely literary, way of explaining gospel origins.

In my consideration of Bart's schema of Christological evolution set forth in *How Jesus Became God*, I will address a major objection to Jesus Mythicism, namely how to explain the seeming progression from Markan adoptionism to Matthean and Lukan depiction of Jesus as a virgin-born demigod, to the incarnationism of John—if, as Mythicists hold, the gospel Jesus represents a fictional historicization of an originally purely celestial Jesus-deity. I will also discuss and defend Bart's advocacy of the notion that early Christians believed Jesus was an angel. And I will suggest that it actually implies Mythicism.

Bart's great book (right up there with *The Orthodox Corruption of Scripture* as far as I am concerned) *Forgery and Counterforgery* explodes the attempt of apologists to depict the ancient practice of pseudepigraphy as innocent and acceptable. Then I will consider whether he does not stop short when he accepts the authenticity of the seven Pauline letters conventionally received by mainstream critical scholars, doubts concerning which he finds literally laughable. And I will go a bit farther to scrutinize particular elements in the canonical gospels as to whether they ought to be ranked as cases of fraud and imposture.

Many readers of my books and listeners to my Bible Geek podcast are also avid fans of Bart Ehrman's work. Sometimes I am asked about our differences. We are both ex-evangelicals. We are both outspoken and controversial in our exercise of biblical criticism. My primary motive in writing this book, a very enjoyable process, has been to clarify things for these readers. Where, how, and why do Bart and I differ? This book attempts to answer those questions. I am not trying to refute Bart's work or to win an argument with him, but rather simply to account for our differing opinions.

And this brings up an important point about biblical scholarship in general: though the evidence we sift and weigh is quite voluminous, it is also fragmentary and susceptible to a range of interpretations. There are very many ways to put the puzzle pieces together. If a definitive answer to our questions were readily available, the debates would be long over. They're not. Acquainting oneself with the many approaches, theories, and opinions not only is endlessly fascinating but also enriches one's own ongoing synthesis. The quest for the historical Jesus, the central message of the New Testament, the authorship of the epistles, etc., is a long and exciting journey, filled with discoveries. And that had better be enough of a reward since it seems pretty unlikely we will ever reach any definitive destination.

I highly respect Bart Ehrman and his work, as I think will be evident throughout. He is also a friend and a great guy. I hope he finds that I have treated him fairly.

Robert M. Price
February 8, 2017

BART EHRMAN INTERPRETED

CHAPTER ONE
APOPLECTIC PROPHET

THE SKY IS FALLING!

In his breakout book, *Jesus, Apocalyptic Prophet of the New Millennium*,[1] Bart Ehrman sets forth and defends an understanding of the historical Jesus first catapulted into prominence by Albert Schweitzer in his book *The Quest of the Historical Jesus*.[2] For Ehrman as for Schweitzer, Jesus must be acknowledged to have been a failed apocalyptic seer, whipping up excitement about the imminent end of the world and predicating upon that false prophecy his demand for repentance. Both Jesus scholars showed great courage in refusing to euphemize or sugarcoat the shocking truth. Both refused to cover up or to rationalize the gross embarrassment that, despite his reputation of infallible Godhood, Jesus was a colleague of Chicken Littles ancient and modern who electrified, then disappointed, their mesmerized followers and exposed them to a fusillade of scorn and jeers from their skeptical neighbors who had not been foolish enough to heed their dour warnings.

What? You mean Jesus Christ was a first-century Harold Camping? The

---

1. Bart D. Ehrman, *Jesus: Apocalyptic Prophet of the New Millennium* (New York: Oxford University Press, 1999).

2. Albert Schweitzer, *The Quest of the Historical Jesus: A Critical Study of its Progress from Reimarus to Wrede*. Trans. W. Montgomery (New York: Macmillan, 1961).

ostensible Son of Jehovah was as much of a washout as Jehovah's Witnesses? 'Fraid so! The historical Jesus, an "apocalyptic prophet of a new millennium" that never materialized, was, Schweitzer says, seconded by Ehrman, "an offense to [modern] religion,"[3] whether of liberal or conservative stripe. Schweitzer was by no means the very first to draw such a picture of Jesus, as he himself readily acknowledged (just as Ehrman gives due credit to Schweitzer). One of Schweitzer's predecessors, the German Deist Hermann Samuel Reimarus,[4] mercilessly drove home the fatal implications for Christian theology: of all the claims Jesus is said to have made about the unseen world of God, the only one empirically testable was the prediction that the Millennium would dawn in his own generation. And when it came to the test, the calendar rudely debunked it. And, well, if *this* one proved false, what conceivable reason remains for believing anything *else* Jesus said?

Obviously, Jesus is on record as saying many wise things and making many stirring appeals to one's conscience, and their validity in no way depends on his false belief that the world was soon to come to a crashing halt. But that is not the point. Christianity is much more than wisdom and morality. There is such a thing as Christianity at all because of the status of Jesus as a revealer of heavenly secrets, an oracle of divine truths unobtainable by mere human reason. And chief among these revelations was the way of salvation. On such a key issue, we cannot be satisfied with hypotheses and opinions. As fundamentalists like to say, Christianity offers good *news*, not good *views*. But Jesus turns out to have had nothing more than good views to offer, or rather, bad views, since his crucial tenet of belief was rudely debunked. "The time is fulfilled. The kingdom of God is at hand. Repent and believe the good news!" (Mark 1:15). Yikes!

Despite Bart Ehrman's acknowledged debt to Albert Schweitzer's work, he is by no means merely recycling the earlier scholar. Schweitzer thought, for instance, that Jesus believed himself to be the destined Son of Man, or, more strictly speaking, that he should soon *become* the Son of Man via a supernatural (Enoch-style) transfiguration at the conclusion of the impending Tribulation. Until then, he refrained from publicly preaching his secret identity, hence his frequent third-person references to the Son of Man. (In the same way, and I

---

3. Schweitzer, *Quest*, p. 401.

4. *Reimarus: Fragments*. Ed. Charles H. Talbert. Trans. Ralph S. Fraser. Lives of Jesus Series (Philadelphia: Fortress Press, 1970).

don't think he got it from reading Schweitzer, the Reverend Sun Myung Moon was careful not to refer to himself as the Lord of the Second Advent, that is, until he judged that he had completed the necessary works to justify the title.)[5] Schweitzer pictured Jesus as trying to prepare his disciples to hunker down and endure the coming Trial. One day he sent them out, two by two, to visit village after village, warning people to repent before it was too late and dodging expected persecutors as they went. Jesus thought they would not complete their mission before the Last Trumpet rang out. But here they came, no persecution to report, and Jesus still wearing solid flesh. Then he concluded that the End Times would zero in on him by himself. John had died in mundane, ignominious circumstances, and Jesus decided he, too, must suffer such a death, taking, Atlas-like, the burden of eschatological woe on his drooping shoulders, like a rough cross beam. The Tribulation should be his alone to undergo, suffering and dying in the place of his disciples. Only then should he be transfigured by a resurrection from the dead. None of this reappears in Ehrman's *Apocalyptic Prophet of the New Millennium*, though he does seem to like Schweitzer's theory that what Judas betrayed to the Sanhedrin was Jesus' hitherto-secret of his messiahship.[6]

Any way you cut it, Schweitzer's schema is speculative, and not just in the sense that all attempts at historical reconstruction are. The very ingeniousness of Schweitzer's suggestions is a measure of their speculative character. Bart will not permit himself the degree of speculativeness upon which Schweitzer's view depends. Also, Albert Schweitzer allowed himself a larger database than Ehrman does; Schweitzer did not go in for theories of Synoptic interdependence. He simply decided that Matthew and Mark were substantially accurate sources, while Luke and John were inferior. He rejected the approach of William Wrede (*The Messianic Secret*)[7] because he could

---

5. Frederick Sontag, *Sun Myung Moon and the Unification Church* (Nashville: Abingdon Press, 1977), p. 99; George D. Chryssides, *The Advent of Sun Myung Moon: The Origins, Beliefs and Practices of the Unification Church* (London: Macmillan Professional and Academic, 1991), pp. 44, 119, 124. Sontag wrote before Reverend Moon had attained the status of Lord of the Second Advent, Chryssides after.

6. Albert Schweitzer, *The Mystery of the Kingdom of God: The Secret of Jesus' Messiahship and Passion*. Trans. Walter Lowrie (New York: Schocken Books, 1964), pp. 216–217; Ehrman, *Jesus: Apocalyptic Prophet*, p. 218.

7. William Wrede, *The Messianic Secret*. Trans. J.C.G. Greig. Library of Theological Translations (Cambridge: James Clarke, 1971).

not brook Wrede's skepticism. Wrede anticipated the method of redaction criticism and read Mark as far from an unvarnished report of Jesus. Instead, Wrede argued, Mark's gospel was already a pretty sophisticated narrative treatise in theology. This meant that the historical Jesus would be very difficult to detect behind the text. Schweitzer called Wrede's approach "thoroughgoing skepticism," necessitating dead-end agnosticism *vis-à-vis* Jesus. Wouldn't it be better all around to accept Schweitzer's alternative, "thoroughgoing eschatology,"[8] the result of his reading of Mark and Matthew as basically accurate? All right, you might not be able to stomach the knowledge of what Jesus was really all about, but at least you could know. I guess you could sum up the basic difference between Bart's approach and my own this way: he opts for "consistent eschatology" and I choose "consistent skepticism." As we continue, you'll see what I mean.

SOURCE AND SORCERY

Bart Ehrman returns to the question of our surviving sources of information about Jesus in his book *Did Jesus Exist?* where it assumes a different sort of importance. I will deal with that in a later chapter, but for the present, let's just discuss the number and value of the gospel sources, within and without the canon of scripture. The first is, collectively, the epistles of Paul. Here Bart and I find almost no common ground because he, with the huge majority of scholars, considers at least the "lucky seven" (Romans, 1 and 2 Corinthians, Galatians, Philippians, 1 Thessalonians, and Philemon) to be authentically Pauline and thus earlier than the earliest gospel, while I think the whole lot of them are late-first, early-second-century patchworks of Paulinist (Marcionite and Gnostic) and Catholicizing fragments. Thus, in my eyes, the relation between the Pauline epistles and a historical Paul is exactly analogous to that obtaining between the gospels and a historical Jesus. The documents may be as much an obscuring barrier as a door of access. But this issue, too, is moot in the present connection, as Bart admits that the epistles tell us precious little about Jesus anyway. There is no citation of Jesus' sayings even on subjects germane to his arguments. If he knew the sayings, wouldn't they have pretty

---

8. I switch back and forth between two synonymous translations of Schweitzer's German original, "thoroughgoing" meaning the same as "consistent." I have heard/ read both and like both.

quickly settled the issues he was arguing?[9] If we had nothing but the epistles we should never suspect that Jesus was supposed to be a teacher. Nor should we guess that Jesus was believed to have been a miracle-worker. It strikes me as a bit puzzling that Bart would not take these silences in a supposedly earlier source to undermine the credibility of such representations of Jesus in the gospels. The silences of the epistles speak eloquently, don't they? But Bart is quite willing to interrogate the miracle stories of the gospels once he gets to them, as we will see.

Dr. Ehrman briefly comments on an odd note in Galatians: "Paul tells us that Jesus was born of a woman (Gal. 4:4; this, of course, is not a particularly useful datum—one wonders what the alternative may have been!)"[10] I think the alternative was the Marcionite belief that Jesus descended from heaven in the form of an adult, with a celestial body, a form of docetism (the notion that Jesus only *appeared* to be a flesh-and-blood human). I think that Galatians 4:4 is an interpolation to counteract the proto-Marcionite character of the epistle, on display in Galatians 3:19–20. Otherwise, why on earth *would* anybody assert that Jesus had a mother? It must have been up for dispute—as it was in the second century.

Bart accepts, as do I, the Two Document Hypothesis of Synoptic relations. To wit: Matthew and Luke overlap so much of Mark because they each incorporate most of Mark's gospel, already a widely known work. Each of these second-generation evangelists omitted some material from Mark (sometimes the same stuff) and edited much else. But Matthew and Luke also overlap one another where they did *not* derive material from Mark. The kind of editorial changes seen in their treatment reappear in the non-Markan material they share. This naturally implies the use of a second pre-Matthean, pre-Lukan source document. Scholars call it Q, for *Quelle*, German for "source." There are other theories, but since Bart and I are both Q partisans, there seems to be little point in going into these alternative theories here.

What about the material in Matthew and Luke that is unique to each? Many scholars theorize that this material represents two more Q-like sources, dubbed M and L. Others regard them as the contributions (creations) of Matthew and Luke. Each batch of material is characterized by certain themes, interests, and

9. G.A. Wells, *The Jesus of the Early Christians: A Study in Christian Origins* (London: Pemberton Books, 1971), pp. 131–135.

10. Ehrman, *Jesus: Apocalyptic Prophet*, p. 79.

ethical-theological tendencies. M is more interested in Judaism and Torah-observance, Luke more occupied with the poor and apostolic authority. Each uses distinctive vocabulary. These facts would fit with either option: M and L as distinct source documents or as redactional layers. I incline toward the latter, though, because it looks to me as if the same interests, vocabulary, and ideas can be spotted in the redactional changes Matthew and Luke have made in the material they got from Mark and Q. Thus M and L belong to a younger gospel stratum, after Mark and Q, not contemporary with them. "M" simply *is* Matthew; "L" is identical with Luke.

This question will come up again in my discussion of Bart's book *Did Jesus Exist?* There he argues that one solid reason for thinking there was a historical Jesus is that, if there weren't, we wouldn't have such a multitude of pre-Synoptic source documents, i.e., Q, M, and L, bridging the gap between the written gospels and the oral traditions embodied in their sources. But these supposed sources seem to me to be purely hypothetical. They represent heuristic devices for interpreting the possible interrelationships between the actual source documents we do know we have: Mark, Matthew, and Luke. To treat Q, M, and L as independent early sources seems to me to place them in the wrong frame of discourse. It is to try to ground one hypothesis upon the shaky foundation of another (mere) hypothesis.

Bart joins most scholars in accepting the verdict of David Friedrich Strauss[11] and Albert Schweitzer[12] that the Gospel of John is an almost purely literary work. It may be free creation, or it may have been a thorough rewrite of the Synoptics (sometimes critiquing them). For our purposes it doesn't really matter which theory is correct. Either way, it is exceedingly dubious to appeal to John for historical information about Jesus, as Bart sometimes does.

Of the once-popular Gospel of Peter, Bart has this to say.

An author living perhaps at the beginning of the second century did what others had done before him and yet others would do afterward, collecting the stories he had heard, or possibly read, and creating out of them a narrative of the words, deeds, and experiences of Jesus. The result is that this Gospel may

---

11. David Friedrich Strauss, *The Life of Jesus Critically Examined.* Trans. George Eliot [Mary Ann Evans]. Lives of Jesus Series (Philadelphia: Fortress Press, 1972), pp. 85–87.

12. Schweitzer, *Quest*, p. 238.

provide some independent verification of some of the accounts found in our earlier Christian sources, the New Testament Gospels.[13]

To me, the Gospel of Peter reads like a stringing together of bits and pieces from the four canonical gospels embellished with apocryphal, legendary elements like the friendship between Herod Antipas and Pontius Pilate, the heightened anti-Semitism, and the spectacular depiction of the resurrection. But John Dominic Crossan[14] shows to my satisfaction that there is more to it. He makes an intricate but powerful case that Peter and the canonical evangelists made use of a "Cross Gospel," a bare-bones crucifixion account consisting largely of Old Testament "testimonia," commonly used proof-texts supposedly predicting the sufferings of Jesus. "Peter," Crossan argues, fleshed out this skeleton with passages from the canonical gospels, and, later still, other scribes added apocryphal embellishment. If Crossan is correct, the only pre-gospel source underlying the Gospel of Peter is this Cross Gospel, which looks to be a collection of the Old Testament building blocks that were rewritten as gospel episodes, i.e., not historical information about Jesus.

Bart regards the Gospel of Thomas as independent of the canonical gospels. The numerous parallels to them he chalks up to independent oral tradition, a view many scholars share: "if Thomas did use the Synoptics, we would be hard-pressed to explain why he left out most of their sayings of Jesus, many of them relevant to his agenda."[15] But I think differently. There's no way to know for certain, but I get the impression that whoever compiled Thomas wrote down what he remembered of Jesus-sayings he had heard read in church. No written copy of the gospels was available to him, so he had to rely on his imprecise recollections (as we still do today in informal conversation). In Thomas the sayings found in the gospels had returned to the oral-traditional stream. In any case, the possible independence of Thomas seems too debatable for us to rely upon that gospel as an additional source of information for the historical Jesus.

---

13. Ehrman, *Jesus: Apocalyptic Prophet*, p. 71.

14. John Dominic Crossan, *The Cross That Spoke: The Origins of the Passion Narrative* (San Francisco: Harper & Row, 1988).

15. Ehrman, *Jesus: Apocalyptic Prophet*, p. 77

CRITERIA AND THE CHRIST

Where on earth did the sayings and stories in the gospels come from? And how does their possible/probable origin bear on their historical accuracy/ authenticity? Bart Ehrman thinks that the gospels grew from eyewitness testimony, but that this doesn't mean that witness is accurate, since it must have been distorted along the line through oral transmission.

> I suppose everyone would agree that the Gospels of the New Testament in some way or another go back to the reports of eyewitnesses.[16] [. . .] For many people, who possibly haven't thought much about it, such a claim—that a story is based on an eyewitness account—provides a kind of guarantee of its accuracy. A moment's reflection, though, shows that nothing could be farther from the truth [. . . because] even stories based on eyewitness accounts are not necessarily reliable, and the same is true a hundredfold for accounts that—even if ultimately stemming from reports of eyewitnesses—have been in oral circulation after the fact.[17]

It is striking that Bart invokes the theory of eyewitness testimony, not to defend gospel accuracy as Christian apologists like to do, but instead to argue the very opposite! "Eyewitness testimony? *Uh*-oh!" This is because he envisions what the process must have been like, given a realistic picture of early Christianity's spread. Apologists[18] insist that the transmission of Jesus

---

16. Well, maybe not everyone . . .

17. Ehrman, *Jesus: Apocalyptic Prophet*, p. 47

18. F.F. Bruce, *The New Testament Documents: Are They Reliable?* (Grand Rapids: Eerdmans, 1960), p. 30; John Warwick Montgomery, *History & Christianity* (Downers Grove: InterVarsity Press, 1974), pp. 30–31. The same old futile arguments for accurate oral transmission of eyewitness testimony in the gospels have themelves become a matter of oral tradition, as the same arguments are tirelessly (and tiresomely) repeated decade after decade by each new generation of apologist spin doctors. Timothy Paul Jones, for instance, in his *Misquoting Truth: A Guide to the Fallacies of Bart Ehrman's* Misquoting Jesus (Downers Grove: InterVarsity Press, 2007), makes a wishful case for the faithful eyewitness content of the gospels that is one more exercise in striving to conquer one's own doubts. His virtually explicit approach is to construct a chain of mere possibilities which, if true, would allow him to keep on believing in supernaturalist evangelicalism. The "convincing" character of his argument lies in the imagined permission it gives Jones to keep clinging to his teenage faith.

material *must* have been carefully supervised by eyewitness apostles, preventing and censoring the slightest instances of careless or inventive Christian embellishment, distortion, or (God forbid!) fabrication. By contrast, Bart begins with realistic conditions "on the ground."

> The new converts tell the stories; and since the faith necessarily grows exponentially, most of the people telling the stories were not eyewitnesses and indeed had never laid eyes on an eyewitness or even on anyone else who had. These stories were then circulated year after year after year, primarily among people who had no independent knowledge of what really occurred. It takes little imagination to realize what happened to the stories.[19]

It is quite revealing that one evangelical New Testament scholar genuinely friendly to mainstream biblical criticism, George Eldon Ladd,[20] admitted that the historical skepticism of form critics like Bultmann was perfectly justified except for God's supervision of the Jesus material's transmission. In other words, it would have taken a miracle for the sayings and stories *not* to become distorted and embellished during their pre-literary stage! This is of course one more case of the discredited "God of the gaps"[21] gimmick, invoking the supernatural to get your theory out of a tight spot.

Given the high likelihood that the Jesus tradition has grown, really mutated, in the telling, we have to wonder if there is any way, so to speak, to restore the original portrait. The gospels would seem to be comparable to ancient palimpsests, reused sheets of parchment. Scribes would wash off the writing of a document nobody wanted to read anymore, wait for it to dry, and write new text on it. Historians are more interested in the original writing than in the newer stuff. In recent years infrared techniques have enabled them to read the erased writing after all. Well, that is kind of like the task facing Life of Jesus scholars: can we read the original history of Jesus beneath the over-writing of the canonical gospels? How does Bart Ehrman propose to do it?

---

19. Ehrman, *Jesus: Apocalyptic Prophet*, p. 51; cf., Strauss, *Life of Jesus*, p. 74.

20. George Eldon Ladd, *The New Testament and Criticism* (Grand Rapids: Eerdmans, 1967), pp. 152–153.

21. Dietrich Bonhoeffer, *Letters and Papers from Prison*. Trans. Reginald H. Fuller (New York: Macmillan, 1962), p. 190.

we will need to think carefully about how to mine such theologically interested documents for historical data, how to decide which features of the Gospels represent Christianizations of the tradition and which represent the life of Jesus as it can be historically reconstructed.[22]

Obviously, Bart Ehrman thinks it is possible. Not everyone thinks so. I think he would second Adolf Harnack's opinion.[23]

We now know that it is not after they have been long dead, nor even after the lapse of many years, that miracles have been reported of eminent persons, but at once, often the very next day. The habit of condemning a narrative, or of ascribing it to a later age, only because it includes stories of miracles, is a piece of prejudice.

I, on the other hand, share the caution of David Friedrich Strauss:[24] the story is no better than its most unreliable elements for the sake of which it was originally told.

Every narrative, however miraculous, contains some details which might in themselves be historical, but which, in consequence of their connexion with the other, supernatural, incidents, necessarily become equally doubtful. . . . It is at once apparent that that which is credible in itself is nevertheless unhistorical when it is so intimately connected with what is incredible that, if you discard the latter, you at the same time remove the basis on which the former rests.

Though I will elaborate on this theme in a subsequent chapter, let me just note here that this approach of assuming there is some "historical core," however modest,[25] strikes me as a subspecies of ancient Euhemerism, the attempt of ancients like Herodotus and Plutarch to recover a hypothetical

22. Ehrman, *Jesus: Apocalyptic Prophet*, p. 53.

23. Adolf Harnack, *What Is Christianity?* Trans. Thomas Bailey Saunders. Harper Torchbooks (New York: Harper & Row, 1957), p.2.

24. Strauss, *Life of Jesus*, p. 90.

25. Gerd Lüdemann, *Early Christianity according to the Traditions in Acts: A Commentary* (Minneapolis: Fortress Press, 1989) is another example of this "textual distillation" approach.

historical, nonsupernatural core beneath the myths of Hercules, Osiris, Ares, etc. It is also the approach of apologists to preserve a more modest "original," pre-interpolated version of the *Testimonium Flavianum*. I consider the whole approach to be a species of apologetics.

When were the four gospels written? Here is Bart's account:

> most historians think that Mark was the first of our Gospels to be written, sometime between the mid-60s to early 70s. Matthew and Luke were probably produced some ten or fifteen years later, perhaps around 80 or 85. John was written perhaps ten years after that, 90 or 95. These are necessarily rough estimates, but almost all scholars agree within a few years. Perhaps the most striking thing about these dates for the historian is the long interval between Jesus' death and the earliest accounts of his life.[26]

My opinion on this issue definitely does not conform to that of most scholars. I think all four gospels originated in the second century. But for our purposes, that is neither here nor there, because Bart recognizes that a much shorter tunnel period between the ostensible time of Jesus and the production of the gospels in no way guarantees, nor even implies, their historical accuracy. And he's right. Even a span of four decades between Jesus and the earliest gospel affords plenty of room for mischief. David Friedrich Strauss explained why. He refuted

> the objection . . . that the space of about thirty years, from the death of Jesus to the destruction of Jerusalem, during which the greater part of the narratives must have been formed; or even the interval extending to the beginning of the second century, the most distant period which can be allowed for the origin of even the latest of these gospel narratives, and for the written composition of our gospels;—is much too short to admit of the rise of so rich a collection of myth[s]. But . . . the greater part of these myth[s] did not arise during that period, for their first foundation was laid in the legends of the Old Testament, before and after the Babylonish exile; and the transference of these legends with suitable modifications to the expected Messiah, was made in the course of the centuries which elapsed between that exile and the time of Jesus. So that for the period between the formation of the first Christian community and the writing of the Gospels, there remains to be effected only

---

26. Ehrman, *Jesus: Apocalyptic Prophet*, p. 48.

the transference of Messianic legends, almost all ready formed, to Jesus, with some alterations to adapt them to Christian opinions, and to the individual character and circumstances of Jesus; only a very small proportion of myth[s] having to be formed entirely new.[27]

DISSIMILARITY AND DISSIMULATION

For a long time, one of the most important criteria for sifting sayings ascribed to Jesus was that of *dissimilarity*. Norman Perrin[28] was perhaps the most prominent exponent of the technique, but it was very widely used. Applying it to gospel sayings about the end of the age, Bart Ehrman aptly sums up the principle: "some of the ways Jesus talks about the coming end do not coincide with the way his followers later talked about it, suggesting that these particular sayings are not ones they would have invented."[29]

In my opinion, the dissimilarity criterion faces an insurmountable objection. It assumes that all early Christians were of one mind. "They" are said to have abandoned or transcended the teachings of Jesus in favor of subsequent notions they came to like better. But there was no monolithic "they." It seems to me that we would not be reading these "dissimilar" sayings at all if they didn't still represent the views of the Christians who preserved them, which is *why* they preserved them in the first place. Apologist John Warwick Montgomery once quipped that "practically everything Jesus said was offensive to somebody in the early church, and this is no criterion at all for selectivity."[30] And, conversely, everything in the gospels must have *pleased* somebody in the early church or the sayings wouldn't be there. All we can say is that gospel sayings pointing in different directions reflect a variety of early Christians' beliefs, all ascribed to Jesus. Look at the variety of opinions attributed to Jesus on the topic of fasting.

---

27. Strauss, *Life of Jesus*, p. 86. Cf., Schweitzer, *Quest*, p 79: "Even though the earthly life of the Lord falls within historic times, and even if only a generation be assumed to have elapsed between His death and the composition of the Gospels; such a period would be sufficient to allow the historical material to become intermixed with myth. No sooner is a great man dead than legend is busy with his life."

28. Norman Perrin, *Rediscovering the Teaching of Jesus* (New York: Harper & Row, 1976).

29. Ehrman, *Jesus: Apocalyptic Prophet*, p. 135.

30. John Warwick Montgomery in *The Altizer-Montgomery Dialogue: A Chapter in the God Is Dead Controversy* (Chicago: Inter-Varsity Press, 1967), p. 64.

Do Christians no longer fast (Mark 2:18, 21–22)? Or is it only a temporary moratorium (Mark 2:19–20)? Or do they practice fasting, just not like the hypocrites (Matt. 6:16)? Which one goes back to Jesus, *if any*? Maybe you are beginning to see the reason for "thoroughgoing skepticism." Let's review some examples discussed in *Jesus: Apocalyptic Prophet of the New Age.*

Why would anyone make up the idea that Jesus had lived in a podunk burg like Nazareth? Why not a more appropriate birthplace, like Jerusalem or Washington D.C,? It's like making him "Jesus of Camden." Bart explains:

> with respect to dissimilarity, it is difficult to imagine why Christians would have wanted to make the tradition up. Nazareth was a little, unknown, and completely insignificant village. . . . If you wanted to speak about the powerful Messiah of Israel, surely you'd have him come from the center of power, Jerusalem, or possibly Bethlehem. There is little doubt that the tradition of Jesus coming from Nazareth is so firmly entrenched in the tradition precisely because it's historically accurate.[31]

I think it is not that difficult to explain. Let's assume for the sake of argument, that there *was* an inhabited Nazareth in the ostensible time of Jesus, though the matter remains in dispute.[32] It has long been suggested that "Jesus the Nazorean" originally denoted Jesus' membership in the Nazorean sect of Judaism,[33] whose name meant "the Keepers" of the Torah or of esoteric secrets, an epithet equivalent to that of the Gnostics, initiates into secret knowledge. But eventually Christians came to feel that such a connection ill comported with Jesus' divine uniqueness, the same Christological anxiety that, e.g., led to the belief in the perpetual virginity of Mary, lest the Son of God share DNA with merely human, sinful brothers. And at this point, "the Nazorean/ Nazarene" came to be reinterpreted as "from Nazareth," in just the same way that Mary the mother of James and Joses (Mark 15:40, 47; 16:1) became the *sister* of Mary the mother of Jesus, who was originally thought to be the mother

---

31. Ehrman, *Jesus: Apocalyptic Prophet*, p. 98.

32. Rene Salm, *Nazareth Gate: Quack Archaeology, Holy Hoaxes, and the Invented Town of Jesus* (Cranford: American Atheist Press, 2015).

33. Hugh J. Schonfield, *The Passover Plot: New Light on the History of Jesus* (New York: Bantam Books, 1967), p. 31.

of Jesus, James, Joses, Judas, and Simon (Mark 6:3).[34]

It sounds odd that Jesus is sometimes quoted in the gospels as referring to the apocalyptic Son of Man in the third person. "For whoever is ashamed of me and of my words in this adulterous and sinful generation, of him will the Son of man also be ashamed, when he comes in the glory of his Father with the holy angels" (Mark 8:38). "When the Son of man comes, will he find faith on the earth?" (Luke 18:8). Traditionally gospel readers have thought Jesus did intend to refer to himself even in these sayings, a parallel, as some have pointed out, with Buddhist scriptures in which Gautama Buddha speaks of himself in the third person as "the Tathagatha" (the "Thus-Come One"). Bultmann and others[35] suggested that in these texts Jesus is referring to an apocalyptic deliverer distinct from himself, in the same way that John the Baptist predicted the Coming One. Bart Ehrman agrees. And that implies these sayings are pre-Christian, authentic sayings of Jesus. In view of the emerging Christology that understood Jesus himself as the Son of Man, these old third-person Son of Man sayings were rendered obsolete.

> [S]ince Christians thought *Jesus* was the Son of Man, it seems unlikely that they would make up a saying in such a way as to leave it in question whether he was referring to himself. This means Jesus probably did say the words now found in Mark 8:38.[36]

But then why were they preserved? Personally, I find Gerd Theissen's suggestion[37] quite compelling. The third-person Son of Man sayings would

---

34. Robert Eisenman, *James the Brother of Jesus: The Key to Unlocking the Secrets of Early Christianity and the Dead Sea Scrolls* (New York: Viking Penguin, 1997), pp. 204, 592, 753, 778, 782, 840, 845.

35. Rudolf Bultmann, *The History of the Synoptic Tradition*. Trans. John Marsh (New York: Harper & Row, 1968), p. 122; Bultmann, *Jesus and the Word*. Trans. Louise Pettibone Smith and Erminie Huntress Lantero (New York: Scribners, 1958), pp. 30, 38–39; Ferdinand Hahn, *The Titles of Jesus in Christology: Their History in Early Christianity*. Trans. Harold Knight and George Ogg (New York: World Publishing, 1969), pp. 29, 33–34; H.E. Tödt, *The Son of Man in the Synoptic Tradition*. Trans. Dorothea M. Barton. New Testament Library (Philadelphia: Westminster Press, 1965), pp. 57, 60, 93, 114, 226.

36. Ehrman, *Jesus: Apocalyptic Prophet*, p. 135.

37. Gerd Theissen, *Sociology of Early Palestinian Christianity*. Trans. John Bowden (Philadelphia: Fortress Press, 1978), p. 27.

have originated on the lips of the itinerant charismatics, the wandering "brethren" who walked the dusty roads from village to village, preaching the gospel. They were the earthly mouthpieces of the exalted Son of Man. "Whoever hears you hears me" (Luke 10:16). On the one hand, this means that "whoever is ashamed of *me*" referred to the preacher himself, while "the Son of Man" invokes their heavenly patron who will avenge them and vindicate their message. On the other, the very fact that the words of the messenger should be received as though spoken by the exalted Christ himself made it natural, almost inevitable, that these sayings should sooner or later be attributed to Jesus himself. They would be the classic examples of the phenomena Bultmann[38] highlighted: the unwitting slippage of sayings from the category of "Christian prophetic sayings" to that of "historical Jesus sayings."[39] And the third-person Son of Man sayings enable us almost to see the process at work. This would also explain why the sayings were preserved. Once people did ascribe the words of his prophets to him as their ultimate source, they naturally treated them as words of Jesus. And of course, if Theissen is right, we can forget about these as sayings of any historical Jesus. And I do.

More about the title Son of Man:

> And the fact is that there are lots of places in our tradition—independently attested all over the map—that Jesus himself does use the phrase in this way, as a title for a future cosmic judge from heaven. *Someone* coined the phrase; it would be pretty bizarre to think that it couldn't have been Jesus, the one to whom all of these sayings are attributed in independent sources, or someone living before him.[40]

Though our evidence suggests the phrase was not used exactly as a title, Daniel and 1 Enoch establish "the Son of Man" as a kind of epithet for a heavenly being. Daniel, in an apocalyptic vision, mentions "one like a son of man" (Dan.7:13), while 1 Enoch refers to the ascended patriarch as "that son of man," "the son of man who is born unto righteousness," etc. (1 Enoch

---

38. Bultmann, *History of the Synoptic Tradition*, pp. 127–128.

39. M. Eugene Boring, *Sayings of the Risen Jesus: Christian Prophecy in the Synoptic Tradition*. Society for New Testament Studies Monograph Series 46 (New York: Cambridge University Press, 1982).

40. Ehrman, *Jesus: Apocalyptic Prophet*, p. 146.

41:1:2; 45:1–2; 46:1, 3; 48:3–6; 51:3; 55:4, 12; 61:8–9; 62:7, 14; 69:27, 46–47). Rabbinic sources cite the Danielic passage as a kind of shorthand reference to the coming of King Messiah, so the eventual use of "Son of Man" as a title was surely a natural development.[41] But then who developed it? I tend to agree with Norman Perrin[42] that the apocalyptic Son of Man sayings of the gospels were originally a product of an early Christian tradition of midrash, including the grafting together of phrases snipped from this and that scripture passage, in this case Psalm 110:1, Daniel 7:13, and Zechariah 12:10, and reflected most fully in Revelation 1:7; John 19:27; Matthew 24:30; Luke 21:27.

According to Bart, some gospel passages have a different slant on eschatology from that embraced by "the" early Christians. And such non-conforming texts, he reasons, stand a good chance of going back to Jesus himself.[43] But again, who do we think transmitted these sayings? Who do we think wrote the gospels in which they now appear? Presumably Christians who accepted the eschatology contained in these texts. An example, Bart says, is the famous parable/prophecy of the Sheep and the Goats.

> When the Son of man comes in his glory, and all the angels with him, then he will sit on his glorious throne. Before him will be gathered all the nations, and he will separate them one from another as a shepherd separates the sheep from the goats, and he will place the sheep at his right hand, but the goats at the left. Then the King will say to those at his right hand, "Come, O blessed of my Father, inherit the kingdom prepared for you from the foundation of the world; for I was hungry and you gave me food, I was thirsty and you gave me drink, I was a stranger and you welcomed me, I was naked and you clothed me, I was sick and you visited me, I was in prison and you came to me." Then the righteous will answer him, "Lord, when did we see thee hungry and feed thee, or thirsty and give thee drink? And when did we see thee a stranger and welcome thee, or naked and clothe thee? And when did we see thee sick or in prison and visit thee?" And the King will answer them, "Truly, I say to you,

---

41. Maurice Casey, *Son of Man: The Interpretation and Influence of Daniel 7* (London: SPCK, 1979); Geza Vermes, *Jesus the Jew: A Historian's Reading of the Gospels* (London: Fontana/Collins, 1976), Chapter 7, "Jesus the son of man," p. 160–186.

42. Norman Perrin, *A Modern Pilgrimage in New Testament Christology* (Philadelphia: Fortress Press, 1974), Chapter II, "Mark 14:62: The End Product of a Christian Pesher Tradition?" pp. 10–22.

43. Ehrman, *Jesus: Apocalyptic Prophet*, p. 137.

as you did it to one of the least of these my brethren, you did it to me." Then he will say to those at his left hand, "Depart from me, you cursed, into the eternal fire prepared for the devil and his angels; for I was hungry and you gave me no food, I was thirsty and you gave me no drink, I was a stranger and you did not welcome me, naked and you did not clothe me, sick and in prison and you did not visit me." Then they also will answer, "Lord, when did we see thee hungry or thirsty or a stranger or naked or sick or in prison, and did not minister to thee?" Then he will answer them, "Truly, I say to you, as you did it not to one of the least of these, you did it not to me." And they will go away into eternal punishment, but the righteous into eternal life.

Many of today's readers, chafing at the "salvation by grace through faith" dogma of Protestantism, like to invoke this passage to show that good works are required, not necessarily religious belief. Where in the text does Jesus say anything like, "Tough luck, goats! You should have accepted me as your personal savior!"? *Nowhere, that's* where! But that's not the whole story.

I have to say that it makes more sense to me if we take Jesus as praising the nations which accepted the gospel preaching of his itinerant brethren, and damning those nations who rejected it.[44] Remember, Matthew tells his readers they must recruit and baptize "the nations" (Matt. 28:19). He (and the other accounts of the Synoptic Mission Charge) tells the missioners to depend upon the hospitality and generosity of those who are receptive to their preaching. As for those who slammed the door in their faces, the itinerants were to kick the town's dust off their sandals, anticipating the doom that these unbelievers had invited. It is the former, those who welcomed the message and tended to the needs of the gospel heralds, who are to enter into the joy of their Lord. It is the latter who are to be cast into the ever-burning inferno. To reject the messengers is to reject the message. Thus I see no contradiction between this passage and subsequent Christian teaching on the Final Judgment. Jesus *could* have spoken the parable, even if it did match the early Christian eschatology, but there are other reasons to suspect he didn't.[45]

---

44. George Eldon Ladd, "The Parable of the Sheep and the Goats in Recent Interpretation." In Richard N. Longenecker and Merrill C. Tenney, eds., *New Dimensions in New Testament Study* (Grand Rapids: Zondervan, 1974), pp. 197–198.

45. John A. T. Robinson, *Twelve New Testament Studies.* Studies in Biblical Theology No. 34 (London: SCM Press, 1962), Chapter VI, "The 'Parable' of the Sheep and the Goats," pp. 76–93.

Wouldn't Jesus' association with sinners, whores, tax-gatherers and other riff-raff have been embarrassing to Christians who therefore wouldn't have made it up? Bart Ehrman thinks so: "this is not the sort of tradition—our Master particularly enjoyed the lowlifes and hookers—that later Christians would be likely to invent."[46] I don't see why we ought to assume Christians, many possibly recruited from the ranks of the despised, would necessarily have come to despise their former compatriots. Matthew 18:17 does sneer at the "Gentiles and tax-collectors." But was it the rule? "And such were some of you" (1 Cor. 6:11). And, as Jack T. Sanders[47] suggests, following Loisy, the stories of Jesus associating with "sinners" are quite likely polemics on behalf of the Gentile Mission, urging Jewish Christians to share the gospel with "Gentile sinners" (Gal. 2:15).

"He befriends wild demoniacs whom no one else will come near (Mark 5:1–20)."[48] Is the Gerasene Demoniac story (Mark 5:1–20) really to be treated as historical evidence? Are we to whittle away the story to a supposed historical core in which Jesus steps out of the boat and invites the screaming, bleeding, wild-eyed lunatic to a rap session, like Dave Wilkerson ministering to the Jets and the Sharks? This is a great example of Strauss's warning that, if the story as a whole is blatantly fanciful, transparently legendary, the historian simply has no business looking for some diamond in the garbage can, a toy in the Cracker Jack box. So I cannot see any reason to think Jesus was a friend of raving demoniacs.

Judas's betrayal?

This act of betrayal is about as historically certain as anything else in the tradition. For one thing, it is multiply attested (Mark 14:10–11, 43–45; John 18:2–3; Acts 1:16; possibly 1 Cor. 11:23). Moreover, it is not the sort of thing that a later Christian would probably make up (one of Jesus' *closest disciples* betrayed him? He had no more authority over his disciples than *that*?).[49]

---

46. Ehrman, *Jesus: Apocalyptic Prophet*, p. 187.

47. Jack T. Sanders, *The Jews in Luke-Acts* (Philadelphia: Fortress Press, 1987), Chapter 4, "The Pharisees," pp. 84–131.

48. Ehrman, *Jesus: Apocalyptic Prophet*, p. 188.

49. Ehrman, *Jesus: Apocalyptic Prophet*, p. 216.

Is Judas' betrayal "about as historically certain" as it gets in the gospels? Perhaps so, but, then again, that may not be very certain! Would we feel compelled to accept the betrayal of Osiris by Set, of Siegfried by Hagen, and that of Balder by Loki as historical?[50] If it looks like a myth, walks like a myth, and quacks like a myth . . . well, you know. Besides, many of us agree with Frank Kermode,[51] Hyam Maccoby,[52] John Shelby Spong[53] and others that Judas Iscariot is a fictional incarnation of "Christ-rejecting Jews." The seed from which the whole thing grew was the statement in Romans 8:32 that God "gave him up for us all," implying that God sent him to his death for the sake of our salvation. The word for "gave him up," *paradidomai*, can also be translated as "betrayed" depending on the context. It also appears in 1 Corinthians 11:23, "On the night he was . . ." what? Betrayed? That's what you will think it means if you have the gospel narratives in mind as you read it. But without reference to them, you would naturally think it meant "delivered up," by God, for our sins, as in Romans. Well, somebody imagined it meant "betrayed" and asked himself who the betrayer might have been? Some character in the story? And even once he is written into the story, it is not apparent that he has any natural reason for being there. Why do Jesus' enemies need Judas' help? To find him? They could have had him tailed. To point him out in the crowd? The whole reason the guards come to arrest him is that Jesus is so popular that a public arrest must prompt rioting and rebellion. "Which one you guys is Elvis?"

"In independent sources Peter is said to have denied knowing Jesus three times, another tradition that may pass the criterion of dissimilarity (Mark 14:66–72; John 18:15–18, 25–27)."[54] I happen not to see it that way.

---

50. René Girard, *The Scapegoat*. Trans. Yvonne Freccero (Baltimore: Johns Hopkins Press, 1986), pp. 66–70.

51. Frank Kermode, *The Genesis of Secrecy: On the Interpretation of Narrative*. Charles Eliot Norton Lectures 1977–1978 (Cambridge: Harvard University Press, 1979), pp. 84–86.

52. Hyam Maccoby, *The Sacred Executioner: Human Sacrifice and the Legacy of Guilt* (New York: Thames and Hudson, 1982), Chapter 10, "Judas Iscariot," pp. 121–133; Maccoby, *Judas Iscariot and the Myth of Jewish Evil* (New York: Free Press, 1992).

53. John Shelby Spong, *The Sins of Scripture: Exposing the Bible's Texts of Hate to Reveal the Love of God* (New York: HarperOne, 2006), Chapter 23, "The Role of Judas Iscariot in the Rise of Anti-Semitism," pp. 199–204.

54. Ehrman, *Jesus: Apocalyptic Prophet*, p. 219.

Alfred Loisy[55] long ago suggested that the story of Peter's denial was a bit of slanderous propaganda circulated by Paulinists to discredit Peter not merely as a lily-livered coward, but even as an apostate who had been "ashamed of [Jesus] before men" (Mark 8:38) and thus purchased a one-way ticket to Gehenna. Ever since F.C. Baur,[56] it has been apparent to critical scholars that the New Testament writings can be parceled out between Paulinist, Petrinist, and Catholicizing factions. If we accept this, as I do, we cannot say the story of Peter's denial successfully runs the dissimilarity gauntlet.

Did Jesus say he was the Messiah?

> it is almost certain that during Jesus' lifetime, some people, at least, believed that he would be the future leader of Israel. Otherwise it's impossible to explain why they (his followers) thought he was the Messiah after he had died. You can't say that they started to think so only after they became convinced that he was raised from the dead, for the very simple reason that prior to Christianity, there weren't any Jews, so far as we know, who expected that the Messiah was *going* to be raised from the dead. . . . And so, if Jesus' followers called him Messiah later, after his death, they must have already thought of him as Messiah earlier, while he was alive. And yet in our earliest accounts Jesus doesn't teach that he's the Messiah and discourages his disciples from noising it about.[57]

I don't see much of a problem here provided we reckon with the influence of the Mystery Cults upon primitive Christians, many of whom had once belonged to these groups. The great scholars of the *Religionsgeschichtlicheschule* ("History of Religions School") had no trouble providing striking parallels in both theology and mythology between New Testament religion and the faiths of Hellenistic Jews, Gnostics, Mithraists, the Attis cult, the religion of Isis and Osiris, etc. Apologists for Orthodox Judaism and traditional Christianity have always claimed that their religions had been kept insulated from these adjacent

55. Alfred Loisy, *The Birth of the Christian Religion*. Trans. L.P. Jacks (London: George Allen & Unwin, 1948), p. 102. More recently, see Robert H. Gundry, *Peter: False Disciple and Apostate according to Saint Matthew* (Grand Rapids: Eerdmans, 2015).

56. Ferdinand Christian Baur, *The Church History of the First Three Centuries*. Trans. Allan Menzies. Theological Translation Fund Library (London: Williams & Norgate, 1878).

57. Ehrman, *Jesus: Apocalyptic Prophet*, pp. 218, 222–223, 234.

faiths. It was all about "the anxiety of influence" on the part of believers who wanted their own religions to appear as pure revelations from the true God, unpolluted by the "false" religions of the benighted heathens and heretics. This apologetical tendency continues today, even among scholars from whom one might least expect it, e.g., Jonathan Z. Smith.[58] Whatever the motivation, one can readily detect the tendency of the arguments offered. They're still quite unconvincing to me, even when offered by people who are not evangelical apologists.[59]

And I think that the whole idea of Jesus as the Jewish Messiah is a function of the Judaizing of a pagan Mystery Religion or perhaps a reinterpretation of the ancient Sacred King mythology of Israel and Judah. In the context of the former, "messiah" ("anointed one") would have referred to the anointing of the slain Savior (originally Osiris) to raise him from the dead. Thus I posit a more circuitous route between belief in Jesus' resurrection and his being deemed Messiah.

Bart raises another aspect of the problem: how could Jesus come to be considered Messiah if he had not made such a claim in the earliest traditions? I think Bultmann made sense of this when he judged it impossible for a pre-Easter Jesus to have claimed Messiahship because that would make it impossible to explain the presence of early adoptionism on display in Romans 1:3–4; Acts 2:36; 13:33–34. Is it possible that Jesus taught his disciples that he was the anointed Messiah, but that early Christians thought he *hadn't* been, at least until the resurrection? Oh, that would be "dissimilarity," all right, but of a self-torpedoing kind! Surely the way to explain this disparity is what William Wrede proposed: Jesus had not claimed to be the Messiah, but only predicted the near advent of the messianic Son of Man. After some had visions of a risen Jesus, they thought he had been elevated to divine/messianic honors (just as Romulus had when he appeared after his death glorified as the new god Quirinus). Henceforth they expected Jesus to appear again, this time as newly crowned Messiah. But, alas, deadlines passed and he never showed up. Somewhere along the line some Christians began to "messianize" the only coming of Jesus available to them, the one that (they believed) had already

---

58. Jonathan Z. Smith, "Dying and Rising Gods." In Mircea Eliade, ed., *Encyclopedia of Religion* (New York: Macmillan Library Reference, 1986), Volume 4, pp. 521–527.

59. Bart's mentor in textual criticism, Bruce Metzger, a pious evangelical scholar, used this approach, and I have to wonder if Bart might have learned it from him.

happened. "I guess he was already the Messiah, appearing incognito! None of us recognized him! Boy, do I feel silly!" (Remember Matthew 25:37–39.) In this way the Christian concept of the Messiah and his mission began to veer off from the Jewish. What their stories of Jesus said he did (healing, exorcizing, teaching, suffering, rising from the dead) now became the "predicted" job description of the Messiah. This is how Christians came to believe Jesus was the Messiah. Sounds pretty reasonable to me.

BASIC FACTS?

Do we know for sure that Jesus spoke Aramaic? "There are multiply attested traditions that Jesus spoke Aramaic. Sometimes, for example, the Gospels quote his words directly without translating them into Greek (see Mark 5:41; 7:34; John 1:42)."[60] There's no particular reason to think a historical Jesus would not have been speaking Aramaic. But the problem here is that Jesus would not have been *the only one who did.* Jeremias used to award points to gospel sayings (all in Greek) which could be successfully "reverse-translated" into Aramaic (not all can be). Such sayings, he figured, were pretty good candidates for genuine words of Jesus.[61] But isn't that jumping the gun? Sure, you might rule out sayings that didn't sound like translations from Aramaic, but that doesn't mean the rest are safe. There were plenty of Aramaic-speaking Christians around who might have fabricated these sayings.

> It is generally assumed that the Gospel writers didn't make up these stories from whole-cloth (they certainly *may* have; but given their use of other sources for their accounts, it seems somewhat unlikely). If not, then they must have gotten them from someplace—either written documents that no longer survive or oral traditions that they had heard.[62]

---

60. Ehrman, *Jesus: Apocalyptic Prophet*, pp. 99–100

61. Joachim Jeremias, *New Testament Theology*. Trans. John Bowden (London: SCM Press, 1971), p. 8. Despite providing a couple of cautions, Maurice Casey seems to me to favor the same fallacy: Aramaic? Genuine Jesus! Maurice Casey, *Jesus: Evidence and Argument or Mythicist Myths?* (London: Bloomsbury Academic, 2014), pp. 68, 73–74. See also Burton L. Mack, *A Myth of Innocence: Mark and Christian Origins* (Philadelphia: Fortress Press, 1991), p. 254, for a criticism of this approach.

62. Ehrman, *Jesus: Apocalyptic Prophet*, pp. 82–83.

But this may be a false choice. What if the Jesus stories were literary creations but based on pre-existent sources?

> [M]any of the legends respecting him had not to be newly invented; they already existed in the popular hope of the Messiah, having been mostly derived with various modifications from the Old Testament, and had merely to be transferred to Jesus, and accommodated to his character and doctrines. In no case could it be easier for the person who first added any new feature to the description of Jesus, to believe himself its genuineness, since his argument would be: Such and such things must have happened to the Messiah; Jesus was the Messiah; therefore such and such things happened to him. (David Friedrich Strauss)[63]

Was Jesus a carpenter like his father Joseph? Bart thinks so. "About the only thing said about Joseph in the Gospels, outside the birth narratives, is that he was a common laborer (Matt. 13:55)."[64] As for me, I am persuaded Geza Vermes is correct in understanding the Nazareth homecoming passage Mark 6:3 in light of a rabbinic maxim. When faced with a particularly knotty passage of scripture, the sages would exclaim, "There is no carpenter, nor a carpenter's son, to explain it." Or "This is something that no carpenter, son of carpenters, can explain."[65] That, in case it's not obvious, is exactly what's going on in that Jesus episode, right? He is guest preaching in a synagogue. Visitors were commonly invited to address the congregation, commenting on the scripture reading assigned for that day (cf., Acts 13:14–16). Jesus would be expounding scripture, as Luke knew when he expanded the Markan original in Luke 4:16–30. Mark tells us the audience was delighted! "And they spoke well of him." We rush past this because Mark suddenly reverses course and has the crowd heckle Jesus, which Mark does in order to squeeze in the proverb about a prophet being honored everywhere but in his home town.[66] In the original conclusion, Mark 6:3a, the people are saying, "Wow! What an interpreter of Scripture!"[67] Did Jesus pick up the scroll with hands calloused by woodworking?

---

63. Strauss, *Life of Jesus*, p. 84.

64. Ehrman, *Jesus: Apocalyptic Prophet*, p. 99.

65. Vermes, *Jesus the Jew*, p. 22.

66. Bultmann, *History of the Synoptic Tradition*, p. 31.

67. Okay, it's a pretty distant parallel, but I can't help thinking of a line from Gene

Such a reading ignores the cultural context. Again, there is nothing far-fetched about a guy being a carpenter. But is there really evidence that Jesus (or Joseph) was one"? I'm afraid not.

Since we're on the subject, was Jesus rejected in his town and by his family? "He was rejected by his own family, by people living in his hometown."[68] I think not. As I just suggested, it is only the tacked-on ending that misleads readers into thinking so. But what about the "independent traditions" Bart appeals to?[69] In view here is Luke 4:16–30.

> And he came to Nazareth, where he had been brought up; and he went to the synagogue, as his custom was, on the sabbath day. And he stood up to read; and there was given to him the book of the prophet Isaiah. He opened the book and found the place where it was written,
>
>> "The Spirit of the Lord is upon me,
>> because he has anointed me to preach good news to the poor.
>> He has sent me to proclaim release to the captives
>> and recovering of sight to the blind,
>> to set at liberty those who are oppressed,
>> to proclaim the acceptable year of the Lord."
>
> And he closed the book, and gave it back to the attendant, and sat down; and the eyes of all in the synagogue were fixed on him. And he began to say to them, "Today this scripture has been fulfilled in your hearing." And all spoke well of him, and wondered at the gracious words which proceeded out of his mouth; and they said, "Is not this Joseph's son?" And he said to them, "Doubtless you will quote to me this proverb, 'Physician, heal yourself; what we have heard you did at Capernaum, do here also in your own country.'" And he said, "Truly, I say to you, no prophet is acceptable in his own country. But in truth, I tell you, there were many widows in Israel in the days of Elijah, when the heaven was shut up three years and six months, when there came a great famine over all the land; and Elijah was sent to none of them but only to Zarephath, in the land of Sidon, to a woman who was a widow. And there were many lepers in Israel in the time of the prophet Elisha; and none of them was cleansed, but only Naaman the Syrian." When they heard this, all

---

Shepherd's movie *A Christmas Story*: "My father worked in profanity the way other artists might work in oils or clay. It was his true medium. A master."

68. Ehrman, *Jesus: Apocalyptic Prophet*, pp. 200–201.

69. Ehrman, *Jesus: Apocalyptic Prophet*, p. 201.

in the synagogue were filled with wrath. And they rose up and put him out of the city, and led him to the brow of the hill on which their city was built, that they might throw him down headlong. But passing through the midst of them he went away.

Is this really independent tradition?[70] I can only say it makes much more sense to me as Lukan redaction/creation. The additional material seems to be an attempt to rationalize the sudden change in the crowd from appreciative audience to angry lynch mob (cf., Acts 7:54, 57–58), unexplained by Mark. Why Jesus would have purposely goaded the congregation in this way still makes no narrative sense, but that's okay: the whole thing is aimed at the reader, to anticipate Jewish anger at the successful missionary work of Christians among Gentiles (Acts 13:45, 50; 14:2, 5, 19; 17:5; 18:5–6; 19:9; 20:3; 22:21–22).

But Jesus appears to have been Mister Unpopular over the whole region. "Not only in his own town and the surrounding areas, but also in a place like Gergesa on the other side of the Sea of Galilee, he is clearly not welcomed, at least according to our earliest Gospel (Mark 5:17)."[71] Excuse me, but I just cannot see relying on a wild tale (probably based on Homer's *Odyssey* [72]) in which Jesus bargains with a Legion of demons, sending them into a herd of pigs who stampede over a cliff into the sea, as a source of any kind of facts about the historical Jesus. Shall we cast aside virtually the whole story just to retain the concluding note that the villagers, now freed of the demoniac, kicked Jesus out for no stated reason? That's the pointed tail wagging the three-headed dog if you ask me. This is like Dale Gribble denying that Lee Harvey Oswald assassinated President Kennedy but nonetheless using the story to prove that Oswald had once visited Dallas.

"This would make sense of . . . his claims, in a completely independent source, that he is 'hated by the world' (John 15:18)."[73] Again, I just do not see

70. Christopher M. Tuckett, "Luke 4, 16–30, Isaiah and Q." In Joel Delobel, ed., *Logia: Les parables de Jesus—The Sayings of Jesus*. Memorials Joseph Coppens. Bibliotheca Ephemeridum Theologicarum Lovaniensium LIX (Leuven: Leuven University Press, 1982), pp. 343–354.

71. Ehrman, *Jesus: Apocalyptic Prophet*, p. 201–202.

72. Dennis R. MacDonald, *The Homeric Epics and the Gospel of Mark* (New Haven: Yale University Press, 2000), Chapter 8, "Speluncular Savages," pp. 63–76.

73. Ehrman, *Jesus: Apocalyptic Prophet*, p. 202.

how a critical scholar can cherry pick an item out of the fantasyland of the Gospel of John and use it as historical evidence. But who knows? Maybe I'm wrong.

Was he *persona non grata* in Bethsaida, Chorazin, and Capernaum, too?[74]

> Then he began to upbraid the cities where most of his mighty works had been done, because they did not repent. "Woe to you, Chorazin! Woe to you, Bethsaida! For if the mighty works done in you had been done in Tyre and Sidon, they would have repented long ago in sackcloth and ashes. But I tell you, it shall be more tolerable on the day of judgment for Tyre and Sidon than for you. And you, Capernaum! Will you be exalted to heaven? You shall be brought down to Hades! For if the mighty works done in you had been done in Sodom, it would have remained until this day. But I tell you that it shall be more tolerable on the day of judgment for the land of Sodom than for you." (Matt. 11:20–24; cf., Luke 10:13–15).

Did the historical Jesus say this? I can't say yes. Did he actually have clairvoyant powers? We never give the benefit of the doubt to "predictions" in other apocalyptic texts.[75] Don't we know by now that passages like this are *vaticinia ex eventu* ("predictions" after the fact)? Surely this passage is Christian gloating over the destruction of these towns by the Romans in the Jewish War (66–73 C.E.). Were these burgs unreceptive to Christian evangelism? I assume so. That's why somebody coined this saying so as to give Jesus the last laugh. Remember, my goal is by no means to "refute" Bart, just to illustrate the difference between our approaches.

Did Jesus discount purity rules based on Mark chapter 7?[76] Red flag. Notoriously, this altercation between Jesus and the scribes is predicated on the wording of the Greek Septuagint translation of Isaiah 29:13. Jesus' critics descend on him for allowing his hillbilly Galilean disciples to eat lunch without first washing their hands in a ritual fashion, not for reasons of hygiene, but to render them ceremonially pure. Jesus flies off the handle and blasts them for obscuring the plain sense of scripture passages in the fog of their "tradition of the elders."

---

74. Ehrman, *Jesus: Apocalyptic Prophet*, p. 201.

75. James Barr, *Fundamentalism* (Philadelphia: Westminster Press, 1978), pp. 237–238.

76. Ehrman, *Jesus: Apocalyptic Prophet*, p. 204.

Well did Isaiah prophesy of you hypocrites, as it is written, "This people honours me with their lips, but their heart is far from me; in vain do they worship me, *teaching as doctrines the precepts of men.*" You leave the commandment of God, and hold fast the tradition of men. (Mark 7:6–8)

The trouble is that it doesn't read this way in the Hebrew original: "This people draw near with their mouth and honour me with their lips, while their hearts are far from me, and their fear of me *is a commandment of men learned by rote.*" You need the Greek in order to make the desired point. Palestinian Jews held a public funeral when the Septuagint was published! Can we really picture Jesus debating with these guys based on the Greek Bible?

Besides, as Bultmann[77] argued, when the gospel stories have Jesus getting criticized for what *his disciples* do, not what *he* does, it is very likely the story was first told by Christians to defend themselves in debate (probably against other, stricter Christians). I just can't regard Mark 7 as a mine from which dominical diamonds may be extracted. There are just too many strikes against it.

And there's the little matter of the opinion attributed here to the scribes (precursors of the rabbis). Did they really allow a man to yank the rug out from under his aged parents and divert their support to the Temple treasury instead? Not as far as our Jewish sources tell us. Apparently some idiots thought it was a good idea and asked their rabbis if they thought it was okay. So the issue does come up. But every time it does, the rabbis rule it out. So Mark actually has Jesus give the opinion his "opponents" probably would have held. It all sounds like anti-Jewish slander, not history. I don't think we can take it as evidence that Jesus was a scofflaw vis-à-vis the purity laws of the Torah. But that's just me.

JESUS AT THE END OF TIME

Bart Ehrman advocates essentially the "consistent eschatology" position of Albert Schweitzer and Johannes Weiss.[78] It is, as I have long thought, a strong reading of the evidence. It does make plenty of sense of plenty of passages when employed as an interpretive pattern or paradigm. It has in its favor that

---

77. Bultmann, *History of the Synoptic Tradition*, p. 16.

78. Johannes Weiss, *Jesus' Proclamation of the Kingdom of God.* Trans. Richard Hyde Hiers and David Larrimore Holland. Lives of Jesus Series (Philadelphia: Fortress Press, 1971).

it does depend on known ancient thought. There are very many apocalyptic texts from the New Testament period. We know that plenty of Jews believed that the world (especially Jews) languished under the terroristic regime of Satan and his henchmen the Principalities and Powers, the fallen sons of God from Genesis 6:1–4. They expected an imminent intervention by God and his Messiah and/or his angels. This Age must soon give way to the Age to Come. By contrast, certain other, more recent historical Jesus paradigms seem to depend upon modern ideological constructs like feminism and community organizing. These often produce strained interpretations and reinterpretations that give the impression of opportunistic propaganda. To his credit, Bart sees these anachronistic schemes for what they are.[79]

But it must be admitted that the recent trend of interpreting gospel materials as reflecting ancient Cynicism is also based on an authentically ancient option. Bart doesn't buy this one, but I find myself more sympathetic to it once we take one more factor into consideration, and that is the role of the itinerant charismatics, the wandering "brethren" of the Son of Man who have already popped up more than once in this chapter. They, just like the Cynics, were homeless wanderers, having renounced family, livelihood, and possessions, treading the roads to preach that one ought to live simply, in accord with nature via reason. Such was the rule of Zeus (= kingdom of God).

What I want to do next is to review the major gospel passages Bart cites to establish and to illustrate the "consistent eschatological" character of Jesus' message. I want to ask if each text fits most naturally into such a frame of reference, or if it is perhaps equivocal in its reference.

"The time is fulfilled, and the kingdom of God is at hand; repent, and believe in the gospel" (Mark 1:15).[80] As many have pointed out, this is Mark's own summation of Jesus' preaching. It is indirect discourse. It might be better rendered, "Jesus came into Galilee preaching that the time is fulfilled and the kingdom of God is at hand; that people should repent and believe the gospel." So it is not even a quote, whether authentic or not. Plus, the use of the phrase "gospel" (here and elsewhere) seems to reflect Christian terminology.

What about this one?

---

79. Ehrman, *Jesus: Apocalyptic Prophet*, p. ix.

80. Ehrman, *Jesus: Apocalyptic Prophet*, p. 142.

But in those days, after that tribulation, the sun will be darkened, and the moon will not give its light, and the stars will be falling from heaven, and the powers in the heavens will be shaken. And then they will see the Son of man coming in clouds with great power and glory. And then he will send out the angels, and gather his elect from the four winds, from the ends of the earth to the ends of heaven. . . . Truly, I say to you, this generation will not pass away before all these things take place. (Mark 13:24–27, 30)[81]

Many scholars, me included, accept the suggestion of Timotheé Colani[82] that Mark chapter 13 originated as a "Little Apocalypse" circulated on the eve of the Fall of Jerusalem in 70 C.E. It was subsequently incorporated either by the evangelist Mark or some early scribe. Thus inserted, the passage interrupted the question of the disciples about when the Temple should be destroyed and Jesus' reply that no one knows exactly when. The point of the "this generation" in the original tract would have been to measure the temporal distance between the envisioned time of Jesus' Passion and the impending Roman victory forty years afterward. It might be a real saying of a historical Jesus. Bart may be right, but in my opinion there is serious and irresolvable doubt.

"For whoever is ashamed of me and of my words in this adulterous and sinful generation, of him will the Son of man also be ashamed, when he comes in the glory of his Father with the holy angels." And he said to them, "Truly, I say to you, there are some standing here who will not taste death before they see that the kingdom of God has come with power." (Mark 8:38–9:1)[83]

This text makes the most sense to me as a butt-covering "correction" of the "this generation" deadline imposed once the Little Apocalypse had been inserted into the gospel. Time went by, and no Parousia (Second Advent of Jesus) occurred. Very few individuals belonging to the generation in question

---

81. Ehrman, *Jesus: Apocalyptic Prophet*, pp. 129, 144, 160.

82. Timotheé Colani, "The Little Apocalypse of Mark 13." An excerpt from Colani, *Jesus-Christ et les croyances messianiques de son temps*, 1864, pp. 201–214. Trans. Nancy Wilson. *Journal of Higher Criticism* (10/1) Spring 2003, pp. 41–47; Hermann Detering, "The Synoptic Apocalypse (Mark 13 par): a Document from the Time of Bar Kochba." Trans. Michael Conley and Darrell J. Doughty. *Journal of Higher Criticism* (7/2) Fall 2000, pp. 161–210.

83. Ehrman, *Jesus: Apocalyptic Prophet*, p. 129.

still survived. Only "some," and so this passage restricts the original reference to these old geezers. It is hypertext to Mark 13. And its placement just before the Transfiguration means to make even this more modest prediction refer to something other than the non-existent Parousia. The original point was simply to extend the apocalyptic deadline to accommodate the passing of the first-envisioned generation. Now every member of that generation was dead. So who are the "some standing here," i.e., those standing there alongside Jesus, who are to see the coming of the kingdom of God? The, ah, disciples! That's the ticket! But then why only "some"? Jesus excludes three quarters of them for no stated reason. But the reason seems clear: to accommodate the re-purposing of the text.

> For as the lightning flashes and lights up the sky from one side to the other, so will the Son of man be in his day. . . . As it was in the days of Noah, so will it be in the days of the Son of man. They ate, they drank, they married, they were given in marriage, until the day when Noah entered the ark, and the flood came and destroyed them all . . . so will it be on the day when the Son of man is revealed. (Luke 17:24, 26–27, 30; cf., Matt. 24:27, 37–39)[84]

The problem here is that nothing is said about any time-frame. Nothing about it happening soon, just that, whenever it does, it will bring everything to a screeching halt. "In the midst of life we are in death."

"But know this, that if the householder had known at what hour the thief was coming, he would not have left his house to be broken into" (Luke 12:39). "Therefore you also must be ready; for the Son of man is coming at an hour you do not expect" (Matt. 24:44).[85] This Q material certainly does presuppose that the advent of the Son of Man might occur at any moment. But that does not have to mean that it must happen soon. In fact, you have to wonder if perhaps "at an hour you do not expect" is not a reference to the delay of the Parousia. "You expected him to show up by the end of the generation, but he didn't. But don't give up on him!" This would of course make it not only post-Jesus but second-generation material.

---

84. Ehrman, *Jesus: Apocalyptic Prophet*, pp. 129, 144.

85. Ehrman, *Jesus: Apocalyptic Prophet*, pp. 129, 161.

Just as the weeds are gathered and burned with fire, so will it be at the close of the age. The Son of man will send his angels, and they will gather out of his kingdom all causes of sin and all evildoers, and throw them into the furnace of fire; there men will weep and gnash their teeth. Then the righteous will shine like the sun in the kingdom of their Father. He who has ears, let him hear. (Matt. 13:40–43)[86]

Again, the kingdom of heaven is like a net which was thrown into the sea and gathered fish of every kind; when it was full, men drew it ashore and sat down and sorted the good into vessels but threw away the bad. So it will be at the close of the age. The angels will come out and separate the evil from the righteous, and throw them into the furnace of fire; there men will weep and gnash their teeth. (Matt. 13:47–50)[87]

The hell-fire element of these uniquely Matthean ("M") passages is a borrowing from the Q passage Luke 13:29 (cf., Matt. 20:16). In Q the weeping and gnashing of teeth described the anguish felt by pious Jews in the moment they realize they have been supplanted by God-fearing Gentiles. Nothing is said of what may ensue. But Matthew has repeated and reapplied the phrase to describe the ongoing torment of the damned. In any case, neither of these Matthew 13 parables says a thing about the time of the Final Judgment. "This is what's going to happen some day."

Matthew 19:28[88] ("Jesus said to them, 'Truly, I say to you, in the new world, when the Son of man shall sit on his glorious throne, you who have followed me will also sit on twelve thrones, judging the twelve tribes of Israel'") and Luke 22:30 ("that you may eat and drink at my table in my kingdom, and sit on thrones judging the twelve tribes of Israel") speak of the future exaltation of Jesus' followers. Here the reference is to the twelve disciples, but I think the original promise was made to Christians in general, which is the way it reads in 1 Corinthians 6:2–3; Revelation 2:26–27; and 2 Timothy 2:12a, and that by the time it made it into the gospels, ascribed to Jesus, its scope was restricted to the twelve. But even if the reference was originally to Peter, James, John and the rest, this does not imply that they were being promised it was right around

---

86. Ehrman, *Jesus: Apocalyptic Prophet*, pp. 129, 145.

87. Ehrman, *Jesus: Apocalyptic Prophet*, p. 145.

88. Ehrman, *Jesus: Apocalyptic Prophet*, p. 143.

the corner. Think of the similar promise that righteous Gentiles would find themselves on the (pretty big!) banquet dais with the Israelite Patriarchs. This scene would be played out many hundreds of years after the Patriarchal Age. It seems no more unlikely to imagine the (newly resurrected) disciples/apostles would occupy "the chief seats" even if their reign began in the remote future. No soon-coming End is mentioned or even implied.

Is there any reference to the imminence of the Judgment in Mark 8:38; cf., Luke 12:8–9; cf., Matt. 10:32–33[89]? "For whoever is ashamed of me and of my words in this adulterous and sinful generation, of him will the Son of man also be ashamed, when he comes in the glory of his Father with the holy angels." True, there is a clear reference to the generation of Jesus' contemporaries, but this says nothing about when unbelievers will be facing the music. Instead, "this generation" need simply refer to Jesus' audience, responsive or unreceptive, and the judgment they will sooner or later face. Why would he talk about the damning sins of past or future generations? At any rate, the Christian theological language ("his Father and the holy angels") hints at a churchly origin. One might suggest that these phrases are garnishes added to an originally simpler statement of the historical Jesus, but that seems gratuitous to me. Isn't that just editing the text to make it fit a theory better?

Luke 21:34–36[90] stands in contrast to many of the passages we have considered so far.

> But take heed to yourselves lest your hearts be weighed down with dissipation and drunkenness and cares of this life, and that day come upon you suddenly like a snare; for it will come upon all who dwell upon the face of the whole earth. But watch at all times, praying that you may have strength to escape all these things that will take place, and to stand before the Son of man.

Here it *is* clear that the coming Tribulation is near at hand. But I do have a couple of minor qualms. For one thing, the saying appears only in Luke. For another, the very dangers warned against here, i.e., drunkenness, loose living, and mundane preoccupations, are elsewhere connected with the loss of apocalyptic enthusiasm in the face of the delay of the Parousia (cf., Matt. 24:48–49; 25:5). If that is presupposed here, we have a later, post-Jesus saying.

---

89. Ehrman, *Jesus: Apocalyptic Prophet*, pp. 144, 160.

90. Ehrman, *Jesus: Apocalyptic Prophet*, p. 144.

Does not the possibility of lapsing into worldly distraction imply a longer period of waiting than Schweitzer's "consistent eschatology" permits?

Does Mark 10:29–31 tell us that the historical Jesus preached the soon-coming end of the age?

> Truly, I say to you, there is no one who has left house or brothers or sisters or mother or father or children or lands, for my sake and for the gospel, who will not receive a hundredfold now in this time, houses and brothers and sisters and mothers and children and lands, with persecutions, and in the age to come eternal life. But many that are first will be last, and the last first. (Mark 10:29–31[91])

Personally, I cannot see that it does, and this for four reasons. First, the promise of recompense does presuppose a time reference, but it is not quite apocalyptic, more like the promises of today's Prosperity preachers or the Melanesian Cargo Cults: the prospect of great wealth *during the present age*. Perhaps it anticipates the sharing of money, possessions, and real estate in a communal lifestyle, as in Acts 2:44–45; 4:32–37. How this state of affairs is compatible with persecutions is not clear, since, *a la* Hebrews 10:34, persecutions begin with the seizure of property. And then, secondly, would Jesus be warning his followers about persecution during his public ministry when he was enormously popular? Surely this saying looks *back* from a later period when Christianity was an outlaw sect. It is anachronistic, as is its language: persecuted on account of "the gospel"? Third, "the age to come" is not said to be anytime soon. It may be no more than your typical "pie in the sky" promise. Fourth, "the first will be last, and the last first" not only lacks a time reference but also may well refer (anachronistically) to the subsequent Gentile Mission, as it certainly does in Luke 13:29–30: "And men will come from east and west, and from north and south, and sit at table in the kingdom of God. And behold, some are last who will be first, and some are first who will be last."

These next three passages certainly refer to the apocalyptic return of Jesus, but that's just the problem.

> Take heed, watch; for you do not know when the time will come. It is like a man going on a journey, when he leaves home and puts his servants in charge,

---

91. Ehrman, *Jesus: Apocalyptic Prophet*, pp. 148–149.

each with his work, and commands the doorkeeper to be on the watch. Watch therefore—for you do not know when the master of the house will come, in the evening, or at midnight, or at cockcrow, or in the morning—lest he come suddenly and find you asleep. And what I say to you I say to all: Watch." (Mark 13:33–37[92])

Watch therefore, for you know neither the day nor the hour. (Matt. 25:13[93])

Be like men who are waiting for their master to come home from the marriage feast, so that they may open to him at once when he comes and knocks. (Luke 12:36[94])

I don't think these texts can be extracted from their contexts in which they are naturally to be understood as referring to the expectation of Jesus' second coming. The gospels seem to me not to picture the situation of Jesus as one in which he had explained the details of Christian theology. Instead, they give the impression that the disciples did not clearly grasp the fact of Jesus' upcoming death, much less his resurrection. Only in the wildly unreliable Gospel of John, at the Last Supper, does Jesus even broach the question of his leaving and returning, and even there the matter is far from clear. What is he talking about? The resurrection or the Second Advent? Isn't it obvious that in these three passages "Jesus" is talking over the heads of the characters in the story directly to the readers who already know good and well about the Parousia?[95] If any of this stuff does go back to a historical Jesus, I'd be very surprised.

A pair of parallel parables are sometimes invoked to illustrate Jesus' apocalyptic expectation, though I think interpreters are really trying to reconcile the parables with a piece of theology they do not readily fit.

With what can we compare the kingdom of God, or what parable shall we use for it? It is like a grain of mustard seed, which, when sown upon the ground, is the smallest of all the seeds on earth; yet when it is sown it grows up and

92. Ehrman, *Jesus: Apocalyptic Prophet*, p. 160.

93. Ehrman, *Jesus: Apocalyptic Prophet*, p. 161.

94. Ehrman, *Jesus: Apocalyptic Prophet*, p. 161.

95. Robert M. Fowler, *Let the Reader Understand: Reader-Response Criticism and the Gospel of Mark* (Minneapolis: Fortress Press, 1991), pp. 21, etc.

becomes the greatest of all shrubs, and puts forth large branches, so that the birds of the air can make nests in its shade. (Mark 4:30–32)

Bart explains: "Thus the Kingdom was like a mustard seed: a small beginning in Jesus' ministry, but an immense outcome on the day of judgment."[96]

"The kingdom of heaven is like leaven which a woman took and hid in three measures of flour, till it was all leavened" (Matt. 13:33; cf. Luke 13:20–21). Bart says it means the same thing: "The Kingdom of God is like that: inauspicious beginnings with enormous consequences."[97] I always felt a little uneasy with this interpretation but felt like I was stuck with it once I had embraced Schweitzer's "consistent eschatology." My better judgment (and of course I realize how subjective this is) was that the Puritans and Postmillennialists had been correct: the parables predicted the gradual growth of Christianity through the centuries.[98] But it is a prediction after the fact, as James Breech notes, a bit of retrospective triumphalism.[99] It has to be pretty late.

The parable of the Seed Growing Secretly, unique to Mark, is another that does not seem to me compatible with apocalyptic expectation.

The kingdom of God is as if a man should scatter seed upon the ground, and should sleep and rise night and day, and the seed should sprout and grow, he knows not how. The earth produces of itself, first the blade, then the ear, then the full grain in the ear. But when the grain is ripe, at once he puts in the sickle, because the harvest has come. (Mark 4:26–29)[100]

---

96. Ehrman, *Jesus: Apocalyptic Prophet*, p. 179; George Eldon Ladd, *The Presence of the Future: The Eschatology of Biblical Realism* (Grand Rapids: Eerdmans, 1974), pp. 222, 234–238; Joachim Jeremias, *The Parables of Jesus*. Studies in Biblical Interpretation (New York: Scribners, 1972), p. 149.

97. Ehrman, *Jesus: Apocalyptic Prophet*, p. 179.

98. Henry H. Halley, *Halley's Bible Handbook: An Abbreviated Bible Commentary* (Grand Rapids: Zondervan Publishing House, 1965), p. 440, gives this traditional interpretation, attesting the wide popularity of the idea.

99. James Breech, *The Silence of Jesus: The Authentic Voice of the Historical Man* (Philadelphia: Fortress Press, 1983), p. 71.

100. Ehrman, *Jesus: Apocalyptic Prophet*, p. 180.

This imagery implies a process of gradual building, the opposite of cataclysmic intervention.[101]

INTERIM ETHICS?

Albert Schweitzer[102] spoke of Jesus teaching an "interim ethic," the placing of moral demands in a higher key. The absolute standards , the moral principles which we ordinarily relativize, employing them as distant stars to navigate by, must, in view of the imminent End of the Age, be brought down to earth and obeyed in literal terms. No mundane concerns must be allowed to mitigate them, because no mundane factors *need* concern us anymore. There will be no worldly future to plan for. Bart Ehrman agrees.

> His entire proclamation consisted in a call to prepare for the coming Kingdom, which would be brought in by a final judgment through the appearance of the Son of Man. Jesus' teaching of what we might call "ethics" was advanced to show people how they could be ready.[103]

"Give unto every one who asks of you!" Sounds good! Ideally, I would! But, ah, I have my family to provide for! I have to pay for my kids' college. Well, you *did*, but no more! The kingdom of God is about to dawn. In the meantime, on the edge of forever, the only thing your money's good for is to feed the poor during the narrow window of opportunity that remains. Besides, since the Final Judgment is right around the corner, a few charitable acts might increase your chances of surviving it!

Turn the other cheek? Inherently noble, to be sure, but if everybody did it, violence and rapine would reign unopposed! Social order would be destroyed! I've got news for you: it's going to be wiped out very shortly anyway, when the Son of Man touches down to destroy the sinners! Till then, better do your Gandhi imitation! This is perhaps the greatest strength of Schweitzer's thorough-going eschatology. This interpretation makes sense of the gospels' otherwise crazy-sounding, Tolstoy-like ethics of total vulnerability in an

---

101. Ehrman, *Jesus: Apocalyptic Prophet*, p. 190.

102. Schweitzer, *Mystery of the Kingdom of God*, p. 103.

103. Ehrman, *Jesus: Apocalyptic Prophet*, p. 177.

ongoing world. Bart sees this strength. But I am no longer so sure this approach makes the only, or even the best, sense of the relevant gospel texts.

As in Mark 10:29–31, the disciples are said to have given up everything including jobs and families,[104] and Bart says they were simply doing what Jesus told all his hearers to do.[105]

> Does, then, seeking the Kingdom above everything else also mean leaving even one's family behind? Yes indeed. The common sense shared by modern proponents of "family values" notwithstanding, Jesus was quite unambiguous that even parents, siblings, spouses, and children were to be of no importance in comparison with the coming Kingdom. Consider the words preserved in Q: "If anyone comes to me and does not hate his own father and mother and wife and children and brothers and sisters and even his own life, he is not able to be my disciple." (Luke 14:26; Matt. 10:37 [NRSV])."[106]

If it is to be read as an apocalyptic saying, it must presuppose an *immediate* coming of the kingdom, within days or weeks. But that would seem to undermine the notion of a new lifestyle in an ongoing society, even a sectarian one. There are two other, equally natural, ways to take these sayings. Walter Schmithals[107] contends that such texts are envisioning the sacrifices required for the faithful in a time of persecution. "Let goods and kindred go, this mortal life also." As I've already said, this would seem anachronistic for Jesus to be saying to his audiences during his public ministry.[108] Surely so premature given their present situation, fully as anachronistic as the summons to follow Jesus carrying one's own cross, as if anyone on the scene could possibly have understood what he was talking about, namely the events of Good Friday. Again, in these sayings the Jesus character is speaking over the heads of the characters on stage and directly to readers who are already Christians in a later day.

---

104. Ehrman, *Jesus: Apocalyptic Prophet*, pp. 170–171.

105. Thaddée Matura, *Gospel Radicalism: The Hard Sayings of Jesus*. Trans. Maggi Despot and Paul Lachance (Maryknoll: Orbis Books, 1984), pp. 42, 51, 56, 58, 60, 64–65, 73–74, etc.

106. Ehrman, *Jesus: Apocalyptic Prophet*, p. 170.

107. Walter Schmithals, *The Theology of the First Christians*. Trans. O.C. Dean (Louisville: Westminster John Knox Press, 1997), p. 345.

108. Tödt, *Son of Man*, p. 340; Matura, *Gospel Radicalism*, p. 35.

Gerd Theissen[109] suggests with equal plausibility that these sayings are aimed at those considering joining the ranks of the itinerant Christian prophets and "brethren." It would have been the same sort of warnings Jesus gave to would-be recruits, that they must become homeless wanderers freed from family duties (Matt. 8:19–22). Their needs would be met by divine Providence at the hands of those sympathetic to their preaching.[110] Their ministry need not have faced an apocalyptic deadline, though it does in Matt. 10:23, "When they persecute you in one town, flee to the next; for truly, I say to you, you will not have gone through all the towns of Israel, before the Son of man comes."

In fact, that passage carried quite a lot of weight in Albert Schweitzer's historical Jesus portrait. Schweitzer, you'll recall, believed that Mark and Matthew were substantially accurate as they stand. He did not really reckon with form criticism which views the gospels as collections of originally independent units of oral tradition. Thus he took Matthew 10:23 to have actually been spoken by Jesus on the occasion described, namely as part of his pep talk to the disciples as he sent them on their preaching tour. This, of course, implied that Jesus did not expect to see his men again in this age. When they gathered once again, he should greet them in transfigured, superhuman form as the Son of Man, the very Eschaton having erupted onto the world. When Bartholomew, Lebbaeus, Thomas, the Iscariot and the rest came back, all wearing the same old aching flesh, Jesus knew something was amiss. Like William Miller and Harold Camping, he must have miscalculated. It now occurred to him that God's will was for him to bear the brunt of the Great Tribulation by himself on everyone else's behalf.

The whole picture, however, was built on exegetical sand. Form criticism allows us to recognize that Matthew 10:23 represents one of several post-Jesus "mission charges," some of which are explicitly attributed to a "post-historical Jesus." For instance, Matthew 28:19–20 has the resurrected Jesus, in a statement dripping with signature Matthean vocabulary and bits from Daniel, deliver the

---

109.   Gerd Theissen, *Social Reality and the Early Christians: Theology, Ethics, and the World of the New Testament.* Trans. Margaret Kohl (Minneapolis: Fortress Press, 1992), Chapter 1, "The Wandering Radicals: Light Shed by the Sociology of Literature," pp. 33–59.

110.   Joachim Jeremias, *The Sermon on the Mount.* Trans. Norman Perrin. Facet Books. Biblical Series—2 (Philadelphia: Fortress Press, 1963), p. 25: "the long section [Matt.] 6:25–34 ... forbids anxiety for oneself and was very possibly originally addressed to the departing missionaries, who were to learn to depend entirely upon God."

Great Commission for evangelizing the Gentiles, a command that can never have been issued by Jesus, especially as his parting words, or we should never see anything like the controversy in Acts chapters 10–11. Why should it have been like pulling teeth without Novocain to get the early Jewish Christians off their butts and preaching to Gentiles? In Acts 13:1–3, the Holy Spirit (virtually synonymous with the "Spirit of Jesus" in Acts) fingers Saul and Barnabas to undertake a preaching mission outside Palestine. Acts 9:15 has the risen Jesus appoint Ananias of Damascus to initiate Saul into the faith in order that he may serve as Jesus' premiere emissary to the Gentile world. In Acts 22:17–21, Jesus appears in a vision to Paul, telling him he will reap a great harvest among the Gentiles.

Well, what we are seeing in Matthew 10:23 belongs to the same category and, like the rest, was at first posthumously placed on the lips of Jesus.[111] Note that Matthew has added it onto Mark's mission charge (Mark 6:7–11). Like the Great Commission of Matthew 28:19–20, Matthew 10:23 says the apostolic mission will culminate in the End of the Age. As I have argued elsewhere,[112] the Gospel of Matthew is a compromise document consisting of elements reflecting at least three different Antiochene viewpoints, those counting Peter, Paul, and James the Just as their figureheads. The Matthew 28 Commission represents the Paulinist position on Gentile evangelism, while Matthew 10:23 (not to mention Matthew 23:15) counters it, representing the view of Peter's critics in Acts 11:1–3. Furthermore, Matthew 10:23 does not merely command a preaching mission to Israel; it protests the Gentile/Samaritan Mission already underway. You don't tell people not to do something they're already not doing. This is a piece of intra-Christian polemic. Apocalyptic or not, the saying doesn't go back to Jesus. At least I don't think it does.

Why would one classify Mark 9:35[113] ("And he sat down and called the

111. Here and elsewhere I do not assume there was a historical Jesus. Rather, I am simply arguing, for the moment, in the terms of the post-Schweitzer discussion. As a Mythicist, I think *all* sayings ascribed to Jesus are "posthumous," so to speak, first coined in the absence of any historical Jesus.

112. Robert M. Price, "Antioch's Aftershocks: Rereading Galatians and Matthew after Saldarini." In Alan J. Avery-Peck, Daniel Harrington, and Jacob Neusner, eds., *When Judaism and Christianity Began. Volume One: Christianity in the Beginning. Essays in Memory of J. Saldarini.* Supplements to the Journal for the Study of Judaism (Leiden: Brill, 2004), pp. 231–250.

113. Ehrman, *Jesus: Apocalyptic Prophet*, p. 149.

twelve; and he said to them, 'If any one would be first, he must be last of all and servant of all') as an apocalyptic saying? Schweitzer[114] thought it was. He thought Jesus meant that the best way to secure oneself a good position in the Age to Come would be to take the lowest place on the totem pole now, since fortunes will get reversed when the kingdom of God comes. Seems pretty cynical to me, but that does not mean Schweitzer was wrong. In any case, I think the interpretation is gratuitous. Unless you have the "consistent eschatology" bug up your butt, I'm guessing you would naturally think Jesus simply meant to define true greatness as self-giving servanthood (like Schweitzer himself, Dr. King, Gandhi, or George Bailey in *It's a Wonderful Life*).

The same can be said of the Q saying Luke 18:14; Matthew 23:12.[115] "Every one who exalts himself will be humbled, but he who humbles himself will be exalted." It hardly need refer to the Eschaton. "Pride goeth before a fall" (cf., Proverbs 16:18).

The similar passage Mark 10:42–44[116] does not particularly strike me as presupposing thoroughgoing eschatology either.

> And Jesus called them to him and said to them, "You know that those who are supposed to rule over the Gentiles lord it over them, and their great men exercise authority over them. But it shall not be so among you; but whoever would be great among you must be your servant, and whoever would be first among you must be slave of all."

This version is even more problematical for the eschatological model, since it appears to be what Bultmann called a community rule. Somehow it doesn't seem compatible both to expect the imminent end of the world *and* to set the terms for an ongoing religious community. It reminds me of an old *Peanuts* strip in which Peppermint Patty is touring a summer camp run by a TV evangelist well known for predicting the soon-coming End. Her guide points out a grove of saplings planted to form a beautiful canopy in some twenty years' time. Patty quips, "The world may be ending tomorrow, but I wasn't born yesterday!" Or, if you prefer the Old Testament to *Peanuts* (and not everyone does), the situation might be compared to that of the two Decalogues (lists

---

114. Schweitzer, *Quest of the Historical Jesus*, p. 366.

115. Ehrman, *Jesus: Apocalyptic Prophet*, p. 150.

116. Ehrman, *Jesus: Apocalyptic Prophet*, pp. 149–150.

of Ten Commandments) in Exodus chapters 20 and 34. The laws stipulated in both simply do not apply to the desert nomads to whom Moses ostensibly delivered them. The commandments presuppose a settled, agricultural society. Thus anachronistically ascribing them to Moses is just a way of reinforcing their authority in a later time, the actual time of writing. It's the same with crediting community life principles to an apocalyptic Jesus.

Is Jesus' practice of associating with sinners part and parcel of an avid expectation of the soon-coming Final Judgment?[117] Obviously, a belief that the Great Assize is coming right up would provide a pretty good motivation to urge sinners to repent.[118] But such doom-saying is hardly a necessary pretext for preaching repentance. Or for infiltrating the ranks of the sinners, Dave Wilkerson-style.[119] A great rabbinical tale[120] tells that the high priest Aaron, no apocalypticist, used to befriend robbers and hooligans so that when they began to plot some crime, they'd stop and think, "How can I face Aaron again if I do this? Aw, to hell with it!"

Bart Ehrman understands the Beatitudes (Matt. 5:3–12)[121] as eschatological in reference. "They describe what certain groups of people are experiencing in the present and what they *will* experience in the future. *Will* experience? When? Not in some vague, remote, and uncertain moment—sometime in the sky by and by; it will happen when the Kingdom arrives."[122] I don't think so. Yes, I know some of the Beatitudes speak of "the kingdom of heaven," but I am no longer so sure these verses refer to apocalyptic salvation in the near future. It is admittedly clear that in some instances "kingdom of God" denotes the *reign* of God more than the *realm* of God, the Age to Come as opposed to the Great Beyond. But context has to be the deciding factor, and in the Beatitudes it is not self-evident that the intended meaning is "reign" rather than "realm." Another thing to keep in mind is that, while Matthew usually changes Mark's

---

117. Ehrman, *Jesus: Apocalyptic Prophet*, p. 151.

118. A boy spots his grandfather on a park bench reading a Bible and religious pamphlets. This is uncharacteristic of the old man, so the kid asks his mom, "What was grandpa doing?" She replies, "He's cramming for his finals!"

119. David Wilkerson with John and Elizabeth Sherrill, *The Cross and the Switchblade* (New York: Pyramid Books, 1967).

120. *Fathers according to Rabbi Nathan* 12.

121. Ehrman, *Jesus: Apocalyptic Prophet*, p. 153.

122. Ehrman, *Jesus: Apocalyptic Prophet*, p. 253.

"kingdom of God" to "kingdom of heaven" out of reverent reticence in the use of "God," these Beatitudes have no Markan parallels/originals. If they are original to Matthew, we have even less reason to suppose they do not mean "the realm of heaven," you know, up in the sky.

"Blessed are the poor in spirit, for theirs is the kingdom of heaven" (Matt. 5:3). There is no reason at all that this should not mean to describe the postmortem fate of beggars like Luke's Lazarus (Luke 16:22). They need not wait for the Last Trumpet to sound, whether sooner or later. If they starve to death, they will wake up in heaven.

"Blessed are those who mourn, for they shall be comforted" (Matt. 5:4). That's pretty terse—and equally vague. Eschatological comfort as in Revelation 7:17? Could be! But maybe it just refers to the comfort we receive from God through those who share our sufferings as in 2 Corinthians 1:3–4. Eschatology may be an over-interpretation.

"Blessed are the meek, for they shall inherit the earth" (Matt. 5:5). Again, it would make sense if it promised land redistribution in the Millennial kingdom, as when a friend of mine learned that local Jehovah's Witnesses were already divvying up his large estate for when Jesus returned! But I am tempted to think the saying is a wry comment to the effect that the meek and passive, now oppressed by competing empires, will be left to possess the earth by default once, e,g., the Romans and Parthians kill each other off.

"Blessed are those who hunger and thirst for righteousness, for they shall be satisfied" (Matt. 5:6). How did we read this verse before we learned about eschatology? We thought it was a promise to those who, like the Rich Young Ruler, have kept the commandments yet sense the need for something more. God will not disappoint them. They sing "Fill my cup, Lord; I lift it up, Lord! Come and fill this longing of my soul!" And they hear a still, small voice reassuring them that this very longing *is* spiritual fulfillment.

"Blessed are the merciful, for they shall obtain mercy" (Matt. 5:7). When? When the Word of God, clad in blood-stained vesture, shall descend from the sky astride a blinding white stallion? Could be, but I take it to mean that other people will be more inclined to give you a break if you are known to go easy on others. Who's going to want to help or to forgive you if you are a hard-hearted son of a bitch? To jump ahead for a moment, we can say the same thing about the saying, which Bart quotes:

"Don't judge, so that you won't be judged" (Luke 6:37; Matt. 7:1 [NRSV]). I probably don't need to add that that the teaching is clearly linked to an apocalyptic notion of the future comeuppance; in Matthew, for example, the saying continues: "for you will be judged [i.e., in the coming judgment!] with the measure that you yourself use to judge" (Matt. 7:2 [NRSV]).[123]

Is it "clearly linked" to apocalyptic? Even Bart has to insert the eschatological element into the text in brackets, as an interpretive gloss. But does it mean more than that people are more likely to be quick to judge you if you are known to be quick to judge others? Yes, I know all about the so-called "divine passive" which Jeremias[124] sees in such texts, implying that it is *God* who will judge, satisfy, show mercy, etc. The point would be, again, to piously avoid throwing around the divine name unnecessarily. But *must* the reference be to God? When Cato used to demand, "Carthage must be destroyed!" did he mean Jupiter had to do it? If my wife tells me, "Those clothes have to be washed!" is she demanding God put 'em into the Maytag? Of course not. Context decides the case. But the context of the Beatitudes in no way demands God as the implied subject. I think it is more like the Book of Proverbs where virtue is the shrewdest calculation. Maybe God arranged life that way, but there is no need for apocalyptic intervention.

"Blessed are the pure of heart, for they shall see God" (Matt. 5:8). When the Son of Man appears amid the clouds, "*every* eye shall see him." But why not think the saying simply means that only the pure in heart, the mature in character, the righteous like Noah, Enoch, and Job will arrive in heaven to be welcomed by their old Friend? Want to be in that number when the saints go marching in? It's up to you.

"Blessed are the peacemakers, for they shall be called sons of God" (Matt. 5:9) or, presumably, daughters of God. This assumes that God is a peacemaker (not exactly the impression one would get from reading the Old Testament, but what the heck). If we are inclined to try to talk down angry antagonists, to negotiate solutions, to tender a soft answer in order to turn away wrath (Prov. 15:1), we will be known as "godly," "sons of God," "those who are like God" in this important respect. Where is any reference to the End of the Age?

---

123. Ehrman, *Jesus: Apocalyptic Prophet*, p. 174.

124. Jeremias, *New Testament Theology*, pp. 9–14.

"Blessed are those who are persecuted for righteousness' sake, for theirs is the kingdom of heaven" (Matt. 5:10). Once martyred, these courageous souls have secured their position in heaven, but not necessarily in the earthly Millennium. It might be the latter, as in Revelation 20:4–6. But then it might be the former, as in Revelation 6:9–11.

"Blessed are you when men revile you and persecute you and utter all kinds of evil things against you falsely on my account. Rejoice and be glad, for your reward is great in heaven, for so men persecuted the prophets who were before you" (Matt. 5:11–12). "In heaven" sure sounds like the treasury of merit in the sky (cf., 2 Cor. 5:1; 1 Pet. 1:4). Besides, did Jesus ever say this? No, it is another anachronism, just like John 9:22, where the Sanhedrin has already decreed that any partisan of Jesus will be excommunicated from the synagogue, despite the fact that the very same gospel admits that such a measure lay yet in the future (John 16:1–4). Why should Jesus' listeners imagine there was a danger of persecution at this point? Of course, Jesus is talking to Matthew's readers.

Mark 9:43–48[125] warns that, unless radical steps of self-reformation are taken, eliminating the sins of hand, foot, and eye, the sinner will one day find himself thrown bodily into Gehenna, the fiery netherworld. Isn't it worth any sacrifice, any disadvantage, to avoid such a fate and to enter God's kingdom? This saying speaks of the opposite destinies of the righteous and the wicked, but where is there any mention of the Day of Judgment being any time soon?

Does the story of the Rich Young Ruler (Mark 10:17–22; Luke 18:18–23; Matt. 19:16–22)[126] teach or even imply that the eschatological kingdom is speedily approaching? I don't see it. The seeker asks how he may "inherit" eternal life (Mark 10:17), an image that seems to me to imply receiving it *after death*. In verse 21, Jesus speaks of the man's "having treasure in heaven," i.e., *up there*. The subsequent comment speaks of the destiny of the righteous as "entering the kingdom of God" (Mark 10:23). In light of the preceding, this phrase would suggest "going to heaven." Doesn't the idiom "entering" the kingdom imply passage into an already existing state—or *place*?

Why does the Pearl of Great Price (Matt. 13:44)[127] have anything to do with consistent (or any other kind of) eschatology? "The kingdom of heaven is

125. Ehrman, *Jesus: Apocalyptic Prophet*, p. 154.

126. Ehrman, *Jesus: Apocalyptic Prophet*, pp. 165, 166.

127. Ehrman, *Jesus: Apocalyptic Prophet*, p. 167.

like treasure hidden in a field, which a man found and covered up; then in his joy he goes and sells all that he has and buys that field." The kingdom of God is worth any sacrifice, to be sure, but does the parable necessarily refer, like the preaching of John the Baptist, to the impending Eschaton? The point *may* be that a ticket to the End-Time kingdom[128] is worth everything and more. But it may just as well simply refer to "going to heaven." And in no case is entrance into the kingdom said to be immediately in the offing.

What does the Golden Rule[129] have to do with consistent eschatology? Luke 6:31: "And as you wish that men would do to you, do so to them." Matthew 7:12: "So whatever you wish that men would do to you, do so to them; for this is the law and the prophets." Was it eschatological when Rabbi Hillel gave his version ("What you hate, do not do to another") a century earlier?

Does Matthew 7:24–27 (cf., Luke 6:47–49) refer to the Final Judgment?

> Every one then who hears these words of mine and does them will be like a wise man who built his house upon the rock; and the rain fell, and the floods came, and the winds blew and beat upon that house, but it did not fall, because it had been founded on the rock. And every one who hears these words of mine and does not do them will be like a foolish man who built his house upon the sand; and the rain fell, and the floods came, and the winds blew and beat against that house, and it fell; and great was the fall of it.

In my opinion, to understand the buffeting storm as the apocalyptic baptism of fire robs the saying of its valuable point, a sapiential one. Isn't the message that those who take seriously Jesus' words and put them into practice will live a wise and successful life that can withstand all cruel (though mundane) vicissitudes?

Professor Ehrman opines that miracles (though they only "allegedly" happened!) were acted parables of the coming of the kingdom. "They were parables of the Kingdom." [130] Bart accepts the contention of an earlier generation of scholars like Reginald H. Fuller[131] that Jesus' miracles were signs

---

128. Just as Don Imus's character Reverend Billy Saul Hargis used to peddle airline tickets to heaven on the Wings of Him. "Most Protestants go coach!"

129. Ehrman, *Jesus: Apocalyptic Prophet*, p. 168.

130. Ehrman, *Jesus: Apocalyptic Prophet*, pp. 180, 212–213.

131. Reginald H. Fuller, *Interpreting the Miracles* (London: SCM Press, 1963), pp. 39–42.

of the rapid advance (or anticipatory presence) of the kingdom of God. But what is it in the miracle stories that connects them with the coming kingdom? One text[132] is always cited in this connection: "And if I cast out demons by Beelzebul, by whom do your sons cast them out? Therefore they shall be your judges. But if it is by the finger of God that I cast out demons, then the kingdom of God has come upon you" (Luke 11:20). But this is, I venture to say, an obvious midrashic rewrite of Exodus 8:19 where, unable to reproduce Moses' latest miracle, "the magicians said to Pharaoh, 'This is the finger of God.' But Pharaoh's heart was hardened, and he would not listen to them; as the Lord had said." Moses becomes Jesus. Pharaoh's magicians become "your sons." And in both, the miracles are wrought by "the finger of God." Come on! Let's face it: this is no statement of the historical Jesus.

But whether or not they were a function of eschatology, did Jesus actually perform miracles?

Jesus' exorcisms are among the best-attested deeds of the Gospel traditions. Individual accounts are scattered throughout the first part of Mark (1:21–28; 5:1–20), and L (Luke 13:10–14; cf. 8:2). Moreover, the sources themselves consistently summarize Jesus' activities as involving exorcisms (e.g., Mark 1:32–34, 39; 3:9–12; see also Acts 10:38), and the theme that Jesus could and did cast out demons is documented in multiply attested forms throughout the sayings materials, for example, Mark, Q, and L (Mark 3:22; Matt. 12:27–28; Luke 11:15, 19–20; 13:32).[133]

I see a problem here. The particular gospel episodes of exorcism are all fanciful. As in *The Exorcist*, the demoniacs are not mere schizophrenics but possess preternatural knowledge of Jesus' true, hidden identity (Mark 1:23–24, 34; 5:7). The mighty Gerasene Demoniac (Mark 5:1–13) is obviously based on the Cyclops Polyphemus from Homer's *Odyssey*, while the stampede of the "Legion" of deviled ham comes from Odysseus' soldiers transformed into pigs by Circe.[134] Jesus' long-distance exorcism of the Syro-Phoenician Woman's daughter (Mark 7:24–30) seems like a parable on behalf of the Gentile Mission, symbolizing Jesus' saving power that can save *distant* Gentiles of a *subsequent*

132. Ehrman, *Jesus: Apocalyptic Prophet*, p. 198.

133. Ehrman, *Jesus: Apocalyptic Prophet*, pp. 197–198.

134. MacDonald, *Homeric Epics*, pp. 63–76.

generation. Is this liable to be real historical data? The story of the Deaf-Mute Epileptic (Mark 9:14–29) implicitly has the possessed lad's indwelling devil recognize Jesus via supernatural knowledge (verse 20). These stories, taken individually, seem to be fictitious. What sum do you get when you add a bunch of zeroes? And as for the summaries ("Yeah, he did loads of these"), they are rhetorical generalizations, implying not a larger number of cases from which the individual tales have been selected, but rather an attempt to cover up the paucity of specific examples available. Though there certainly were ancient exorcists, and Jesus (as Bultmann[135] thought) might have been one of them, I don't see sufficient evidence of it.

One of Bart's most impressive arguments for Jesus having been an apocalypticist is that John the Baptist was clearly a preacher of the impending End and that Jesus was his follower, so Jesus can hardly have held a different view.[136] But Mark 2:18, Luke 11:1, and Matthew 11:18–19 (cf., Luke 7:33–34) imply Jesus had broken with John. He conspicuously flouted the ascetical regimen of John, which must have been penitential preparation for the Eschaton. Why did Jesus reject this stance? Because he believed the kingdom of God had already dawned, albeit in a figurative sense? "Being asked by the Pharisees when the kingdom of God was coming, he answered them, 'The kingdom of God is not coming with signs to be observed; nor will they say, "Lo, here it is!" or "There!" for behold, the kingdom of God is within you." (Luke 17:20–21). I think it is not certain that Jesus parroted John's eschatological enthusiasm.[137]

Jesus is said to have had twelve disciples, to whom he promised elite positions in his regime: "Truly, I say to you, in the new world, when the Son of man shall sit on his glorious throne, you who have followed me will also sit on twelve thrones, judging the twelve tribes of Israel" (Matt. 19:28; cf. Luke

---

135. Bultmann, *Jesus and the Word*, p. 173.

136. Ehrman, *Jesus: Apocalyptic Prophet*, pp. 184–185.

137. Bart D. Ehrman, *Forgery and Counterforgery: The Use of Literary Deceit in Early Christian Polemics* (New York: Oxford University Press, 2013), pp. 231–232, insists that Luke 17:20–21 must be translated "The kingdom of God is *in your midst*," not "within you," since Jesus, in the Lukan context, is speaking to black-hearted, horn-sporting, villainous Pharisees, who in the nature of the case, cannot possibly be said to harbor the divine kingdom within themselves. At any rate, the (usually artificial) narrative setting is irrelevant when we are trying to work from individual sayings back to a historical Jesus.

22:30). Bart thinks the twelve were conceived as a new twelve tribal patriarchs, corresponding to the sons of Jacob. What would this make Jesus? Implicitly, the Messiah.[138] But wouldn't it fit the imagery better for Jesus to be a new *Jacob*? Not that I think that's what he thought. But if having twelve subordinates makes one the Messiah, was this equally true at Qumran? There was a council of twelve there, too, but as far as we know, the sectarians did not regard the Teacher of Righteousness as the Messiah.

Was the Cleansing of the Temple an apocalyptic sign?

> Jesus not only preached this message upon arriving in Jerusalem, he acted it out, entering the Temple and engaging in a kind of symbolic action of destruction as a warning of what was to come, overturning tables and causing a mild ruckus.[139]

Forgive me, but this inference strikes me as completely gratuitous. It would only make sense if we brought to it the assumption that, for Jesus, everything was eschatology, as it was for Schweitzer. Besides, what kind of dramatization of the apocalypse is "a mild ruckus"?

What was Jesus' stance on the Jewish Torah? The gospels certainly depict him as a loyal partisan of the Law (though holding more flexible interpretations of it than some). He deems it more likely that the very cosmos should perish than that the least detail of the Torah should be abrogated.[140] Matthew 5:18 has Jesus say, "Truly, I say to you, till heaven and earth pass away, not an iota, not a dot, will pass from the law until all is accomplished" (cf., Luke 16:17). This seems to be the product of post-Jesus polemic. What sense would it make for Jesus to assert the perpetuity of the Law in the Jewish context in which the gospels place him? It would be like him saying, "God exists!" Was this, or the lasting authority of the Torah, in question? The statement instead fits better into the controversy over legal observance in the Gentile Mission. This becomes absolutely clear when we widen the camera angle to take in the redactional material into which Matthew has placed the Q saying. Here is the full Matthean version:

---

138. Ehrman, *Jesus: Apocalyptic Prophet*, pp. 217.

139. Ehrman, *Jesus: Apocalyptic Prophet*, pp. 208.

140. Ehrman, *Jesus: Apocalyptic Prophet*, pp. 165.

Think not that I have come to abolish the law and the prophets; I have come not to abolish them but to fulfil them. For truly, I say to you, till heaven and earth pass away, not an iota, not a dot, will pass from the law until all is accomplished. Whoever then relaxes one of the least of these commandments and teaches men so, shall be called least in the kingdom of heaven; but he who does them and teaches them shall be called great in the kingdom of heaven. For I tell you, unless your righteousness exceeds that of the scribes and Pharisees, you will never enter the kingdom of heaven. (Matt. 5:17–19)[141]

Jesus is not speaking in a vacuum, is he? The text presupposes that some *Christians* teach that "Jesus came to abolish Scripture (the Law and the Prophets)." The "I came to / The Son of Man came to" language, often met with in the gospels, is theological language defining in retrospect the significance of the mission of Jesus,[142] and we know that Marcionites advocated Christian rejection of the Law and the Prophets. Paul's teaching was, fairly or not, taken to imply the same thing when he taught that "For Christ is the end of the law, that every one who has faith may be justified" (Rom. 10:4).

Moreover, to stress the perpetuity of the Torah, especially contrasting it with the passing away of heaven and earth, is incompatible with any notion that the present age was soon to end. What need could there possibly be for all those "Thou shalt nots" in a new world without sin?[143] If the Law is never to pass away, mustn't that mean there will always be a need for it? For instance, the divorce discussion (e.g., Mark 10:4–12; Luke 16:18)[144] assumes ongoing mundane history.

Bart admits we can't be sure that every one of these gospel statements on the Torah is historically authentic but that the picture they create must be historical anyway.[145] Isn't this a chain of weak links? Perhaps the weakest link is John 10:34–35. "Jesus answered them, 'Is it not written in your law, "I said, you are gods"? If he called them gods to whom the word of God came (and

---

141. Ehrman, *Jesus: Apocalyptic Prophet*, pp. 165.

142. Bultmann, *History of the Synoptic Tradition*, pp. 155–156.

143. Gershom Scholem, *On the Kabbalah and Its Symbolism*. Trans. Ralph Manheim (New York: Schocken Books, 1969), pp. 68–75.

144. Ehrman, *Jesus: Apocalyptic Prophet*, pp. 173.

145. Ehrman, *Jesus: Apocalyptic Prophet*, pp. 165, 188.

scripture cannot be broken),'" etc. This is like throwing an asbestos log on the fire. John's gospel simply does not qualify.

So was Jesus an apocalyptic prophet of the new millennium, as fine scholars like Schweitzer, Weiss, Bultmann, Jeremias, and Ehrman have contended? Perhaps. All I can say is, "Now we see in a glass darkly."

CHAPTER TWO
AGNOSTIC APOLOGIST

IS THERE A MAN BEHIND THE CURTAIN?

When Bart Ehrman's book *Did Jesus Exist?* appeared, it generated a range of reactions. His usual critics were relieved to see him defending at least the existence of a historical Jesus. But many of his well-deserved fans suggested he was being inconsistent: given the skeptical estimate of the gospels in his previous works, how could he now make such an about face and defend the gospels as sources of knowledge about a historical Jesus? But a more patient scrutiny of both *Jesus: Apocalyptic Prophet of the New Millennium* and *Did Jesus Exist?* shows that there is no inconsistency. Think of when they weigh you at the doctor's office: you step on the scale, and the nurse adjusts the counters on the upper and the lower calibrated bars, one to the left, the other to the right, and thus they reckon the extent to which your carcass burdens the earth. (In my case, I'm always surprised when the scales don't crash through the floor.) Well, that's kind of what Bart is doing between these two books: pushing the one metal peg away from the "historical" side, then balancing it off with the other one as he pushes it in the other direction.

Did Jesus Exist? is an attempt to demonstrate the folly of Jesus Mythicism, the theory that there was no historical Jesus, that behind the gospels stands no historical figure. Bart regards it as a crackpot opinion like unto the belief in Roswell aliens, Holocaust denial, and 9/11 Trutherism. His criticisms are refreshingly blunt. Though I am one of his chief targets, I must say he has treated me respectfully, and I plan on doing the same here as I attempt to reply to his refutation. I'm going to be suggesting that Bart, though now an agnostic, seems to retain a good bit of the outlook and approach of conservative evangelicals, resulting in an ironically apologetical[1] treatment. He has, so to speak, moved over several notches but is still playing by the same basic rules.

I guess you might say I think not only that there is no great and powerful Oz, but that there's not even a man behind the curtain. Bart, on the other hand, agrees Oz is an illusion, but if you pull back the curtain, you'll find the anti-climactic Professor Marvel.

THINKING INSIDE THE BOX

Is Christ Mythicism some kind of novelty, dreamed up by skeptics living far enough after the events to be able to get away with it? Bart and many others think so. "The idea that Jesus did not exist is a modern notion. It has no ancient precedents."[2] "Even the enemies of the Jesus movement thought [that Jesus had existed]; among their many slurs against the religion, his nonexistence is never one of them."[3] I'm not so sure of that. Justin Martyr ascribes to his dialogue partner Trypho (perhaps to be identified with the historical Rabbi Tarfon) the allegation, "You have received a futile rumour, and have created some sort of Christ for yourselves."[4] We always hear apologists explain this away as if it meant, "You Christians have nominated your own Christ/Messiah." "You Christians pretend your Jesus was the Christ." But that's rather different. Would Trypho have said the partisans of Simon bar Kochba had "created" their "own messiah"? I don't think so. It seems less contrived to take Trypho as charging that the Christian Savior was a figment of pious imagination. Bart

---

1. I prefer the old-style "apologetical" (in this connection) to the now more common "apologetic" because the former is less likely to be mistaken as denoting "apologizing."

2. Bart D. Ehrman, *Did Jesus Exist? The Historical Argument for Jesus of Nazareth* (New York: HarperOne/HarperCollins, 2012), p. 96.

3. Ehrman, *Did Jesus Exist?*, pp. 171–172.

4. R.P.C. Hanson, ed. and trans., *Selections from Justin Martyr's Dialogue with Trypho, a Jew.* World Christian Books No. 49. Third Series (New York: Association Press, 1964), p. 23.

points out that throughout the *Dialogue*, Trypho acknowledges that Jesus did exist but declines to accept him as the Messiah. Is that so clear? To me it sounds as if Trypho is being made to grant the reality of the crucified Jesus purely for the sake of argument: could such an individual as you describe have qualified as the Christ?

> Trypho: Let Him be recognised as Lord and Christ and God, as the Scriptures declare, by you of the Gentiles, who have from His name been all called Christians; but we who are servants of God that made this same [Christ], do not require to confess or worship Him. (Chapter 64)[5]

Similarly, Celsus, the second-century critic of Christianity, says, "It is clear to me that the writings of the Christians are a lie, and that your fables have not been well enough constructed to conceal this monstrous fiction." Does he elsewhere speak of Christ as a historical figure? Not necessarily. Origen says,

> Celsus pretends to grant that the scriptures may be true when they speak of "cures or resurrection or a few loaves feeding many people, from which many fragments were left over, or any other monstrous tales," as he thinks, "related by the disciples." And he goes on to say: "Come, let us believe that these miracles really were done by you." Then he puts them on a level with "the works of sorcerers who profess to do wonderful miracles." (*Contra Celsum* I:68)[6]

And then there's 2 Peter 1:16–18, "We did not follow cleverly devised myths when we told you of the power and coming of our Lord Jesus Christ." Let me get this straight: the author, by pretending to be an eyewitness apostle, is perpetrating the very deceit he is trying to refute! But his fraudulent claim about being on-site at the Transfiguration is not the only thing at issue. Some are alleging that "we," "Simeon Peter" and his colleagues, were devising myths about the *coming* of Jesus. That sounds to me like an accusation that the apostles fabricated the whole business.

I read Bart as accepting the "Jesus as a committee product" model of

---

5. Trans. Marcus Dods and George Reith, rev. Kevin Knight. http://www.newadvent.org/fathers/01285.htm.

6. Origen, *Contra Celsum*. Trans. Henry Chadwick (Cambridge: Cambridge University Press, 1965), p. 62. Chadwick italicized the portions of Celsus' text quoted by Origen, but I have instead placed them in quotation marks.

mythicism. I consider this a straw man (though some mythicists do, I think, espouse it). I think Bart's assumption creates a fault line running beneath his whole argument. What do you make of these excerpts from *Did Jesus Exist?*

all within a generation or so of Jesus himself, assuming he lived.[7]

Aramaic Jews in Jesus' native land were telling stories about him well before Paul wrote his letters in the 50s of the Common Era, arguably from within a few years of the traditional date of his death.[8]

some of these traditions must have originated in Aramaic-speaking communities of Palestine, probably in the 30s CE, within several years at least of the traditional date of the death of Jesus.[9]

And so the book of Acts provides further evidence from outside the Gospels that Christians from earliest times believed that Jesus actually lived.[10]

at least seven Gospel accounts of Jesus, all of them entirely or partially independent of one another, survived from within a century of the traditional date of his death.[11]

And it is important to remember that Jews were saying that Jesus was the crucified messiah in the early 30s . . . this belief in the crucified messiah goes all the way back to a short time after Jesus' death.[12]

---

7. Ehrman, *Did Jesus Exist?*, p. 76.

8. Ehrman, *Did Jesus Exist?*, p. 91.

9. Ehrman, *Did Jesus Exist?*, p. 92–93. "There is very little dispute that some of the Gospel stories originated in Aramaic and that therefore they go back to the earliest stages of the Christian movement in Palestine" (p. 88). Couldn't they have originated in Antioch, Syria? They spoke Aramaic there, too. And Antiochene traditions need not be so old.

10. Ehrman, *Did Jesus Exist?*, p. 109. Interestingly, Bart elsewhere dismisses Acts as a fiction and a forgery, in Bart D. Ehrman, *Forgery and Counterforgery: The Use of Literary Deceit in Early Christian Polemics* (New York: Oxford University Press, 2013), pp. 263–282. How confident should we be that Acts, then, is a source of *any* facts about early Christianity?

11. Ehrman, *Did Jesus Exist?*, p. 97.

12. Ehrman, *Did Jesus Exist?*, p. 164.

We are talking about a large number of sources, dispersed over a remarkably broad geographical expanse, many of them dating to the years immediately after Jesus's alleged life.[13]

These oral traditions about Jesus . . . started in the early 30s, a year or two after Jesus allegedly died.[14]

our Gospel sources . . . spoke of the historical Jesus already by the early 30s, within at least a year of the traditional date of his death.[15]

Palestinian traditions that can readily be dated to 31 or 32 CE, just a year or so after the traditional death of Jesus.[16]

Plainly, Bart supposes that mythicists think the Jesus figure did pop up at the time assigned by Christian tradition to a historical Jesus, but that this Jesus was a committee fabrication by the apostles who had in fact never seen or known such a person. Did somebody "invent" Jesus[17] at the same point in history when the gospels depict Jesus appearing on the scene?

But if there was no historical Jesus, as we wild-eyed, tinfoil hat-wearing Mythicists suggest, the bottom falls out of the whole thing. The emergence of Jesus Christ looks to me more like that moment when, in the process of evolution, enough small mutations accumulate to cross the taxonomical line to count as a new species. It was a long process of myths morphing and mutating. There is no way to determine when the timeline began, no way to say what or when is "early." This is why it is way off target to say, for instance, "In nearly all our sources Peter was Jesus's most intimate companion and confidant for his entire public ministry after his baptism."[18] That presupposes the factual character of the narrative, which is just the point at issue. Invoking the possibly

---

13. Ehrman, *Did Jesus Exist?*, p. 171.

14. Ehrman, *Did Jesus Exist?*, p. 206.

15. Ehrman, *Did Jesus Exist?*, p. 248.

16. Ehrman, *Did Jesus Exist?*, p. 251.

17. Ehrman, *Did Jesus Exist?*, p. 221.

18. Ehrman, *Did Jesus Exist?*, p. 145.

fictive Peter character[19] to attest the historicity of Jesus is like using the empty tomb *story* as evidence for the factuality of the resurrection *story*. The portrayal of Peter in the gospels is likely no more historical than that in 2 Peter.

CUTTING JESUS DOWN TO SIZE[20]

Bart addresses the common Mythicist objection to Jesus' historical existence: how could contemporary writers have failed to record a Jesus who worked the amazing feats the gospels describe? Their crashing silence implies there was no such historical figure to report on. But does it have to be all or nothing? Contemporaries would probably not have taken much notice of any historically plausible Jesus, an itinerant sage and faith healer, which would have been a dime a dozen. How much coverage do you think Oral Roberts is going to get in American History textbooks?

> [A]nyone as spectacular as Jesus allegedly was, who did so many miracles and fantastic deeds, would certainly have been discussed or at least mentioned in pagan sources if he really did exist. Surely anyone who could heal the sick, cast out demons, walk on water, feed the multitudes with only a few loaves, and raise the dead would be talked about! The reason this line of reasoning is in error is that we are not asking whether Jesus really did miracles and, if so, why they (and he) are not mentioned by pagan sources. We are asking whether Jesus of Nazareth actually existed. Only after establishing that he did exist can we go on to ask if he did miracles. If we decide that he did, only then can we revisit the question of why no one, in that case, mentions him. But we may also decide that the historical Jesus was not a miraculous being but a purely human being. In that case it is no surprise that Roman sources never mention him, just as it is no surprise that these same sources never mention any of his uncles, aunts, cousins, nieces, or nephews —or in fact nearly any other Jew of his day.[21]

---

19. Arthur Drews, *The Legend of Saint Peter*. Trans. Frank R. Zindler (Austin: American Atheist Press, 1997).

20. I'm shamelessly stealing this subtitle from G.A. Wells, *Cutting Jesus Down to Size: What Higher Criticism Has Achieved and Where It Leaves Christianity* (Chicago: Open Court, 2009).

21. Ehrman, *Did Jesus Exist?*, pp. 43–44.

But isn't this like asking whether the historical Superman really had superhuman powers "beyond those of mortal men"? Should we decide that there was indeed a historical Superman but that he was merely Clark Kent?[22] "And if Saint George had killed a dragonfly instead of a dragon, who would remember him?"[23]

Bart continues this line of reasoning (or, should we say, of "Rationalism"?).

> If you can find stories that are independently attested in multiple sources *and* that pass the criterion of dissimilarity, you can establish, then, a higher level of probability that you are dealing with a historical account. It may have legendary features, but the heart of the story may be historical.[24]

> You can shape a tradition about Jesus any way you want so that it looks highly legendary. But that has no bearing on the question of whether beneath the legendary shaping lies the core of the historical event.[25]

Let's try to imagine what these hypothetical pre-legendary originals might have looked like.

> On that day, when evening had come, he said to them, "Come, let us go to the other side." And leaving the crowd, they took him with them, just as he was, in the boat. And other boats were with him. And a great storm of wind arose, and the waves beat into the boat so that the boat capsized. But the other boats

---

22.   Dennis R. MacDonald, *Mythologizing Jesus: From Jewish Teacher to Epic Hero* (Lanham: Roman & Littlefield, 2015), "Introduction: The Christian Superhero," pp. 1–11.

23.   Movie version of Jerome Lawrence and Robert E. Lee, *Inherit the Wind* (New York: Bantam Books, 1963), p. 26.

24.   Ehrman, *Did Jesus Exist?*, p. 188.

25.   Ehrman, *Did Jesus Exist?*, p. 190. In our debate on October 21, 2016, Bart denied that he meant to suggest that individual stories about Jesus grew in the telling, but rather that *on the whole* the Jesus figure generated stories that were legendary to the core. But this seems to represent a change of opinion compared with the passage from *Did Jesus Exist?* I have quoted here, where the evolution/embellishment of particular stories is in view. Also see Bart D. Ehrman, *How Jesus Became God: The Exaltation of a Jewish Preacher from Galilee* (New York: HarperOne/ HarperCollins, 2014), p. 13: "Scholars have had to ... determine which stories, and which parts of stories, are historically accurate ... and which represent later embellishments ..."

stayed afloat, and Jesus and the disciples swam to them and, climbing aboard, were saved. (The historical core of Mark 4:35–41?)

They came to the other side of the sea, to the country of the Gerasenes. And a great herd of swine was grazing on the hillside. But immediately some wild dogs began to bark, and the swine took fright and stampeded down the steep hillside, and they were drowned in the sea. (The original story behind Mark 5:1–13?)

And when Jesus had crossed again in the boat to the other side, a great crowd gathered about him; and he was beside the sea. Then came one of the rulers of the synagogue, Jairus by name; and seeing him, he fell at his feet, and besought him, saying, "My little daughter is at the point of death. Come and lay your hands on her, so that she may be made well, and live." While he was still speaking, there came from the ruler's house some who said, "Your daughter is dead. Why trouble the Teacher any further?" And Jesus said to him, "Poor man! You have my sympathies. Now who's up for lunch?" (The historical core of Mark 5:21–23, 35?)

And they went away in the boat to a lonely place by themselves. Now many saw them going, and recognized them, and they ran there on foot from all the towns and got there ahead of them. As he went ashore he saw a great throng, and he had compassion on them, because they were like sheep without a shepherd; and he began to teach them many things. And when it grew late, his disciples came to him and said, "This is a lonely place, and the hour is now late; send them away to go into the country and the surrounding villages and buy themselves something to eat." And he answered them, "You have said it." And he dispersed the crowd. And they all ate and were satisfied. (The historical core of Mark 6:32–44?)

Immediately he dismissed the crowd and he made his disciples get into the boat to go to the other side, to Bethsaida. And he got into the boat with them. And when evening came, the boat was out on the sea. (The historical core of Mark 6:45–51?)

On the third day there was a marriage at Cana in Galilee, and the mother of Jesus was there; Jesus also was invited to the marriage, with his disciples. When her wine gave out, the mother of Jesus said to him, "Have they no more wine?" Now six stone jars were standing there, each holding twenty or thirty gallons of wine. Jesus said to them, "Now draw some out, and take it to the steward of the feast." So they took it. When the steward of the feast tasted the wine, he called the bridegroom and said to him, "Every man serves the good wine first; and when men have drunk freely, then the poor wine; but you have kept the good wine until now." (The historical core of John 2:1–11?)

What's left? Who would have even remembered these unremarkable incidents if they in fact happened? *And why would it have occurred to anyone to embellish them?* In terms of evolution, these tepid anecdotes would have had no survival value. To treat such gospel episodes the way Bart suggests is to trim away the element that would have caused the story to be passed on in the first place. Unless of course the whole thing *began* as a fiction or legend. It sounds like the old time Protestant Rationalism ridiculed by D.F. Strauss.[26] Boiling the spectacular down to the mundane, just to provide a toehold on historical reality. This is a modern version of ancient Euhemerism: the attempt to salvage the myths of gods and demigods by positing they were mythologized versions of ancient celebrities. Osiris was a king, Ares a mighty warrior, Asclepius a doctor, Hercules a weight-lifter, Apollo the owner of a tanning salon.

I am reminded of Martin Kähler's wholesale repudiation of the Liberal scholarly quest for the historical Jesus. He believed that the gospel Jesus, the Christ of faith, was the same as the Jesus who lived in history. The records of him might not be flawlessly accurate, but their depiction of Jesus Christ had to be substantially sound because, without such an entity at the beginning, Christianity could never have begun. The cause had to be adequate to the effect.

How can this figure of Jesus—this tentative residue remaining after the work of critical subtraction—which must now, for the first time, be ingeniously evoked from the mist of the past, be the object of faith for all Christians? And finally, how can this figure have been the object of faith hitherto in spite of this disguise which we are now so "fortunate" as to be able to strip away?[27]

26. David Friedrich Strauss, *The Life of Jesus Critically Examined*. Trans. George Eliot (Mary Ann Evans) Lives of Jesus Series (Philadelphia: Fortress Press, 1972).

27. Martin Kähler, *The So-called Historical Jesus and the Historic Biblical Christ*. Trans. Carl E. Braaten. Seminar Editions (Philadelphia: Fortress Press, 1964), p. 103. Similarly, Friedrich Schleiermacher, *The Life of Jesus*. Trans. S. Maclean Gilmour. Lives of Jesus Series (Philadelphia: Fortress Press, 1975), p. 82: "it is clear that those who take their

Again, Kähler was practically as far as one could get from Bart Ehrman's position, the very position against which he fought. And he was not on my side either. But I think he was on to something here. Could the Christian religion have begun with the modest historical figure Bart and his colleagues have whittled from the oak of the gospels' Jesus Christ? But Kähler was wrong, too: there was no such historical figure. Jesus possesses the grandeur of the mythical demigods because that's what he was. *That's* why no contemporary historian mentions him.

Likewise, evangelical scholar F.F. Bruce sees a particular advantage of form criticism for apologetics. This, he says, is the result: "no matter how far back we may press our researches into the roots of the gospel story, no matter how we classify the gospel material, we never arrive at a non-supernatural Jesus."[28] But if, like Bart Ehrman and myself, you deem the gospel miracles to be legendary, what does a Jesus who is supernatural to the core imply? A mythical hero like Hercules, that's what.

THE HERESY OF HEARSAY

Did Jesus come in for mention by ancient historians? Bart regards the well-known statements of Pliny the Younger and Cornelius Tacitus about "Christos" and/or "Chrestus" as textually authentic (as they may well be). But, as he readily admits, these writers quite likely learned what they said about "Christ" (not "Jesus") from Christians.[29] Here are multiple attestations—of hearsay. "Tacitus . . . shows that high-ranking Roman officials of the early second century knew that Jesus had lived and had been executed by the governor of Judea."[30] Wait a second. Tacitus "knew"? Again, "it is completely possible that they themselves had simply heard stories about Jesus. Indirectly, then, Tacitus and (possibly) Josephus provide independent attestation to Jesus's existence from outside the

---

departure from the attempt to represent the life of Christ completely as a genuinely human life usually end up by conceiving Christ in such a way that no intelligible reason remains for making him in any way such an object of faith."

28. F.F. Bruce, *The New Testament Documents: Are They Reliable?* (Grand Rapids: Eerdmans, 1960), p. 33.

29. Ehrman, *Did Jesus Exist?*, pp. 52, 55–56.

30. Ehrman, *Did Jesus Exist?*, p. 56.

Gospels."[31] If you ask me, "possibly" and "indirectly" add up to a pretty slim reed. The weakness and scantiness of these "attestations" only accentuate the paucity of the supposed non-Christian documentation of a historical Jesus. "Is that all you've got?"

And then we have to ask, why are the gospels' witness to Jesus any *better* founded? "Within a couple of decades of the traditional date of his death, we have numerous accounts of his life found in a broad geographical span."[32] And

> stories about Jesus circulated widely throughout the major urban areas of the Mediterranean from a very early time. Otherwise it is impossible to explain all the written sources that emerged in the middle and end of the first century. These sources are independent of one another. . . . Where did all these sources come from? They could not have been dreamed up independently of one another by Christians all over the map because they agree on too many of the fundamentals. Instead, they are based on oral traditions.[33]

In other words, hearsay, just like Pliny and Tacitus. Thomas Arnold famously said the resurrection of Jesus was "the best-attested fact in history. But, replied the critics, its being well attested only proves that a lot of people believed it, not that it happened."[34]

TESTIMONIUM FLIMSIANUS

Bart has just added our old friend Flavius Josephus to the mix. The famous (notorious?) passage in Josephus' *Antiquities of the Jews*, the so-called *Testimonium Flavianum*, is longer than the brief snippets from Tacitus and Pliny, so there is more to argue about. Here's the passage.

> *About this time* there lived *Jesus, a wise man* if indeed one ought to call him a man. For he was one who wrought surprising feats and was a teacher of such people as accept the truth gladly. He won over *many Jews and many* of the

31. Ehrman, *Did Jesus Exist?*, p. 97.

32. Ehrman, *Did Jesus Exist?*, pp. 82–83.

33. Ehrman, *Did Jesus Exist?*, p. 86.

34. R.G. Collingwood, *The Idea of History* (New York: Oxford University Press, 1946), pp. 135–136.

Greeks. *He was the Messiah.* When *Pilate,* upon hearing him accused by men of the highest standing among us, *had condemned him to be crucified,* those who had in the first place come to love him did not *cease.* On the third day *he appeared to them* restored to *life.* For *the prophets* of God had prophesied these and myriads of other *marvellous* things *about him.* And the tribe of *the* Christians, so called after him, has still up to now, not disappeared.[35]

"The majority of scholars of early Judaism, and experts on Josephus, think . . . that one or more Christian scribes 'touched up' the passage a bit. If one takes out the obviously Christian comments, the passage may have been rather innocuous, reading something like this:

> At this time there appeared Jesus, a wise man. He was a doer of startling deeds, a teacher of people who receive the truth with pleasure. And he gained a following both among many Jews and among many of Greek origin. When Pilate, because of an accusation made by the leading men among us, condemned him to the cross, those who had loved him previously did not cease to do so. And up until this very day the tribe of Christians, named after him, has not died out.[36]

Bart ventures that "The pared-down version of Josephus . . . , contains very little that could have been used by the early Christian writers to defend Jesus and his followers from attacks by pagan intellectuals."[37] His point is that the unspectacular version cannot have begun as a wholesale Christian interpolation, so it must be genuine to Josephus, right? But my question would be: Why would *Josephus* mention such a nonentity? Who does *The Daily Planet* report on, Superman or Clark Kent? Bart comes very close to realizing this when he says,

> There is certainly no reason to think if Jesus lived that Josephus must have mentioned him. He doesn't mention most Jews of the first century. . . . Josephus does not mention 99 percent of them—or rather, more than 99 percent. So why would he mention Jesus? You cannot say that he would have

---

35. Josephus, *Antiquities of the Jews* 18.63, Tr. I. H. Feldman, Loeb Classical Library, vol. 9, pp. 49ff.

36. Ehrman, *Did Jesus Exist?*, pp. 60–61.

37. Ehrman, *Did Jesus Exist?*, p. 62.

mentioned Jesus because anyone who did all those amazing miraculous deeds would surely be mentioned. As I pointed out earlier, the question of what Jesus actually *did* has to come after we establish that he lived, not before.[38]

But what this tells me is that the scaled-down version of the passage makes as little sense as the authentic words of Josephus as they do as a Christian interpolation. I haven't taken a survey to determine the majority opinion on the question, but I suspect it is changing. Paul J. Hopper, an authority on the linguistics of Classical literature, has, in my opinion, decisively refuted the "scaled-down non-interpolation" theory. He compares the *Testimonium* treatment of Pilate with the adjacent Pilate episodes in the context and concludes that the *Testimonium* is after all a Christian interpolation intended to rehabilitate the image of Jesus and to shift the blame for his death from Pilate to the Jews. (I ask your indulgence for a pretty long quotation.)

> Typically, a narrative moves along in short segments consisting of a cluster of aorist and imperfect verbs and supported by explanatory states and actions presented through participles, which may be present, aorist, or imperfect, and infinitives (nonfinite verb forms), and, quite often, nominalized verb forms. The Pilate episodes in Book 18 of the *Jewish Antiquities* generally adhere to these same principles.[39] The various narrative forms described above also appear in the *Testimonium Flavianum*, and the differences between their normal functions in Josephus's account of the doings of Pontius Pilate and their apparent use in the *Testimonium* are worthy of comment.[40]

> The finite aorists report in a broad scale the past events concerning Jesus and his followers. That is, unlike the event reporting in the other Pontius Pilate episodes, we are not told in detail what Jesus did. Jesus is throughout a passive participant rather than an active agent. The aorist verbs that are

---

38. Ehrman, *Did Jesus Exist?*, p. 66.

39. Paul J. Hopper, "A Narrative Anomaly in Josephus: *Jewish Antiquities* xviii, 63." https://www.academia.edu/9494231/A_Narrative_Anomaly_in_Josephus, p. 157. See D.M. Murdock's valuable commentary on this important article in her "Josephus's Testimonium Flavianum Examined Linguistically: Greek Analysis Demonstrates the Passage a Forgery In Toto." https://www.academia.edu/10463098/Josephus_s_Testimonium_Flavianum_Examined_Linguistically_Greek_Analysis_Demonstrates_the_Passage_a_Forgery_In_Toto

40. Hopper, "Narrative Anomaly," p. 160.

used to describe Jesus reflect this passivity: *Epēgageto* ["drew over to him"] is a mediopassive (middle voice) verb, and *ephanē* ["appeared"] is passive and also nonvolitional; that is, a supernatural force is at least complicit in Jesus's reappearance. The other two aorists concern not Jesus but his followers, and, curiously, both are in the negative: *ouk epausanto* and *ouk epelipe*. We have seen that aorist verbs typically report single prominent actions associated with the protagonist of the story. They play a crucial role in the event structure of the narrative, and while they cannot alone support the story line, they work to anchor clusters of other kinds of verbs to create episodes. This could hardly be said of the aorists in the *Testimonium*, however. The aorists here seem to belong in a different genre altogether, one which argues and defends rather than reports. The use of the negative in two of the four aorists suggests something else. Negatives point implicitly to the corresponding affirmative. They belong in the contexts of denial, of response to a challenge. They suggest here that the author is contradicting unheard voices that question the truth of the chronicle. There is an element of protest in the voice of the author of the *Testimonium* that is impossible to attribute to Josephus, the sober historian: "There must be some truth in all this, because his followers haven't gone away, in fact they haven't stopped worshipping him."[41]

Whereas in the other Pilate episodes he is the chief protagonist, in the *Testimonium* Pilate's role is unmistakably subordinate. He is mentioned in the genitive absolute construction . . . his name is in the genitive case, and his action in sentencing Jesus is brushed off in four words, one of them a perfect participle, also in the genitive case. Whereas in the other Pilate passages Pilate is depicted as going out of his way to act with premeditation . . . , and as the explicit instigator of acts of repression against Jews, there is now a distinct indirectness. . . . So Pilate, the decisive Roman boss of the other three Pilate episodes, ruthless scourge of the Jews and despiser of their laws, now appears as the compliant puppet of the Jewish hierarchy. But the actions of the elders and Pilate are themselves secondary to the main point of the passage as identified by the aorist verbs, namely Jesus's resurrection and the continued devotion of Jesus's followers, which are presented as skeletal happenings for the entire passage. Again, the grammatical structure of the *Testimonium* is at odds with that of the sequence of Pontius Pilate, in which the chief protagonist is Pilate himself.[42]

---

41. Hopper, "Narrative Anomaly," pp. 162–163.

42. Hopper, "Narrative Anomaly," p. 163.

Who would have wanted to mount such a defense? Another innovative article, this one by Ken Olson, answers that question cogently. The *Testimonium* first appears in Eusebius' *Demonstration of the Gospel*. Our copies of Josephus are centuries later than that, and many scholars have suggested the *Testimonium* was Eusebius' writing, falsely ascribed to Josephus (just the sort of thing Bart discusses in his book *Forgery and Counter-Forgery: The Use of Literary Deceit in Early Christian Polemics*) that crept into our later copies. Olson shows how, whereas the *Testimonium* passage sticks out like a sore thumb in the text of the *Antiquities* where scribes inserted it, thinking they were restoring an accidental scribal omission, the passage fits its Eusebian context so well that, well, you'd think it was made for the purpose. And it was. The particular things said about Jesus in the *Testimonium* all address specific pagan criticisms of Christian beliefs about Jesus current in Eusebius' own day and to which he is responding in the context.

> What Eusebius is seeking to show in Book III is that Jesus has not only a human nature, but a divine one as well. He goes about this by arguing that Jesus' coming as Christ was foretold in prophecy, that he was not a deceiver but a teacher of true doctrines, that he performed superhuman feats, and that he did not perform these feats by sorcery. At the end of Book III, Eusebius concludes that a man who was not a sorcerer but a man of good character (as Porphyry himself allowed he was), yet could perform wonders beyond human ability, must necessarily have been superhuman in his nature. As an ostensibly outside witness to the fact that the man Jesus was not merely human in his nature but evidenced the things foretold of the Christ in prophecy, the *Testimonium* represents an encapsulation of Eusebius' argument. It therefore has its most plausible *Sitz-im-Leben* in the pagan-Christian controversies of the fourth century. This was the period in which the question of whether Jesus was merely a wise man or something more was being debated. The first half of the *Testimonium* seems to address precisely this issue.[43]

And so on.

Bart Ehrman sneers at Mythicist suggestions that this or that "historical

---

43. Ken Olson, "A Eusebian Reading of the *Testimonium Flavianum*," in Aaron Johnson and Jeremy Shott, eds., *Eusebius of Caesarea: Tradition and Innovations* (CHS Research Bulletin, vol. 1.0.11), http://chs.harvard.edu/CHS/article/display/5871

Jesus-leaning" passage in Paul's epistles is a subsequent interpolation (see below): "Here we find, again, textual studies driven by convenience: if a passage contradicts your views, simply claim that it was not written by the author."[44] But aren't "consensus" scholars (Bart's favorite kind) doing the same darn thing with the *Testimonium Flavianum*? They dearly want Josephus to have mentioned Jesus, but the passage as it stands, they admit, cannot have been the work of a non-Christian Jew like Josephus. It's a bad text for their purposes, so they redact it, as Matthew redacted Mark, in order to make it suitable for their use. What the hell? Just exercise the line-item veto: remove the offending passages. *Now* we can use it as evidence to establish a historical Jesus. But no. No you can't.

BUILDING A BRIDGE TO NOWHERE

Bart believes he can build a bridge from the canonical gospels over to the historical Jesus. (Or at least it should go *most* of the way, so that, as Francis A. Schaeffer used to say, it will take only a *step* of faith, not a *leap* of faith). Suppose the gospels themselves are based on prior gospels? That helps. But if we run out of planks, maybe we can close the rest of the distance by tossing sturdy ropes of oral tradition over to the other side. The thinking here matches that of F.F. Bruce:

> If the [early] dates suggested for [the gospels'] composition . . . are anything like correct then no very long space of time separated the recording of the evangelic events from the events themselves. If, however, it can be shown with reasonable probability that these records themselves depend in whole or in part on still earlier documents, then the case for the trustworthiness of the gospel narrative is all the stronger.[45]

In the same vein, Bart enumerates the pre-gospel gospels.

> We are talking about at least four sources: Mark, Q, M, and L, the latter two of which could easily have represented several, or even many, other written narratives. Many leading scholars of Mark think that it, too, was compiled

---

44. Ehrman, *Did Jesus Exist?*, p. 253.

45. Bruce, *New Testament Documents*, p. 30.

not just of oral traditions that had been circulating down to the author's day but of various written sources.[46]

If this is right, then not just our later synoptics but even our earliest surviving Gospel was based on multiple sources.[47]

Matthew and Luke did indeed use Mark, but significant portions of both Gospels are not related in any way to Mark's accounts. And in these sections of their Gospels Matthew and Luke record extensive, independent traditions about Jesus' life, teachings, and death.[48]

But the reality is that Luke inherited oral traditions about Jesus and his connection with Nazareth, and he recorded what he had heard.[49]

A lot of stories are found only in Luke . . . , such as Jesus' parables of the prodigal son and the good Samaritan. Luke must have gotten these from somewhere else: scholars have long offered good reasons for thinking Luke didn't just make everything all up.[50]

By contrast, I think there are quite compelling reasons to think Luke *did* make (almost) everything up, everything he didn't get from Mark and Q. One reason is that his parables share a distinctive authorial voice. They tend to be somewhat detailed, even though brief, narratives. They are often introduced with a note interpreting them in advance (Luke 14:7; 15:1–2; 17:5; 18:1, 9; 19:11). And several times (Luke 12:17–19; 15:18; 16:3–4; 18:5; 20:13 [added to the Markan original]) the protagonists come to a point of crisis and reflect, "What shall I do? I shall . . ." Walter Schmithals[51] demonstrates to my satisfaction that all the uniquely Lukan parables are either drawn from general Hellenistic Judaism (Good Samaritan, Rich Man and Lazarus, Rich Fool) or

---

46. Ehrman, *Did Jesus Exist?*, p. 81.

47. Ehrman, *Did Jesus Exist?*, p 82; cf., Bruce, *New Testament Documents*, p. 45.

48. Ehrman, *Did Jesus Exist?*, p. 75.

49. Ehrman, *Did Jesus Exist?*, pp. 73–74.

50. Ehrman, *Did Jesus Exist?*, p. 81.

51. Walter Schmithals, "The Parabolic Teachings in the Synoptic Gospels." Trans. Darrell J. Doughty. *Journal of Higher Criticism*.4/2 (Fall 1997), pp. 3–32.

composed by Luke himself to serve his special interests in persecution, prayer for deliverance from it, forgiveness for those who fell away and sought readmission to the church, etc. Schmithals argues that all the uniquely Matthean parables are that evangelist's own creations. He notes, too, that, if Luke and Matthew were really drawing on streams of oral tradition, it seems remarkable that we should find no overlaps, i.e., non-verbatim parallels, between them.

In the preface to his narrative, Luke refers to numerous predecessors:

> Inasmuch as many have undertaken to compile a narrative of the things which have been accomplished among us, just as they were delivered to us by those who from the beginning were eyewitnesses and ministers of the word, it seemed good to me also, having followed all things closely for some time past, to write an orderly account for you, most excellent Theophilus, that you may know the truth concerning the things of which you have been informed. (Luke 1:1–4)

According to Bart, "Luke writes his [gospel] simply because he thinks he can do a better job."[52] But is there any note of criticism of his predecessors as inadequate? I don't see one. I think Luke is trying to do what Bart is trying to do, to provide a (possibly fictive) paper trail back to Jesus. The fabricators of Islamic *hadith* (ostensible traditions of the Prophet Muhammad and his teaching) always supplied an attestation chain (*isnad*) for their fabrications. "I heard this from Abdul Alhazred, who heard it from Ras al Ghul, who heard it from Kareem Abdul Jabbar, who heard it from A-hab the A-rab, who heard it from the Sheikh of Araby, who heard it from the Sultan of Swing, who heard it from Abu-bekr, who heard it from the Prophet, peace be upon him." Luke is supplying an *isnad*. It is part and parcel of Luke's apologetic motif of eyewitness apostolic guarantors. As Chares H. Talbert[53] demonstrates, Luke shares the approach of the second-century Apologists[54] who sought to establish their copyright on Christianity, buttressing it with the only legitimate exegesis of scripture against Jewish, Gnostic, and other interpretations. This is why

---

52. Ehrman, *Did Jesus Exist?*, p. 260.

53. Charles H. Talbert, *Luke and the Gnostics: An Examination of the Lucan Purpose* (New York: Abingdon Press, 1966), Chapter I. "The Authentic Witness," pp. 17–32.

54. Richard I. Pervo, *Dating Acts: Between the Evangelists and the Apologists* (Santa Rosa: Polebridge Press, 2006).

Luke portrays the risen Jesus "opening the scriptures" (Luke 24:32), explaining to the apostles all the references to him in the Law, the Prophets, and the Psalms (Luke 24:27, 44).

There is a fine point in the apologetical exploitation of Source Criticism that we shouldn't skip over. Q is a helpful theoretical model for organizing the data of the gospels, but I am not sure it deserves the status of a known pre-gospel source. Ditto M and L. Source Criticism plugs into gospel scholarship in a different way.

> We do not know . . . whether M (or L) was only one source or a group of sources, whether it was written or oral. It could represent a single document available to the author of Matthew (or Luke), or several documents, or a number of stories that were transmitted orally, or a combination of all of these things. Since these sources also predated the Gospels into which they were incorporated, they, too, could provide early access to the sayings and deeds of Jesus.[55]

I think Bart's several brief comments on Q imply the weakness of any appeal to Q as an early document. He calls it a "document that does not exist."[56] He pegs its origin "possibly in the 50s or 60s CE. If so, it represents our earliest—though nonsurviving!—source for the historical Jesus."[57] "Let me repeat: Q is a source that *we don't have*."[58] He claps it on the back: "not bad for a nonexistent source!"[59]

And he seems reluctant to treat Q as a real source document, except as one more link in a hypothetical chain to connect the gospels to a historical Jesus. He does not bother concealing his disdain for the theories of John Kloppenborg, Burton L. Mack, and others that we can stratify Q, the result being an early Cynic or quasi-Cynic collection of sayings with neither Christology nor eschatology in evidence, implying that Q¹ was the product of a Jesus movement who viewed Jesus primarily as a sage, a kind of new Socrates or Diogenes. And presumably the death of Jesus held no particular importance for them.

---

55. Ehrman, *Jesus: Apocalyptic Prophet*, pp. 82–83.

56. Ehrman, *Jesus: Apocalyptic Prophet*, p. 80.

57. Ehrman, *Jesus: Apocalyptic Prophet*, p. 82.

58. Ehrman, *Jesus: Apocalyptic Prophet*, p. 133.

59. Ehrman, *Jesus: Apocalyptic Prophet*, p. 132.

Though Bart's skepticism toward certain trendy historical Jesus theories is commendable, in this particular case, I think he may be selling Kloppenborg and Mack short. At least I take a couple of their arguments more seriously than Bart does.

For instance, Mack notes how, once you try the Q stratification model on for size, something interesting comes into focus, implying that perhaps the stratifiers are onto something. Once you bracket the Christology and eschatology, you get a sequence of seven topical groups of Cynic-flavored sayings.[60] It's a lot like extracting the Exodus 34 set of Ten Commandments from all the adjacent verbiage, which is then seen to be an obscuring thicket of scribal glossing. Sounds okay to me. And if we can differentiate tree rings in the trunk of Q, it is entirely plausible to infer stages of increasing Christianization of the group who first compiled, then inherited, Q, each generation modifying it. We have no problem picking out strata and stages of evolution of the Gnostic communities and the documents they produced, e.g., the Book of Thomas the Contender and Melchizedek. As with Q, The Book of Thomas the Contender gives evidence of an increasingly bitter and defensive posture toward outsiders who rejected their teaching. Melchizedek looks like the result of two Melchizedek sects, one Gnostic, one not, into a unified group, like two failing church congregations merging.

Bart believes we cannot infer from what Q lacks what the compiler did not believe, especially regarding the death of Jesus.

> But to go further and insist that we know what was *not* in the source, for example, a Passion narrative, what its multiple editions were like, and which of these multiple editions was the earliest, and so on, really goes beyond what we can know—however appealing such "knowledge" might be.[61]

All right, but this almost sounds as if he's saying we can assume Q *did* have its own Passion narrative. Apologists want to think "the early Christians" were monolithic,[62] all believing the same things. So even though an early Christian

---

60. Burton L. Mack, *The Lost Gospel: The Book of Q and Christian Origins* (San Francisco: HarperSanFrancisco, 1993), pp. 106–107.

61. Ehrman, *Jesus: Apocalyptic Prophet*, p. 133.

62. Of course, they know about the various "heresies," but they beg the question by ruling out the Ebionites, Naassenes, Gnostics, etc., as not really *part* of "the early

document lacked a Passion narrative as far as we know, we can just assume its compilers believed in the Passion of Jesus anyway. Not that Bart says that, but it does not seem to me much of a leap to think Q lacked a crucifixion account, and that it implies something important about the group. Bart is right, though: this is all speculation. Yet how different is it from the speculative delineation of Synoptic sources? And that's my point.

But Bart casts his net even wider. If he recruits pre-gospel sources, he likewise calls post-canonical gospels to the witness stand. The Gospel of "Thomas . . . is a fifth independent witness to the life and teachings of Jesus."[63] Thomas has nothing to tell us about Jesus' life. It is a collection of sayings. But is it settled that Thomas is independent of the Synoptics? I wouldn't say so. Many scholars think so, but not all (I don't think so, though I'd like to). I doubt everyone will ever agree on the matter, and that is enough to place Thomas under the same shadow as M, L, and Q. It *might* be an independent source, but something that is itself a matter of intense debate can hardly be taken for granted as a building block for one's case. You're just forging a chain of weak links.

The same goes for the Gospel according to Peter:[64] "it is widely thought that Peter preserves an independent narrative, drawn from other, noncanonical sources."[65] Independent? Once at a meeting of the Jesus Seminar Bruce Chilton compared the Gospel of Peter with a guest room in a friend's house. Chilton stayed there once and was amused to note that the bathroom featured a variety of towels emblazoned with the insignias of Marriot, Hilton, Omni, and other hotel chains. What was more likely, Chilton asked us: that these various chains had sent spies to look into this bathroom and that then each chain copied one towel design? Or that Chilton's pal had swiped towels from all these hotels? In the same way, the Gospel of Peter contains many close parallels with the canonical gospels. Bart Ehrman seems not to recognize parallels as important

---

church." In the same way, when apologists maintain that early Christians were scrupulous never to ascribe words to Jesus that he didn't say, they completely ignore the Nag Hammadi texts which are filled with spurious "Jesus" material.

63. Ehrman, *Did Jesus Exist?*, p. 77.

64. Please forgive my covering some of the same ground I did in the previous chapter, but I want the discussion of the Gospels of Peter and Thomas to be fresh in your mind at this point.

65. Ehrman, *Did Jesus Exist?*, p. 77.

in this instance or any other, as we will see. For him, everything is sealed off from everything else.

But John Dominic Crossan does. In his fascinating book *The Cross That Spoke*[66] Crossan acknowledges the obvious (to Chilton and little ol' me) heavy debt Peter owes to the canonical gospels *and* an independent base narrative. He makes a complex but I think strong case that the independent basis for Peter is what he dubs "the Cross Gospel." But this source is by no means historical. Crossan peels away the embellishment drawn from the canonical gospels to lay bare the substratum which turns out to be a skeletal outline linking various "*testimonia*," Old Testament texts understood in the early church as prophecies and typologies anticipating the gospel story. It appears that these *testimonia* were the seeds from which the Passion narrative sprang. This not exactly what Bart seems to have in mind.

"Another independent account occurs in the highly fragmentary text called Papyrus Egerton 2."[67] Let's take a look at the Egerton Gospel.

The Unknown Gospel Egerton Papyrus 2 + Cologne Papyrus 255

Fragment 1: Verso (?)
. . . ? And Jesus said] unto the lawyers, [? Punish] every wrongdoer and transgressor, and not me; . . . And turning to the rulers of the people he spake this saying, Search the scriptures, in which ye think that ye have life; these are they which bear witness of me. Think not that I came to accuse you to my Father; there is one that accuseth you, even Moses, on whom ye have set your hope. And when they said, We know well that God spake unto Moses, but as for thee, we know not whence thou art, Jesus answered and said unto them, Now is your unbelief accused . . .

Fragment 1: Recto (?)
. . . ? they gave counsel to] the multitude to [? carry the] stones together and stone him. And the rulers sought to lay their hands on him that they might take him and [? hand him over] to the multitude; and they could not take him, because the hour of his betrayal was not yet come. But he himself, even

---

66. John Dominic Crossan, *The Cross That Spoke: The Origins of the Passion Narrative* (New York: Harper & Row, 1988).

67. Ehrman, *Did Jesus Exist?*, p. 77.

the Lord, going out through the midst of them, departed from them. And behold, there cometh unto him a leper and saith, Master Jesus, journeying with lepers and eating with them in the inn I myself also became a leper. If therefore thou wilt, I am made clean. The Lord then said unto him, I will; be thou made clean. And straightway the leprosy departed from him. [And the Lord said unto him], Go [and shew thyself] unto the [priests . . .

Fragment 2: Recto (?)

. . . coming unto him began to tempt him with a question, saying, Master Jesus, we know that thou art come from God, for the things which thou doest testify above all the prophets. Tell us therefore: Is it lawful [? to render] unto kings that which pertaineth unto their rule? [Shall we render unto them], or not? But Jesus, knowing their thought, being moved with indignation, said unto them, Why call ye me with your mouth Master, when ye hear not what I say? Well did Isaiah prophesy of you, saying, This people honour me with their lips, but their heart is far from me. In vain do they worship me, [teaching as their doctrines the] precepts [of men] . . .

Fragment 2: Verso (?)

. . . shut up . . . in . . . place . . . its weight unweighed? And when they were perplexed at his strange question, Jesus, as he walked, stood still on the edge of the river Jordan, and stretching forth his right hand he . . . and sprinkled it upon the . . . And then . . . water that had been sprinkled . . . before them and sent forth fruit . . .[68]

I don't know about you, but this text seems to me patently to be derived from at least Mark, Luke, and John, plus a regrettably fragmentary miracle story from some other source. Whatever the Egerton Gospel (named for its discoverer) was, it seems pretty dubious as an independent source of information about a historical Jesus.

PAPIAL BULL

Papias was a bishop of Hierapolis in Asia Minor, a city forming a triad with the biblical Colossae and Laodicea. Around 125 he wrote a work, now lost except

---

68. H.I. Bell and T.C. Skeat, Trans. *Fragments of an Unknown Gospel and Other Early Christian Papyri* (London: Oxford University Press, 1935), pp. 28.

for several quotations by church fathers, called *An Exposition of the Oracles of our Lord*. Eusebius regarded Papias as something of a dim bulb, recording "certain strange sayings of the Savior," including an extravagant apocalyptic prediction of the miraculous fecundity of the vine during the coming Millennium. It looks suspiciously similar to a passage in the Syriac Apocalypse of Baruch, whence it was probably borrowed. In his book *Jesus Before the Gospels* Bart argues that what are usually thought to be inaccurate Papian accounts of the origins of Matthew's and Mark's gospels[69] are really (possibly) accurate accounts of the writing of some other early Christian works credited to these two names. D.F. Strauss[70] suggested the same, and I'm glad to see the theory gain more currency. But even if Papias wasn't erroneously referring to our first and second gospels, it is very difficult to grant any credibility to a man who says he heard from the hearers of the holy apostles that Judas Iscariot had swollen up to the size of a parade balloon, unable to squeeze between two street corners, and urinated live maggots—before he exploded! I don't mean to suggest that Bart is willing to accept such nonsense; he doesn't.[71] But the astonishing thing is that, even in the face of it, he still accepts Papias as an important source. Bart does not hesitate to recruit him to his cause.

---

69. In his attempted refutation, *Misquoting Truth: A Guide to the Fallacies of Bart Ehrman's Misquoting Jesus*, Timothy Paul Johnson mounts a clever but futile argument that the authors of the four gospels must actually have been four guys named Matthew, Mark, Luke, and John because we cannot otherwise account for the fact that these names appear on all extant copies of the gospels. If the authorship ascription had not been transmitted along with the gospels from the start, why would the names appear with complete consistency? Why would we not, e.g., find some copies of our "Matthew" ascribed to Bartholomew or Sven or Mumuwalde? More than likely, the answer is that all our copies represent a single edition, that of the second-century bishop of Smyrna, Polycarp, who named the individual books. See David Trobisch, *The First Edition of the New Testament* (New York: Oxford University Press, 2000); Trobisch, "Who Published the New Testament?" *Free Inquiry* 28/1 (December 2007/January 2008), pp. 30–33.

70. David Friedrich Strauss, *The Life of Jesus for the People*. Theological Translation Fund (London: Williams and Norgate, 1879), vol. 2, p. 76: "with regard to our Gospel of Mark, we cannot tell even whether it had any connection at all with the work of Mark of which Papias speaks."

71. Bart Ehrman, *Jesus Before the Gospels: How the Earliest Christians Remembered, Changed, and Invented Their Stories of the Savior* (New York: HarperOne/HarperCollins, 2016), p. 117.

Intelligent or not, Papias is an important source for establishing the historical existence of Jesus. He had read some Gospels although there is no reason to think that he knew the ones that made it into the New Testament. . . . But more important, he had access to other sources of the sayings of Jesus. He was personally acquainted with people who had known either the apostles themselves or their companions.[72]

Still, on one point there can be no doubt. Papias may pass on some legendary traditions about Jesus, but he is quite specific—and there is no reason to think he is telling a bald-faced lie—that he knows people who knew the apostles (or the apostles' companions). This is not eyewitness testimony to the life of Jesus, but it is getting very close to that.[73]

This from the author of *Forgery and Counter-Forgery: The Use of Literary Deceit in Early Christian Polemics*? I regard Papias' claim to represent the living voice of the apostles as another example of Christian *isnads* for the hadith of Jesus.[74] Given the *Bullgeschichte* he spews, I should think there is plenty of reason to consider Papias a bald-faced liar. Again, to appeal to such a worthless source only underlines the paucity of the evidence.

Up next is Ignatius of Antioch, whom I should imagine to be about as well informed about a historical Jesus as Tacitus was. "Ignatius . . . provides us with yet another independent witness to the life of Jesus."[75] "He cannot be shown to have been relying on the Gospels."[76] But Bart quotes, in this very discussion, Ignatius' reference to Jesus having been "baptized by John that all righteousness might be fulfilled by him" (Smyrnaeans 1). Uh, that's unmistakable Matthean redaction of Mark. Ignatius must have been thinking of Matthew's gospel, not independent oral tradition.

Do 1 Peter 2:21–24; 3:18; 4:1; 5:1 preserve valuable tradition for establishing the historical existence, life, and death, of Jesus? I cannot think so. For one

72. Ehrman, *Did Jesus Exist?*, p. 98.

73. Ehrman, *Did Jesus Exist?*, pp. 100–101.

74. Joseph Schacht, "A Revaluation of Islamic Traditions," in Ibn Warraq, ed., *The Quest for the Historical Muhammad* (Amherst: Prometheus Books, 2000), pp. 358–367.

75. Ehrman, *Did Jesus Exist?*, p. 103.

76. Ehrman, *Did Jesus Exist?*, p. 103.

thing, 2:21–24 is not anyone's historical recollection but rather an allusion to Isaiah 53.[77] (These other verses of 1 Peter merely refer back to this initial one.) But doesn't 5:1 claim that the author himself witnessed Christ's sufferings? Yes, but the epistle is the work of a pious forger, as Bart admits on the very same page.[78] Second Peter 1:16–18 is, of course, yet another forgery, its author lying about being a witness. Bart denies that matters, but how can it not? There is no more any historical memory here than there is in Tacitus, also dependent upon common, late Christian teaching. The same is true of Hebrews.[79]

GRINDING THE AXE OF THE APOSTLES

Bart alleges that "the author of Acts has access to traditions that are not based on his Gospel account so that we have yet another independent witness."[80] But to me this does not quite seem to follow, if only because Luke is after all the author of both works. And consistency does not seem to be one of his main priorities. This is the writer who has Jesus ascend into heaven on Easter evening in his gospel *and* forty days later in Acts. He cannot seem to decide whether Saul's companions saw the light but heard no voice (Acts 22:9) or heard the voice but did not see the light (Acts 9:7) on the Damascus Road. Luke stipulates that an apostle must have been a fellow-traveler with the eleven nonstop since the baptism of Jesus (Acts 1:21–22), even though by his own account not even the eleven would qualify (Luke 5:1–11).

Specifically, Bart is thinking of "nonconforming" Christological patterns in these speeches. He avers that

> the speeches in Acts . . . are, in many instances, based not on Luke's fertile imagination but on oral traditions. The reason for thinking so is that portions of these speeches represent theological views that do not mesh well with the views of Luke himself, as these can be ascertained through a careful reading of his own two-volume work.[81]

---

77. Wells, *Jesus of the Early Christians*, pp. 153–155.

78. Ehrman, *Did Jesus Exist?*, p. 114.

79. Ehrman, *Did Jesus Exist?*, p. 117.

80. Ehrman, *Did Jesus Exist?*, p. 107.

81. Ehrman, *Did Jesus Exist?*, p. 109.

There are, as I see it, two major candidates for passages that sound like left-over "theological fossils" in the Acts speeches, texts that seem to represent different Christologies from that implied elsewhere in Luke-Acts. The first is Acts 2:36, "Let all the house of Israel therefore know assuredly that God has made him both Lord and Christ, this Jesus whom you crucified." Did Jesus become the Messiah only as of his resurrection/ascension (a la the oft-quoted Psalm 110)? How to square this seeming adoptionism with Luke's Nativity story where Jesus is conceived and born Son of God (Luke 1:35; 9:20–22)? J.C. O'Neill points out that these two distinct Christological models could and did coexist in New Testament Christology. Matthew, too, has a Nativity that designated Jesus as God's Son/Messiah from his birth (Matt.2: 2, 4), yet he also tells us that Jesus gained universal cosmic power as of the resurrection (Matt. 28:18).[82] The Epistle to the Hebrews could not be clearer that Jesus was the pre-existent Wisdom of God (Heb. 1:2–3), deserving the adoration of angels from the moment of his birth (Heb. 1:6), while also not hesitating to speak of Jesus in pronouncedly adoptionistic terms (Heb. 1:4, 9; 3:2; 5:5).[83] And William Wrede's theory of the Markan Messianic Secret[84] presupposes pretty much the same situation of two different Christologies circulating side by side: one belief that Jesus would be crowned Messiah only at his resurrection, another that he had become Messiah at his baptism. And if Matthew, Hebrews, and Mark could keep both Christological balls in the air, why not Acts? Thus the adoptionism of Acts 2:36 need not denote a pre-Lukan primitive tradition but rather one of two contemporary Christologies. Maurice Casey says, "In the early speeches of Acts, when pre-existence, sonship and deity had not yet been developed, we find formulations which refer to each possible point of reference correctly left unreconciled."[85]

---

82. J.C. O'Neill, *The Theology of Acts in Its Historical Setting* (London: SPCK, 1961), Chapter 5, "The Titles Given to Jesus," pp. 124–127.

83. John A.T. Robinson, *The Human Face of God* (Philadelphia: Fortress Press, 1973), p. 156.

84. William Wrede, *The Messianic Secret*. Trans. J.C.G. Greig (Cambridge: James Clarke, 1971).

85. Maurice Casey, *From Jewish Prophet to Gentile God: The Origins and Development of New Testament Christology*. The Edward Cadbury Lectures at the University of Birmingham, 1985–85 (Louisville: Westminster/John Knox Press, 1991), p. 106.

The second passage that seems to defy Luke's dominant Christology is Acts 3:19–21.

> Repent therefore, and turn again, that your sins may be blotted out, that times of refreshing may come from the presence of the Lord, and that he may send the Christ appointed for you, Jesus, whom heaven must receive until the time for establishing all that God spoke by the mouth of his holy prophets from of old.

John A.T. Robinson[86] suggested that this text preserves the most primitive Christology of all, that Jesus is not the Christ even from the resurrection/ascension, but waits to be ordained Christ till the time for his Parousia comes. As tempted as I am by this reading, I have to admit that it is unnecessary. The passage, I think, makes perfect sense if we take "the Christ appointed for you" in connection with "establishing all that God spoke by the mouth of his holy prophets of old." In short, Jesus' "appointment" as Messiah consists in his having been anciently prophesied in scripture, precisely as in Luke 24:25–27. This is straight "Lukanism," not a pre-Lukan tradition.

Another specimen of these ostensible pre-Lukan traditions concerns the fate of the Betrayer.

> Luke had an independent tradition of the death of Judas, which was at least as early as the one in Matthew. There are reasons for thinking that at the heart of both stories is a historical tradition: independently they confirm that a field in Jerusalem was connected in some way both with the money Judas was paid to betray Jesus and with Judas's death. Moreover, it was known as the Field of Blood. Matthew calls it a 'potter's field.' Is it possible that it was actually a field of red clay used by potters, and so—because of its color—called the Field of Blood, which is in one way or another was connected with the death of Jesus's betrayer?[87]

Bart has sniffed out a perfect example of an Old Testament–style etiological legend. The actual and original derivation of "Field of Blood"

---

86. John A.T. Robinson, *Twelve New Testament Studies*. Studies in Biblical Theology No. 34 (London: SCM Press, 1962), Chapter X, "The Most Primitive Christology of All?," pp. 139–153.

87. Ehrman, *Did Jesus Exist?*, p. 108.

would have been from the red clay found there. But that wasn't quite good enough for the popular imagination, so it became connected to the death of Judas. For instance, the Old Testament place name *Beer-la-hai-roi* ("Well of the Antelope's Jawbone") originally simply referred to the topography of the place: the well could be found at the low end of a declining row of boulders. But in Genesis 21:9–21 it is reinterpreted as "the Well of One Who Sees and Lives," commemorating the surprise that Hagar beheld God there and survived the shock! And there were more than one version of the Field of Blood etymology, as in Genesis, where, e.g., the name "Isaac" is given no less than four different fictive etymologies (Gen. 17:15–17; 18:9–15; 21:6–7; 21:9). Acts' version is no different from the legend of the Dogwood blossom being marked with a cross after the death of Jesus. Granted, it sounds like a true oral tradition, but it is obviously not historical information. So pre-Lukan tradition may not be worth much.

PAUL: PERSECUTOR OR PRECURSOR?[88]

Bart Ehrman blithely accepts Acts' account of Saul's persecution of early Christians.[89] (As you'll see, this bears on the scandal of a crucified messiah which Bart says no one would have made up.) New Testament chronologies are based on the conversion of Paul,[90] despite the dearth of evidence for it. There is no reference in the Pauline epistles suggesting anything like the Acts account of Paul's conversion, so where *did* Luke derive his inspiration? And why did he feel the need to include such a scene? First, it seems plain, as soon as one reads the texts in question, that Luke has borrowed freely from two well-known literary sources, Euripides' *Bacchae* and 2 Maccabees' story of the conversion of Heliodorus. From 2 Maccabees Luke has borrowed the basic story of a persecutor of the people of God being stopped in his mission by a vision of heavenly beings (3:24–26), thrown to the ground in a faint, blinded (3:27), and cared for by righteous Jews who pray for his recovery (3:31–33), whereupon the

---

88. This section bears a suspicious resemblance to Chapter 1 ("The Legend of Paul's Conversion") of my book *The Amazing Colossal Apostle: The Search for the Historical Paul* (Salt Lake City: Signature Books, 2012). Why bother paraphrasing it?

89. Ehrman, *Did Jesus Exist?*, pp. 156–157.

90. Ehrman, *Did Jesus Exist?*, p. 131. Ah, how different history might have played out had Paul only been wearing his sun glasses!

ex-persecutor converts to the faith he once tried to destroy (3:35) and begins witnessing to its truth (3:36). Given Luke's propensity to rewrite the Septuagint, it seems special pleading to deny that he has done the same in the present case, the most blatant of them all.

From the *Bacchae*, Luke has derived the core of the Damascus Road epiphany, the basic idea of a persecutor being converted despite himself by direct fiat of the god whose followers he has been abusing. King Pentheus has done his best to expel the enthusiastic Maenads of Dionysus from Thebes, against the counsel of Cadmus, Teiresius, and other level heads who warn him not to be found fighting against a god (Teiresias: "Reckless fool, you do not know the consequences of your words. You talked madness before, but this is raving lunacy!" lines 357–360. Dionysus: "I warn you once again: do not take arms against a god." 788–789. "A man, a man, and nothing more, yet he presumed to wage war with a god." 636–637; c.f., Acts 5:33–39).[91] He ought to mark how the Maenads, though they may seem to be filled with wine, are really filled with divine ecstasy ("not, as you think, drunk with wine," 686–687; c.f., Acts 2:15), as witnessed by the old and young among them prophesying ("all as one, the old women and the young and the unmarried girls," 693–694; c.f., Acts 2:17–18) and the harmless resting of tongues of fire upon their heads ("flames flickered in their curls and did not burn them," 757–758; "tongues of fire," 623–624; c.f., Acts 2:3). Pentheus remains stubborn in his opposition, arresting the newly-arrived apostle of the cult, who turns out to be Dionysus himself, the very son of god, in mortal disguise.

After an earthquake frees him from Pentheus' prison (585–603; c.f., Acts 16:25–34), Dionysus strolls into Pentheus' throne room and mocks him ("If I were you, I would . . . not rage and kick against necessity, a man defying god." 793–796; c.f., Acts 26:14), offering Pentheus the chance to find the outlaw disciples in their secret hideaway. Pentheus may see them at their sport, but he must go in drag, wearing their distinctive doeskin costume (912–916; c.f., Acts 9:26–30). He mesmerizes Pentheus into agreeing to the plan (922–924; c.f., Acts 9:17–18), and no sooner does he prettify himself than he has become a

---

91. I am using William Arrowsmith's translation in David Grene and Richard Lattimore, eds., *Greek Tragedies*, Volume 3 (Chicago: University of Chicago Press, Phoenix paperbound edition, 1972), pp. 189–260.

true believer despite himself (929–930).[92] But the joke's on him, since Dionysus sends him to his doom: he knows Pentheus will be detected and torn limb from limb by the frenzied Maenads. Such poetic justice! The poor fool could dish it out but not take it! He wanted to persecute the Maenads? Let him! He'll see how it feels from the standpoint of the persecuted! He becomes a true believer, only to suffer the fate of one. And so does Paul. In light of the parallels with the *Bacchae* (Dionysus to Pentheus: "You and you alone shall suffer for your city. A great ordeal awaits you. But you are worthy of your fate." 963–964), we can at long last catch the awful irony of Acts 9:16, "I will show him how much *he* must suffer for the sake of my name!" Paul, a conscript despite himself, will find his punishment fitting his crime: he will suffer as a member of the same persecuted community against whom he himself had unleashed such violence.

But doesn't the business about Paul having previously persecuted the churches require *some* sort of conversion episode? I believe that every single one of the apparent Pauline references to former persecution is secondary. First, J.C. O'Neill marshals a number of considerations indicating that Galatians 1:13–14, 22–24 did not originally belong to the text of that epistle. "These verses have been interpolated into Paul's argument by a later writer who wished to glorify the apostle. The argument is irrelevant and anachronistic, the concepts differ from Paul's concepts, and the vocabulary and style are not his."[93] "The astounding reversal of roles he underwent, from a fierce persecutor of the Church to an evangelist of the faith, and from a precociously zealous Jew to an opponent of Jewish customs, is no argument in favour of Paul's position,"[94] which seems to be the thread of the passage otherwise.

The reference to "Judaism" is too late for Paul, since it implies that Christianity and Judaism are separate religions, a use analogous to speaking of "Judaism and paganism." Similarly, *pistis* as a reference to "the faith," i.e., the Christian religion, would fit in Acts 6:7 and the Pastorals, but not in Paul. And Paul elsewhere uses the word *ecclesia* for local congregations. The use in 1:13 (cf. 23) smacks rather of the later Church Universal (or even Church Aion) doctrine of Ephesians. The word *anastrophe* is elsewhere to be found over Paul's

---

92. "You don't *believe* me, Doctor Jones? You *will*! You will become a *true believer*! Hahahahaha!"

93. J.C. O'Neill, *The Recovery of Paul's Letter to the Galatians* (London: SPCK, 1972), p. 24.

94. O'Neill, *Recovery of Galatians*, p. 24–26.

name only in Ephesians and 1 Timothy, while *Ioudaismos, porthoo, sunelikiotas,* and *patrikos* do not occur even there. The frequency of the enclitic *pote* (three times) in these few verses is closer to that in Ephesians and the Pastorals (seven) than the other Paulines (once more in Galatians 2:6, nine times elsewhere in the Corpus). Stylistically these verses are un-Pauline, the sentences even and regular, with 20, 19, 12, and 20 words respectively. And there is more.[95]

I have argued at some length elsewhere[96] that Winsome Munro, J.C. O'Neill and others are quite correct in seeing 1 Corinthians 15:3–11, containing another reference to Paul's pre-conversion persecutions, as an interpolation.

First Timothy 1:13 features another reference to the mischief wrought by the pre-Christian Paul, but it is as spurious as the epistle which contains it. The same goes for Philippians 3:6, "as to zeal, a persecutor of the church." As Baur pointed out long ago, Philippians is virtually a fourth Pastoral Epistle, with its anachronistic references to bishops and deacons, the Gnosticizing kabbalism of the Kenosis hymn in 2:6–11, the epistle's unusual vocabulary, and most of all, its heavy hagiographic irony as it has Paul assure his readers that, though he would much rather wing his way to glory and finally attain his crown of perfection, he will continue to minister to them, which of course "he" does by means of this very pseudepigraph. The poignancy depends completely, as it does for the modern reader, on the implied reader knowing that Paul was in fact executed immediately after "he" wrote these sweet sentiments. It is another Acts 19, another 2 Timothy. So no wonder it, too, knows the legend of Paul the persecutor. And note the anti-Semitism whereby it equates Jewish zeal with Christian-hunting. Paul can have written this no more than he can have regarded Judaism as a competing religion he did not belong to (Gal. 1:14) or aimed at fellow Jews the classic anti-Jewish jibe "haters of humanity" (1 Thess. 2:15—and here note yet another variation on the Pauline persecution legend: this time it is Palestinian Jews who persecuted *Paul!*).

Whence the Pauline persecution legend shared by Luke and his fellow Paulinists? I believe it is a late and garbled Gentile Christian version, a turning to hagiographic advantage, of an early and persistent Ebionite reproach of the Christian Paul as an "enemy of the faith," *their* faith, the Torah-gospel of James

95. O'Neill, *Recovery of Galatians*, pp. 24–26.

96. Robert M. Price, "Apocryphal Apparitions: 1 Corinthians 15:3–11 as a Post-Pauline Interpolation," in Price and Jeffery Jay Lowder, eds., *The Empty Tomb: Jesus Beyond the Grave* (Amherst: Prometheus Books, 2005), pp. 69–104.

the Just and the Nazoreans. In the Clementine *Recognitions* we read of attacks led by Paul ("the Enemy") on James and his flock. These are actual physical attacks upon James and the Jerusalem Ebionim, not unlike that attributed to Paul and the Sanhedrin in Acts. But in the Ebionite source underlying this episode of the *Recognitions* it seems doubtful that Paul's attacks presaged a conversion; he is referred to uniformly as "the Enemy" of James throughout, as if nothing ever changed. Now in fact the historical Paul may never have mounted violent attacks on any group of rival religionists. "The legend of Paul's persecution of Christians . . . may have been invented by the Petrine party, as the Paulinists invented the legend of Peter's denial of his Lord."[97]

Was it cut from whole cloth? Not exactly. Paul's reputation as one who, *as a non-Torah Christian*, opposed the "true" (Ebionite) faith and "fought" against it would have eventually crystallized into stories of his actually taking up "worldly weapons of warfare" (2 Cor. 10:4). But the original point was simply that Paul *as a Christian apostle* strove, polemicized, against the Nazorean Christianity of James and Peter. "They have heard concerning you that you teach all the Jews who are among the Gentiles to forsake Moses, telling them not to circumcise their children or observe the customs" (Acts 21:21). Naturally, Gentile, Pauline Christians could never have interpreted his promulgation of the Law-free gospel as opposing the true faith, so when eventually they heard the charge that Paul had been an enemy of the faith they took it to mean he had once persecuted what *they* considered the true faith: their own Hellenized Christianity, which must, in turn, have meant he had previously been a non-Christian and then had undergone a major about-face. As Francis Watson[98] ably shows, there may well have been a Pauline "conversion" of sorts, but only from one sort of Christian mission to another. Paul may have begun preaching a gospel compatible with circumcision among Jews (Gal. 5:11), found only meager results, and turned to the wider Gentile world, trimming back the stringent demands of the Law to make it easier for Gentiles to convert, precisely as his foes alleged (Gal. 1:10).

---

97. L. Gordon Rylands, *A Critical Analysis if the Four Chief Pauline Epistles: Romans, First and Second Corinthians, and Galatians* (London: Watts, 1929), p. 353.

98. Francis Watson, *Paul, Judaism and the Gentiles: A Sociological Approach.* Society for New Testament Studies Monograph Series 56 (New York: Cambridge University Press, 1986), pp. 26–38.

PAUL'S JESUS

"He never mentions Pontius Pilate or the Romans, but he may have had no need to do so. His readers knew full well what he was talking about."[99] Let me get this straight: we can be sure Paul knew the circumstances of Jesus' death despite the fact that he doesn't say so, because his readers already knew about Pilate and the Sanhedrin? Then why not Pilate's wife, or Barabbas, Saint Veronica, Ahasuerus the Wandering Jew, the blind centurion Longinus, and the revived corpses of Matthew 27? Paul never mentions any of these characters. Should we assume the Philippians and the Galatians knew all about *them*, too?

"We don't know how much these people already knew about . . . Jesus. If they were already fully informed about Jesus, then there was no need for Paul to remind them that Jesus walked on water, raised Jairus's daughter from the dead, and was executed in Jerusalem."[100] But suppose his readers *were* familiar with these stories: Bart believes such miracle stories are pure legends.[101] If the Corinthians or the Thessalonians "knew" about these miracles, that doesn't mean they knew anything about a *historical* Jesus.

What is at issue in the question of Paul not mentioning Pilate or the Sanhedrin as the culprits in Jesus' death? Paul never describes the crucifixion as a mundane execution at the hands of earthly governing authorities (though of course nothing he says rules out that possibility). What he does say is that Jesus was done to death by "the rulers (*archons*) of this aeon" (1 Cor. 2:8), "the Principalities and Powers" (Col. 1:16; 2:14–15). Mythicists infer that the author of these epistles was writing at a time when Christians believed in a celestial Man of Light who had not appeared on the earth to teach and heal and die on a Roman cross, but who had been ambushed and slain by the demonic entities (fallen angels, archons, elemental spirits) inhabiting the lower heavens. As we read in various surviving Gnostic texts, this death would have occurred in the primordial past. His slayers harvested the sparks of his Light-body and used them to seed the inert mud-pie creations of the Demiurge, imparting life and motion to them, beginning with Adam. Thus the death of the Primal Light-Man turned out to be a life-giving sacrifice, much like that of the Vedic Purusha, a universe-filling giant (cf., Eph 4:10) who offered himself

---

99. Ehrman, *Did Jesus Exist?*, pp. 124–125.

100. Ehrman, *Did Jesus Exist?*, p. 137.

101. Ehrman, *Jesus Before the Gospels*, pp. 220–221.

as a sacrifice, giving rise to the four castes, the scriptures, animals, heavenly bodies, and everything else (Rig Veda 10.90).[102]

Eventually the Revealer was sent forth from the divine world of light to regather the divine photons, redeeming them from imprisonment in this world of "solid flesh." The Gnostics, naturally, considered themselves to be the elite light-bearers who had heeded the call of the Revealer, manifest among men in the form of Gnostic apostles. At some point some of these Gnostics "historicized" their salvation myth, envisioning the sacrificial death of the Man of Light as taking place down here in the sub-lunar world. At first, the coming of this Christ was understood as what we would call a hologram, an illusion of physical presence among mortal men and women. The enlightened could discern the purely spiritual character of the Savior, while those mired in mundane consciousness took him for a man of flesh. Eventually this unenlightened, genuinely incarnational Christology became normative.[103] The Pauline literature would represent a pre-historicized period of Gnostic Christian belief, or a faction which retained the earlier version when others had adopted a historicized Christology/Soteriology. This is the model that makes most sense to me. And I should note that not all Mythicists would accept my version.

And "one of the most important points Paul makes about Jesus [was] that he was in fact the Jewish messiah."[104] But Bart holds the same opinion as Werner Kramer[105] and Lloyd Gaston:[106] "already by the time of Paul, 'Christ' had become Jesus's name."[107] There is not a single passage in the Pauline epistles where "Christ" must be understood as a title. It would make sense as a title in Romans 9:5, but even there it is not necessary to take it that way: "and of their race, according to the flesh, is the Christ" *or* "is Christ." Since in Greek

102. *The Rig Veda: An Anthology.* Trans. Wendy Doniger O'Flaherty. Penguin Classics (Baltimore: Penguin Books, 1981), pp. 29–32.

103. More discussion of these matters appears in Chapter Five, "No Talk of God Then, We Called You a Man."

104. Ehrman, *Did Jesus Exist?*, p. 119.

105. Werner Kramer, *Christ, Lord, Son of God.* Trans. Brian Hardy. Studies in Biblical Theology No. 50 (Naperville: Alec R. Allenson, 1966), pp. 42, 203–214.

106. Lloyd Gaston, *Paul and the Torah* (Vancouver: University of British Columbia Press, 1987), p. 7.

107. Ehrman, *Did Jesus Exist?*, p. 239.

all proper names have the definite article, it could be translated either way.

Paul "refers on several occasions to Jesus's teachings."[108] He "quotes his teachings on several occasions."[109] What? Where? Of course, Bart is referring to *two* passages from 1 Corinthians. "To the married I give charge, not I but the Lord, that the wife should not separate from her husband . . . and that the husband should not divorce his wife" (1 Cor. 7:10–11). Are we so sure Paul is quoting a saying of the historical Jesus, and not passing on a command vouchsafed him by the ascended Christ? I think the latter is more likely, especially in light of verses 12–16, which begin with "To the rest I say, *not* the Lord, that if any brother has a wife who is an unbeliever, and she consents to live with him, he should not divorce her," *yada yada yada.* I think of the distinction made in the Old Testament between apodictic laws ("Thou shalt not kill." "It is an abomination." "It is unclean.") and casuistic laws ("If two men are fighting, and one man's pregnant wife tries to intervene, and she takes a blow intended for her husband, and then miscarries," etc.)[110] In the same way, the "don't divorce" command "from the Lord" appears to be clear cut, a bulletin from God that we can easily imagine Charlton Heston uttering with appropriate echoes. The "if this, if that" business in 7:12–16 does not fit that description. That one is a law book "hypothetical." It's all a simple matter of form criticism. In 1 Corinthians 7:25 ff., Paul again disclaims revelation. "Now concerning the unmarried, I have no command of the Lord, but I give my opinion as one who by the Lord's mercy is trustworthy." Again, he is dealing with nuanced and complex questions. Not the kind of thing to be dealt with by a bolt from the blue.

We can't be sure Paul does *not* mean he has a historical Jesus quote on hand, but if mine is even a plausible suggestion it is not fair to simply assert Paul is quoting Jesus. The same applies to 1 Corinthians 11:23–26, where Paul quotes the Words of Institution of the eucharist. Bart, like all conservative apologists, contends that the words, "I received from the Lord what I also delivered to you," imply that Paul is repeating an account given him by his

---

108. Ehrman, *Did Jesus Exist?*, p. 130.

109. Ehrman, *Did Jesus Exist?*, p. 139.

110. Johann Jakob Stamm and Maurice Edward Andrew, *The Ten Commandments in Recent Research.* Studies in Biblical Theology Second Series No. 2 (London: SCM Press, 1967), pp. 31–33; Martin Noth, *Exodus: A Commentary.* Trans. John Bowden. Old Testament Library (Philadelphia: Fortress Press, 1962), p. 262.

apostolic predecessors, an account of Jesus' Last Supper. The "received, delivered" language is familiar from Rabbinic tradition. But, especially in Paul, it can just as easily mean the opposite. "I would have you know, brethren, that the gospel that was preached by me is not according to man. For I did not receive it *from* man, nor was I taught it, but it came through a revelation of Jesus Christ" (Gal. 1:11–12). Note the similarity to "I received from the Lord" in 1 Corinthians 11:23. Why doesn't it denote in 1 Corinthians what it most certainly does in Galatians?[111]

Bart makes a pretty good point when he refers us to the Johannine epistles whose author, he thinks, must have known the Gospel of John but nonetheless never explicitly quotes from it:

> the author of 1, 2, and 3 John was living in the same community out of which the Gospel of John was produced, and he shows clear evidence of actually knowing John's Gospel. And how many times does he quote it in his three letters? None at all. How often does he talk about Jesus's parables, his miracles, his trip to Jerusalem, his trial before Pilate? Never. Does that mean he doesn't think Jesus lived?[112]

The problem here is that we cannot determine if these letters were written *before* or *after* the Gospel of John. Are the parallels in vocabulary and subject matter better taken as allusions to the Gospel of John, or as the sort of thing that was subsequently used to compose that gospel? It is precisely parallel to the debate about maxims in the Pauline epistles that sound kind of like Jesus sayings in the gospels. Apologists like James D.G. Dunn[113] maintain (absurdly, to my way of thinking) that these are actually quotes from Jesus but *without attribution*. What, you're going to bring in the big guns to win your argument, the words of the very Son of God, and then neglect to say who you're quoting? Mythicists,[114] on the other hand, suggest that it went in the other direction: the

---

111. Hyam Maccoby, *Paul and Hellenism* (Philadelphia: Trinity Press International, 1991), pp. 91–95.

112. Ehrman, *Did Jesus Exist?*, pp. 137–138.

113. James D.G. Dunn, "Jesus Tradition in Paul," in Bruce Chilton and Craig A. Evans (eds.), *Studying the Historical Jesus* (Leiden: E.J. Brill, 1994), pp. 177–178.

114. And some others, e.g., David Oliver Smith, *Matthew, Mark, Luke, and Paul: The Influence of the Epistles on the Synoptic Gospels* (Eugene: Wipf & Stock, 2011).

evangelist gleaned gems from the epistles (or perhaps collected oracular sayings from the heavenly Christ, e.g., Rev. 1–3[115]) and made them into sayings of Jesus in the process of fleshing out a "historical" Jesus, precisely as some redactor sliced up the text of Eugnostos the Blessed and credited the words to Jesus in another Nag Hammadi document, The Wisdom of Jesus Christ.

We may also compare the situation of the gospels and the Pauline epistles to that regarding the Synoptics versus John. As Maurice Casey[116] notes, it is obvious that the unique and powerful sayings/discourses attributed to Jesus in John's gospel cannot be authentic sayings of a historical Jesus because no such materials (e.g., the numerous "I am" declarations) appear in the Synoptics. Is it reasonable to argue that Jesus really said such things but that *none* of it had reached the ears of the Synoptists? Of course not. As all critical scholars admit, these sayings did not exist, hence were not circulating, in the period when Q, Mark, and Matthew (throw in M and L if you want) were being written. They arose within the sectarian Community of the Beloved Disciple[117] later on. Shouldn't we understand the absence of Jesus material (sayings and stories) from the Pauline literature in the same way? It simply did not yet exist, or we should be seeing some of it in the epistles.

Besides, the words of "Jesus" in the Gospel of John are obviously those of the evangelist himself, so that any distinction between the "Johannine" epistles and their possible allusions to or parallels with the Fourth Gospel becomes meaningless. And the point is not whether the author thought Jesus didn't live on earth in the historical past. Rather, the question is whether he provides us any *evidence* that a historical Jesus existed.

Am I correct in discerning a circular motion in the following?

> But even if Paul knew about the historical Jesus, even if he knew a *lot* about him, there is no reason to think that he therefore must have known about . . . particular sayings of Jesus. Many authors, even those living after Paul, who knew full well that Jesus existed, say nothing about the Lord's Prayer or the

---

115. Rudolf Bultmann, *The History of the Synoptic Tradition*. Trans. John Marsh (New York: Harper & Row, 1968), pp. 127–128.

116. Casey, *From Jewish Prophet to Gentile God*, pp. 25–26.

117. Raymond E. Brown, *The Community of the Beloved Disciple: The Life, Loves and Hates of an Individual Church in the New Testament Period* (New York: Paulist Press, 1979).

injunction to bless those who persecute you. It is striking, for example, that neither of these passages is found in the Gospel of Mark. Did Mark think Jesus existed? Of course he did.[118]

These post-Pauline authors "knew full well that Jesus existed"? Isn't that begging the whole darn question? Besides, this seems a false analogy; we know about Mark what we do not know about Paul, and which is the very point at issue: do we start out with real reason to think Paul envisioned an earthly Jesus?

INTER-PAUL-ATIONS?

Is it possible that any texts in the Pauline epistles that imply belief in a recent historical Jesus might be secondary scribal insertions? Bart Ehrman does not suffer interpolation theories gladly.

> This approach to Paul can be thought of as historical reconstruction based on the principle of convenience. If historical evidence proves inconvenient to one's views, then simply claim that the evidence does not exist, and suddenly you're right.[119]

> It is only the mythicists, who have a vested interest in claiming that Paul did not know of a historical Jesus, who insist that these passages were not originally in Paul's writings. One always needs to consider the source.[120]

The trouble is: these suggestions were not first made by Mythicists.[121] William O. Walker, Jr.,[122] discusses a whole raft of proposed early interpolations, not one of them the proposal of a Mythicist. Each suggestion comes with its own reasoning. Here are a few, from various non-Mythicist scholars.

---

118. Ehrman, *Did Jesus Exist?*, p. 135.

119. Ehrman, *Did Jesus Exist?*, p. 118.

120. Ehrman, *Did Jesus Exist?*, p. 133.

121. But even if they were, wouldn't it be the genetic fallacy to dismiss them for that reason?

122. William O. Walker, Jr., *Interpolations in the Pauline Letters.* Journal for the Study of the New Testament Supplement Series 213 (London: Sheffield Academic Press, 2001).

Galatians 1:18–19:

Unless the allusion is interpolated, Paul had an interview with a brother of Jesus, who was one of the three "pillars" of the Church of Jerusalem (Gal. i, 19). There is a critical case of some slight cogency against the authenticity of Gal. i, 18, 19, which was absent from Marcion's *Apostolicon*; the word "again" in Gal. ii, 1, which presupposes the earlier passage, seems to have been interpolated as it is absent from Irenaeus's full and accurate citation of this section of the Epistle to the Galatians in his treatise against Heretics.[123]

Galatians 4:4:

I conclude that verses 4 and 5 originally comprised a short creedal affirmation in poetic form. It is possible that Paul himself quoted a Jewish Christian hymn to illustrate his point that the coming of God's Son meant adoption as God's sons for men, but I hesitate to believe that Paul was responsible, because I should have expected Paul to make some reference to the fact that what applied to Jews, who were under the Law, applied also to the Gentiles, who were not.[124]

Galatians 4:4 is the one that tells us that God's Son was "born of a woman." Does that mean Paul believed in an earthly, historical Jesus? Perhaps not. Over to you, Bart:

As we have seen, there may be some reason to suspect that Paul held to some such [docetic] views—but it is very difficult to say. Paul does speak about Christ coming in the 'likeness of sinful flesh' (Rom. 8:3) and to have been 'in appearance' as a human (Phil. 2:7). . . . He does, however, say that Christ was actually 'born of a woman' (Gal. 4:4), and that does not sound like the sort of thing most docetists would want to claim.[125]

And that's why it looks more likely to me that the verse is an anti-docetic interpolation aimed at (Paulinist) Marcionism which held, as Bart says, that

123. A. D. Howell Smith, *Jesus Not A Myth* (London: Watts, 1942), p. 76.

124. O'Neill, *Recovery of Galatians*, p. 59.

125. Bart D. Ehrman, *How Jesus Became God: The Exaltation of a Jewish Preacher from Galilee* (New York: HarperOne, 2014), pp. 295–296.

"Jesus came into the world not as a real human being with a real birth."[126]

1 Corinthians 11:23–26:

Concerned to authorize certain innovations to the Eucharistic service,

> the interpolator of 1 Co 11:23–26 put forward an alleged agreement between what the Saviour would have revealed to him and what he taught earlier. Current practice among the Corinthians was therefore a deviation from tradition, though only in part, because the interpolator had to base his narrative on some truth in order to make the falsehood he wanted to impose acceptable.[127]

I have made a case that 1 Corinthians 15:3–11 was interpolated into its present context, but then I don't count, since I'm a crazy Mythicist. But others, not Mythicists, had beaten me to the punch. Winsome Munro "suspects" 1 Cor. 15:1–11 of belonging to a subsequent, post-Pauline stratum of the epistle,[128] while J. C. O'Neill also deems it most probable that "1 Cor. 15.1–11 is a later creedal summary not written by Paul."[129] R. Joseph Hoffmann[130] speaks of "the interpolative character of 1 Cor 15.5–8."

Bart does not linger to examine any of the individual interpolation proposals he scorns. He simply decrees that no literary arguments are sufficient to trump the lack of manuscript evidence. In other words, you would really have to be able to point to actual copies that lacked Galatians 1:18–19; 4:4, etc. Unfortunately (or fortunately?), we have *no* manuscripts from the period during which the interpolations would have been made. None with these

---

126. Ehrman, *How Jesus Became God*, p. 301.

127. Jean Magne, *From Christianity to Gnosis and From Gnosis to Christianity: An Itinerary through the Texts to and from the Tree of Paradise*. Trans. A. F. W. Armstrong. Brown Judaic Studies 286 (Atlanta: Scholars Press, 1993), p. 33.

128. Winsome Munro, *Authority in Paul and Peter, The Identification of a Pastoral Stratum in the Pauline Corpus and 1 Peter*. Society for New Testament Studies Monograph Series 45 (New York: Cambridge University Press, 1983), p. 204.

129. J.C. O'Neill, *Recovery of Galatians*, p. 27.

130. R. Joseph Hoffmann, *Marcion: On the Restitution of Christianity: An Essay on the Development of Radical Paulinist Theology in the Second Century*. AAR Academy Series 46 (Chico: Scholars Press, 1984), p. 131.

verses, none without them. Thus what ought to be agnosticism ("Who the hell *knows* what might or might not have been in those manuscripts?") miraculously transforms into fideism ("We can assume the texts always read as they do now!"). Once again, I am reminded of the apologetical mind games Bart and I have supposedly put behind us. Is there an echo here of Benjamin B. Warfield's fool-proof (but back-firing) defense of biblical inerrancy? If we are unable otherwise to wriggle out of a biblical error or contradiction, we can always assert that the error must be the result of a copyist somewhere along the line. If we could get a peek at the holy Original Autographs, we can be sure (by faith!) that we would not find the error there. But this fideism should turn into agnosticism: if we cannot check the originals as they came from the author's hand, which we cannot do but would *have* to do to be sure we are reading the true inspired text, then we cannot be sure of the true text at *any* point, even when we like what our texts say. Once you open that door it cannot be shut again. Nice going, Benjy! You have destroyed any confidence in our knowledge of the true text of scripture! And indeed we cannot have the old certainty. And that is precisely the skepticism that apologists for both fundamentalist Biblicism and for "consensus" biblical scholarship are stuck with, whether they realize it or not.

> Apart from the mythicist desire not to find such passages in Paul, there is no textual evidence that these passages were not originally in Paul (they appear in every single manuscript of Paul that we have) and no solid literary grounds for thinking they were not in Paul. Paul almost certainly wrote them. Moreover, if scribes were so concerned to insert aspects of Jesus' life into Paul's writings, it is passing strange that they were not more thorough in doing so.[131]

Here Bart is ascribing motives to these hypothetical scribes that Mythicists do not attribute to them. No one claims that ancient copyists were disappointed not to find lots of gospel materials in the epistles and then penciled them in. Why would they? They already had the gospels of Matthew, Mark, Luke, and John just a few pages back. No, if these passages were inserted, it was for different reasons in each case, reasons discussed by Walker, Munro, O'Neill and others but ignored by Bart.

---

131. Ehrman, *Did Jesus Exist?*, p. 133.

BAND OF BROTHERS

Perhaps the major sticking point in the Mythicism debate is the reference in Galatians 1:19 to "James the Lord's brother." Traditionally this is supposed to mean that one of the Jerusalem triad of Pillar apostles was the biological sibling of Jesus Christ, perhaps implying he functioned as a caliph presiding over the church community in Jesus' stead.[132] This is a strong and natural reading. And if it is correct, then we have clear and decisive evidence that Jesus was a historical contemporary of Paul. But it may not be that simple. For this James to be called "the brother of the Lord" might mean the same thing as "the brothers of the Lord" in 1 Corinthians 9:5: "Do we not have the right to be accompanied by a believing wife [literally, "a sister as a wife"] as do the other apostles and the brothers of the Lord and Cephas?" (1 Cor. 9:5). Bart denies that "brothers of the Lord" in this verse means merely "fellow Christians,"[133] as some suggest. He's right; that's ridiculous. But that's not the point.

Nor is it when he rejects G.A. Wells's suggestion that "the brothers of the Lord" were a special group of Jewish-Christian pietists in Jerusalem.[134] You don't need the specific characterization Wells suggests. But the phrase is certainly used in 1 Corinthians 9:5 to denote *itinerant preachers*. Schmithals[135] thinks this is exactly the intent of the reference to "none of the apostles except Cephas and James the brother of the Lord" in Galatians 1:19.

Schmithals deconstructed the later, Lukan, notion of "the twelve apostles," seeing in it a conflation of the earlier notion of "the twelve (disciples)" with the "apostles," i.e., travelling missionaries among whom he numbered Cephas/Peter. He understands Cephas to have been a traveling missionary, but (I think inconsistently) not James, whom he locates in Jerusalem overseeing the order and expansion of the church. But I suggest that, if Cephas is to be seen as a traveling evangelist on the basis of Galatians 1:9, so is James. When Paul says he missed seeing the Jerusalem apostles, he makes two exceptions: Cephas *and* James. Note that later writers assumed something like this when they had

---

132. Ethelbert Stauffer, "The Caliphate of James." Trans. by Darrell J. Doughty. *Journal of Higher Criticism* 4/2 (Fall 1997), pp. 120–143.

133. Ehrman, *Did Jesus Exist?*, pp. 119–120, 146.

134. Ehrman, *Did Jesus Exist?*, pp. 149–150.

135. Walter Schmithals, *Paul and James*. Trans. Dorothea M. Barton. Studies in Biblical Theology No. 46 (Naperville: Alec R. Allenson, 1965), pp. 50–51.

both James and Peter address pseudonymous epistles to Christians in the Mediterranean Diaspora (James 1:1; 1 Pet. 1:1). And I think that the Silas character of whom we read in Acts 15:22–18:5 and who neatly replaces James the Just in the narrative (James retires in 15:22 just before Silas comes onstage and pops up again in 21:18 once Silas disappears from the narrative) is a fictive split-off double of James, since "Silas" seems to be the same as the Koran's prophet "Salih,"[136] whose name signifies "the Just."

My conjecture, then, is that Luke created James' role as the Jewish-Christian Pope, stationed him in the Holy City, and suppressed James' original role as a traveling missionary like/with Paul. Thus, again, James was one of "the brothers of the Lord," i.e., a travelling preacher. The same usage is reflected in Matthew 25:40, where Jesus is made to call his missionaries "my brethren." Third John verses 5–8 also differentiate "the brethren" from the mass of Christians who ought to support these men in their missionary journeys. All this, I think, makes it entirely likely that for James to be referred to as "the brother of the Lord" denoted his prominence among these itinerant missionaries. This is a strong enough possibility to make the identification of James as Jesus' literal brother a tossup. Do you really want to lay such a weighty matter on an ambiguous bit of text?

Is it most natural to take "brother of the Lord" as denoting Jesus' biological brother? Is any other reading special pleading? Let's step back for another look at what's going on in such decisions. Stanley Fish says

something very important about evidence: it is always a function of what it is to be evidence for, and is never independently available. That is, the interpretation determines what will count as evidence for it, and the evidence is able to be picked out only because the interpretation has *already* been assumed.[137]

Similarly, R.G. Collingwood:

The web of imaginative construction is something far more solid and powerful than we have hitherto realized. So far from relying for its validity upon the

136. Robert Eisenman, *James the Brother of Jesus: The Key to Unlocking the Secrets of Early Christianity and the Dead Sea Scrolls* (New York: Viking, 1997), p. 890.

137. Stanley Fish, *Is There a Text in This Class? The Authority of Interpretive Communities* (Cambridge: Harvard University Press, 1980), p. 272.

support of given facts, it actually serves as the touchstone by which we decide whether alleged facts are genuine. . . . It is thus the historian's picture of the past, the product of his *a priori* imagination, that has to justify the sources used in its construction.[138]

Another way of getting this point across might be to say that a bit of data looks very different depending on the heuristic paradigm in which one situates it. This is one reason I am always eager to read unfamiliar approaches to familiar texts. Looking at them from a new perspective, I may come to think the "literal" or "natural" reading is other than I had thought. A particular interpretation may well seem self-evident merely because the interpreter is accustomed to it. As Stanley Fish observes, "A sentence that seems to need no interpretation is already the product of one."[139]

CONFORMED TO THE IMAGE OF HIS SON

Bart dismisses another suggestion of mine about an alternate meaning of "the brother of the Lord," namely that it might have denoted an earthly counterpart of the heavenly Christ by virtue of having attained equal enlightenment. I note how Thomas (which means "the twin") was understood by Syrian Christians to be the twin brother of none other than Jesus Christ himself. Bart rightly muses: "One wonders how the Christians who told such stories could possibly imagine that Jesus had a twin brother. Wasn't his mother a virgin? Then where did the twin come from?"[140] But isn't this in itself a big hint that they *didn't* think Thomas was Jesus' biological brother? In the Acts of Thomas, Thomas is twice addressed as the "twin-brother of Christ"[141] Bart says, "This tale is predicated on the view that Thomas and Jesus really were twins in a physical, not symbolic or spiritual sense."[142] But I think there is much more to it.

---

138. Collingwood, *Idea of History*, pp. 244–245.

139. Fish, *Is There a Text*, p. 284.

140. Ehrman, *Did Jesus Exist?*, p. 153.

141. Edgar Hennecke and Wilhelm Schneemelcher, eds., *New Testament Apocrypha*. Trans. A. Higgins et. al. (Philadelphia: Westminster Press, 1963–1966), vol. 2, pp. 459, 464.

142. Ehrman, *Did Jesus Exist?*, p. 153.

In the Gospel of Thomas the esoteric meaning of this designation as the twin brother of Jesus is explained. "Thomas says to him, 'Master, my mouth can scarcely frame the words of what you are like!' Jesus says, 'I am not your master, because you have drunk, you have become filled, from the bubbling spring which I have measured out'" (saying 13). "Jesus says, 'Whoever drinks from my mouth shall become as I am, and I myself will become he. And the hidden things shall at last be revealed to him'" (saying 108). It is in this sense that Thomas, like all the apostles in the Apocryphal Acts, is the twin of Christ. The apostles are the ones with the secret knowledge of Christ that other men do not share. In every one of the five major Apocryphal Acts of the Apostles Christ sooner or later appears on earth in the guise of one of his apostles.

Drusiana had said, "The Lord appeared to me in the tomb in the form of John and in that of a young man." (Acts of John)[143]

Brother Peter, . . . you began to cry out . . ., "Come, our true sword, Jesus Christ, and do not only cut off the head of this demon, but cut in pieces all her limbs in the sight of all these whom I have approved in thy service." And immediately a man who looked like yourself, Peter, with sword in hand, cut her all to pieces, so that I gazed upon you both, both on you and on the one who was cutting up the demon, whose likeness caused me great amazement. (Acts of Peter)[144]

But Thecla sought for Paul, as a lamb in the wilderness looks about for the shepherd. And when she looked upon the crowd, she saw the Lord sitting in the form of Paul. (Acts of Paul)[145]

Maximilla, the Lord going before her in the form of Andrew, went with Iphidamia to the prison. (Acts of Andrew)[146]

And he saw the Lord Jesus in the likeness of the apostle Judas Thomas. (Acts of Thomas)[147]

143. Hennecke and Schneemelcher, *New Testament Apocrypha*, pp. 225–225.

144. Hennecke and Schneemelcher, *New Testament Apocrypha*, p. 305.

145. Hennecke and Schneemelcher, *New Testament Apocrypha*, p. 358.

146. Hennecke and Schneemelcher, *New Testament Apocrypha*, p. 414

147. Hennecke and Schneemelcher, *New Testament Apocrypha*, p. 448.

If the "twin brother of Christ" language were not already explicit enough, we can refer to two key texts in these Acts. In the Acts of John, in the fascinating Round Dance of the Savior liturgy, we read the words of the Redeemer, "I am a mirror to you who know me . . . Now, if you follow my dance, see yourself in me who am speaking."[148] Similarly, in the Acts of Thomas, in the Hymn of the Pearl, we find the words, "The splendid robe [= the heavenly twin in Gnosticism and the Mystery Religions] became like me, as my reflection in a mirror; I saw it wholly in me, and in it I saw myself quite apart from myself, so that we were two in distinction and again one in a single form."[149] The idea is that of the unification of the enlightened soul with its heavenly twin, the Savior.

If this theory about the meaning of "brother of the Lord" seems entirely too grandiose, just think of James and John, sons of Zebedee, called Boanerges, "upholders of the vault of heaven,"[150] a title of Castor and Pollux, sons of Zeus (which is probably what the epithet "Sons of Thunder" actually means). And "Peter" or "Cephas" reflects the Jewish legend of the Temple altar as the keystone stopping up a hole through which the subterranean ocean, the *tehom*, would otherwise gush.[151] Abraham, too, had been called the world's foundation stone.[152] These myth-bearing titles seem to have originally had much more colorful associations than we are commonly told.[153]

---

148.   Hennecke and Schneemelcher, *New Testament Apocrypha*, p. 230.

149.   Hennecke and Schneemelcher, *New Testament Apocrypha*, p. 502.

150.   John M. Allegro, *The Sacred Mushroom and the Cross: A Study of the Nature and Origins of Christianity within the Fertility Cults of the Ancient Near East* (New York: Bantam Books, 1971), pp. 101–102, 134. Allegro was a controversial Dead Sea Scrolls scholar, and this book pretty much consigned him to the Weirdo File, but you don't have to buy his whole bill of goods to take seriously a particular etymological opinion.

151.   A.T. Hanson, *Studies in the Pastoral Epistles* (London: SPCK, 1968), Chapter 1, "The Foundation of Truth," pp. 5–20; Margaret Barker, *The Gate of Heaven: The History and Symbolism of the Temple in Jerusalem* (London: SPCK, 1991), pp. 18–20.

152.   Solomon Schechter, *Some Aspects of Rabbinic Theology* (New York: Macmillan, 1910), p. 59.

153.   Let me just defend my appeal in my book *The Christ Myth and Its Problems* to the title of Hong Xiuqong, the nineteenth-century Taiping Messiah, who called himself "the Younger Brother of Jesus." Bart ridicules my contention that, if in the one case "brother of Jesus" does not imply a biological sibling, it needn't in the other. I am not implying some far-fetched historical connection, as Bart seems to think, but just the

If the idea that "James the brother of the Lord" as an earthly counterpart of the heavenly Christ seems outlandish, ask yourself if that might simply be because you are not used to thinking that way. I hope I have shown that it fits quite well into an ancient Christian context. Of course that doesn't mean my speculation is correct.

But maybe all these deliberations are beside the point, since, as we have seen, Galatians 1:19 might be an interpolation, too.

THE SCANDAL OF THE CROSS

Was there no Jewish precedent for a suffering messiah?[154] Bart says that "today many Christians appear to think that this is what the messiah was supposed to be, God the savior come to earth. But this is not and never was a Jewish view"[155] "Since no one would have made up the idea of a crucified messiah, Jesus must really have existed, must really have raised messianic expectations, and must really have been crucified. No Jew would have invented him."[156] But maybe they wouldn't have *had* to make up a suffering messiah mytheme. I think the familiar messiah theme itself represents a kind of demythologized remnant of the ancient Sacred King mythology.[157]

Ancient Israel borrowed the whole institution of the monarchy from the surrounding nations, replacing an earlier, much looser tribal confederation (1 Sam. 8:4–5). With it came the accoutrements of the institution. Among these was an ideology exalting the king's authority to that of a god on earth.[158] The

---

opposite: since Hong Xiquong cannot possibly have been claiming to be the biological brother of an earthly Jesus, we can hardly insist that "brother of the Lord" means that in the other case. Hong Xiquong claimed to be the earthly manifestation of a fourth hypostasis of the Christian Godhead. Maybe James had something analogous in mind.

154. Ehrman, *Did Jesus Exist?*, pp. 158–159.

155. Ehrman, *Did Jesus Exist?*, p. 159.

156. Ehrman, *Did Jesus Exist?*, p. 164.

157. The ensuing paragraphs represent a slightly revised version of my article "Myth in the New Testament" (*Christian*New Age Quarterly* (20/1) Summer 2011.

158. Perhaps the greatest students of the Near-Eastern Sacred King mythology are Geo Widengren and Ivan Engnell, though Sigmund Mowinckel, Aubrey Johnson, Helmer Ringgren, and others have made important contributions, too. See, e.g., Geo Widengren, "Early Hebrew Myths and their Interpretation" in S.H. Hooke, ed., *Myth,*

king was Yahweh's vicar (Psalm 45:6; Isa. 9:6), his son (Psalms 2:7; 89:26–27) and anointed, i.e., messiah (Psalms 2:2; 89:20). The king annually renewed his divine mandate to rule, and with it the very vigor of the cosmos and the fertility of the land, by ritually re-enacting the myth of how Yahweh became king of the gods.

The gods were frightened (Job 41:9) by the menace of the Chaos Dragon(s), seven-headed Leviathan (Job 3:8; 26:12–13; Psalm 74:14; Is. 27:1; Rev. 12:3, 7), Nehushtan (2 Kings 18:4), Rahab (Psalm 89:10; Isa. 51:9), Behemoth (Job 40:15–24), Yamm (Psalms 74:13a; 89:9) and/or Tiamat (cf., Gen. 1:2, *"tohu,"* *"tehom"*). Tiamat and Yamm were the sea personified, while Leviathan, or Lotan, was the winding Litani River personified. Then the young war-god (Exod. 15:3) and storm-god (Exod. 19:16; Psalms 18:7–15; 29:3–9; Gen. 9:11) Yahweh stepped forth. Like all his fellow sons of El Elyon (the Most High God) (Psalms 29:1; 89:6–7; Gen. 6:1–4; Job 1:6; 2:1), Yahweh had been in charge of a single nation, Israel (Deut. 32:8), but now he made his bid to take the throne over them all. He volunteered to destroy the dragons if the gods would make him king. They agreed, and he did destroy (Psalms 74:13–14; 89:10; Job 26:10–13; Isa. 27:1; 51:9) or subdue and tame (Job 41:1–5) the monster(s). Then he took the throne (Psalms 74:12; 89:13–14; 93:2a; 95:3; 97:1–2) alongside El Elyon, perhaps as co-regent (Dan. 7:2–7, 9–10, 12a, 13–14). From the carcass of the dragon(s) he created the world (Psalms 74:15–17; 89:11–12; 93:1b).

Eventually, the Deuteronomic theologians decided that the two gods Yahweh and El Elyon were merely different names for a single deity (Gen. 14:22). The sons of El became a council with whom Yahweh consults (Psalm 89:5; 1 Kings. 22:19–22; Gen. 3:22; 11:6–7) in their meeting place on Mt. Zaphon in Lebanon (Isa. 14:13) until he finally condemns them for their

---

Ritual and Kingship: Essays on the Theory and Practice of Kingship in the Ancient Near East and in Israel (New York: Oxford University Press, 1958); Widengren, *Sakrales Königtum in Alten Testament und in Judentum.* Franz Delitzsch-Vorlesungen (Stuttgart: Kohlhammer, 1955); Widengren, "Konungens vistelse I dödsriket" in *Svensk Exegetisk Aarsbok* 10 (1945), pp. 66–81; Ivan Engnell, *Studies in Divine Kingship in the Ancient Near East* (Uppsala: Almqvist & Wiksells Boktryckeri, 1943); Engnell, *A Rigid Scrutiny: Critical Essays on the Old Testament.* Trans. John T. Willis and Helmer Ringgren (Nashville: Vanderbilt University Press, 1969), Chapter 11, "The Messiah in the Old Testament and Judaism;" Adela Yarbro Collins and John J. Collins, *King and Messiah as Son of God: Divine, Human, and Angelic Messianic Figures in Biblical and Related Literature* (Grand Rapids: Eerdmans, 2008), Chapter 1, "The King as Son of God," pp. 1–24.

misrule of their nations and sends them to the Netherworld of Sheol, where their blind stumblings cause earthquakes (Psalm 82). They become both the fallen angels imprisoned underground (2 Pet. 2:4; Jude 6) and the Principalities and Powers ruling this age (Rom. 8:38–39; 1 Cor. 2:6–8; Col. 2:15; Eph. 6:12).

The king could actually be addressed as God (Ps. 45:6–7, a royal wedding song) or as the earthly son of God (Ps. 2:7, a birth oracle or coronation song)—just like the Egyptian Pharaohs, whose names denoted their divine parentage: Thutmose (= Son of Thoth), Ramses (= Son of Ra). When each new king was crowned, he came into possession of his divine status or nature, and hopes were expressed for a reign of perfect righteousness, universal justice and amnesty to prisoners, even peace among animals. Several passages interpreted by New Testament writers as predictions of a messiah were first intended as birth or enthronement oracles, or as coronation anthems. The "messiah" and "son" of Yahweh in Psalm 2 is every new king of Judah. Psalm 110 makes pro forma predictions for military victories by the new sovereign and secures for him the hereditary prerogatives of the old Melchizedek priesthood of pre-Davidic Jerusalem. Psalm 110:3 also makes him, like the king of Babylon (Isa. 14:12), the son of the Semitic dawn goddess Shahar (usually mistranslated as a common noun, "dawn.").

Isaiah 9:2–7 is either a coronation oracle or a birth oracle in honor of a newborn heir to the throne, depending on whether "unto us a child is born, unto us a son is given" (verse 6) refers to the literal birth or the adoption as Yahweh's "son" on the day of coronation ("this day I have begotten thee," Psalm 2:7). The epithets bestowed on the king in Isaiah 9:6, "Wonderful Counselor, Mighty God, Everlasting Father [cf., 1 Kings 1:31: "May my lord King David live forever!"], Prince of Peace," echo the divine titles of Pharaoh. Isaiah 61:1–4 is an inaugural oath, pledging universal justice and amnesty to prisoners. Isaiah 7:14 began as a similar birth oracle, casting the newly conceived or newborn royal heir in the role of the son of the virgin goddess Anath (equivalent to Shahar as in Psalm 110).

Psalms 74 and 89 preserve substantial fragments of the myth of Yahweh's primordial combat with the dragons, the ensuing creation, and his ascension to kingship among the sons of El Elyon. We have seen how the king of Judah must have annually renewed his divine right to rule by ritually reenacting this combat. The ancient Near-Eastern kings, as part of the same ritual, would re-enact the death and resurrection of a god (Tammuz, Baal,

Marduk, etc.). It looks like Yahweh, too, was supposed to have been killed and devoured by the dragon, then rose again (Psalm 18:46, "Yahweh lives!") to defeat him. The king ritually assumed the burden of the fertility of the land and the sins of his people. Sometimes this entailed a mock death or else a mere ritual humiliation, as when the Babylonian high priest publicly removed the king's crown, boxed his ears, and slapped his face. Protesting his innocence, the king would don his robe and crown again and rise to full power once more, having redeemed his people in a ritual atonement in which he himself had played the role of scapegoat. Isaiah 52:13–15; 53:1–12 seems to reflect the Hebrew version of the same liturgy.

Margaret Barker[159] challenges the conventional assumption that Judaism was safely monotheistic ever since the Exile. Barker argues that monotheism was a Deuteronomic novelty imposed with incomplete success onto Israelite faith just before the Exile, and that the suppressed, newly "heretical" traditions continued alongside the newly-minted monotheistic orthodoxy right on through the New Testament period, furnishing the categories, ready-made, for New Testament Christology. In the meantime, the old traditions had taken the forms of Apocalypticism, incipient Gnosticism, Merkabah Mysticism, and Philonic Logos speculation. We have blithely assumed that these various thinkers, schools, and groups hatched hugely complex mythologies *ex nihilo* overnight, like mushrooms after a rain shower. But Barker asks the obvious question of whether it is not *a priori* more likely that they were all variously working with very old traditions and variants of traditions, that their efforts lay mainly in fine-tuning and providing new slants to old mythemes and doctrines, those of ancient Israel outside of Deuteronomic orthodoxy.

Even the later "redeemed redeemer" theology of the Gnostics seems to stem from the pre-Deuteronomic royal ideology. Ancient Babylonian myth depicts Marduk being devoured by Kingu, then escaping and destroying him. Canaanite myth has Baal being devoured by Lotan, then raised by Anath, then triumphing. Centuries later, Manichean myths have the Primal Man of Light devoured by the Darkness Dragon and then being rescued. Thus the older royal ideology has been abstracted into the story of a Gnostic Redeemer, reflecting the role of the Gnostic initiate. This was possible because the dying-and-rising god had already been anciently interpreted as symbolic of (or inclusive of) the

---

159. Margaret Barker, *The Great Angel: A Study of Israel's Second God* (Louisville: Westminster/John Knox Press, 1992).

whole human race. The hardiness of the archaic mythemes is attested by their appearance in the Book of Revelation. Again we meet Leviathan the seven-headed dragon (12:3; 13:1), as well as stray bits of unassimilated Greek myth including Hades (20:13–14), Argus (4:6), Baucus and Philemon (3:12, cf. Acts 14:11–13), and Gaia (12:16). The writer even applies the old myth of Zeus and his father Kronos to the infant messiah in 12:4b-6, 13–14.

The hope of a *future* "messiah," or anointed king, appeared first in ancient Judah after the destruction of the Davidic monarchy by the Babylonian conquerors in 586 B.C.E. For centuries Jews longed for the return of national sovereignty. When Christians proclaimed Jesus as Messiah, the old texts came along with the title, and with them came the associations of the old royal ideology. Thus Jesus the divine king who redeemed his people.

One often reads that the Christology of the New Testament goes far beyond the modest Jewish messianic expectation. Contemporary Jews expected a mortal warrior-king like David, righteous and godly, to be sure, but neither a divine being nor a resurrected sin-bearer. It looks as though the role and character of the sacred king had been cut down to size, its original divine elements trimmed away, so as to safeguard newly-regnant monotheism. They did not want the messiah to be regarded as a second God alongside Yahweh. But Christian belief about Jesus as messiah so closely parallels the outlines of the ancient sacred king mythos that we have to suspect it represents the popular, "underground" survival of the old royal ideology, beyond the grasp of officially sanctioned messianic theology. As such, the New Testament view of the messiah may actually be closer to the Old Testament prototype than the later "official" Jewish one. What Bart says about the absence of "Christian" elements from the messianic job description applies only to the truncated version bequeathed by the Deuteronomic revisionists. And that wasn't the only messianic game in town.

ANXIETY OF INFLUENCE

Studying a number of scholarly works which suggest that this or that gospel story is a Christianization of an Old Testament tale, retold and reapplied to Jesus, I found myself in a position analogous to the two Emmaus disciples as the risen Jesus decoded various scriptures as pertaining to him. "Did not our hearts burn within us as he opened the scriptures to us?" Some of these competing scholarly arguments seemed to me inadequate, but when I had finished reading all of them I was astonished to realize that cogent cases could be made, and had been made, for virtually every gospel narrative being a scriptural rewrite. I compiled all the arguments I found convincing, plus a couple original with me.[160] Bart Ehrman was unimpressed.[161] I guess plausibility is in the eye of the beholder. But it's not as if he doesn't see some of the parallels between Moses, Joshua, David, Elijah, Elisha, et. al., on the one hand, and Jesus on the other. But I still don't think he is letting the one hand know what the other is doing.

> Some of the followers of Jesus believed he was the spokesperson[162] of God like Moses of old, and so they told stories about him to make the connections with Moses obvious. Many other followers considered him to be a prophet of God and the Son of God. And so they naturally talked about him in the ways they talked about other Hebrew prophets, such as Elijah and Elisha and Jeremiah.[163]

I'm tempted to say this is a bit circular, since it seems to take it for granted that there was a historical Jesus who might be painted in scriptural hues. But I guess it would be more fair to say that Bart is simply saying that mine is not the only way to explain the correspondences. He is putting the pieces together in a different way, employing a different paradigm. Yet there is a reason I decline that approach. What Bart envisions is reminiscent of Strauss's dictum that early believers in Jesus' messiahship simply reapplied Old Testament stories

---

160. Robert M. Price, "New Testament Narrative as Old Testament Midrash" in Jacob Neusner and Alan J. Avery-Peck (eds.), *Encyclopaedia of Midrash: Biblical Interpretation in Formative Judaism* (E.J. Brill, 2005), Vol. One, pp. 534–573.

161. Ehrman, *Did Jesus Exist?*, pp. 200–206. He laughs off my claim that the story of Jesus healing Peter's mother-in-law so she can get off her butt and fix Sunday dinner is based on that of Elijah and the Widow of Zarephath, but he is isolating this particular case from a larger complex of gospel Elijah/Zarephath rewrites, with the characters reshuffled in different ways. It is not original with me. I found myself convinced by Thomas L. Brodie, "Luke the Literary Interpreter: Luke-Acts as a Systematic Rewriting and Updating of the Elijah-Elisha Narrative in 1 and 2 Kings." Ph.D. dissertation. Pontifical University of Thomas Aquinas, 1981.

162. Why not "spokes*man*"? Was Jesus of indeterminate gender? But if we must for some reason resort to gender-neutering terminology, I prefer "spokeshole."

163. Ehrman, *Did Jesus Exist?*, p. 200.

to him on the widespread expectation that anything Moses and Elijah did the Messiah would do better.[164] Only Bart wants to have it both ways: the stories are borrowed but they also happened. Take away the Old Testament "color" and what have you got left? What sense does it make to discount the Old Testament elements of a gospel story as mere window dressing? Is there going to be anything left in the window?

Bart finds many of my derivations of gospel tales from Old Testament originals to be far-fetched. "Simply read the stories for yourself. The differences are so pronounced that it is hard to see the one as the source of the other."[165] I think that once again he is making a "critical" methodology out of an old apologist sleight-of-hand trick: "the differences are greater than the similarities." If one story is rewritten into another, they don't have to be identical with only a few names changed. I remember thinking, when I read Peter Straub's celebrated novel *Ghost Story*, that it sounded suspiciously like Stephen King's earlier book *Salem's Lot*. Some years afterward I read that Straub credited reading *Salem's Lot* for showing him how to write a novel.

But I second Bart's suggestion: read the parallel stories for yourself. Here are five of them, beginning with an example he invokes, Mark 2:1–12, which I say was derived from 2 Kings 1:2–17.

> Now Ahaziah fell through the lattice in his upper chamber in Samaria, and lay sick; so he sent messengers, telling them, "Go, inquire of Baalzebub, the god of Ekron, whether I shall recover from this sickness." But the angel of [Yahweh] said to Elijah the Tishbite, "Arise, go up to meet the messengers of the king of Samaria, and say to them, 'Is it because there is no God in Israel that you are going to inquire of Baalzebub, the god of Ekron?' Now therefore thus says [Yahweh], 'You shall not come down from the bed to which you have gone, but you shall surely die.'" So Elijah went. The messengers returned to the king, and he said to them, "Why have you returned?" And they said to him, "There came a man to meet us, and said to us, 'Go back to the king who sent you, and say to him, "Thus says [Yahweh], 'Is it because there is no God in Israel that you are sending to inquire of Baalzebub, the god of Ekron? Therefore you shall not come down from the bed to which you have

---

164. Strauss, *Life of Jesus Critically Examined*, p. 86; Wayne A. Meeks, *The Prophet-King: Moses Traditions and the Johannine Christology*. Supplements to Novum Testamentum Volume XIV (Leiden: E.J. Brill, 1967), pp.211-212.

165. Ehrman, *Did Jesus Exist?*, p. 201.

gone, but shall surely die.'" He said to them, "What kind of man was he who came to meet you and told you these things?" They answered him, "He wore a garment of haircloth, with a girdle of leather about his loins." And he said, "It is Elijah the Tishbite!"

Then the king sent to him a captain of fifty men with his fifty. He went up to Elijah, who was sitting on the top of a hill, and said to him, "O man of God, the king says, 'Come down.'" But Elijah answered the captain of fifty, "If I am a man of God, let fire come down from heaven and consume you and your fifty." Then fire came down from heaven, and consumed him and his fifty. Again the king sent to him another captain of fifty men with his fifty. And he went up and said to him, "O man of God, this is the king's order, 'Come down quickly!'" But Elijah answered them, "If I am a man of God, let fire come down from heaven and consume you and your fifty." Then the fire of God came down from heaven and consumed him and his fifty. Again the king sent the captain of a third fifty with his fifty. And the third captain of fifty went up, and came and fell on his knees before Elijah, and entreated him, "O man of God, I pray you, let my life, and the life of these fifty servants of yours, be precious in your sight. Lo, fire came down from heaven, and consumed the two former captains of fifty men with their fifties; but now let my life be precious in your sight." Then the angel of [Yahweh] said to Elijah, "Go down with him; do not be afraid of him." So he arose and went down with him to the king, and said to him, "Thus says [Yahweh], 'Because you have sent messengers to inquire of Baal-zebub, the god of Ekron,—is it because there is no God in Israel to inquire of his word?—therefore you shall not come down from the bed to which you have gone, but you shall surely die.'" So he died according to the word of [Yahweh] which Elijah had spoken. (2 Kings 1:2–17)

And when he returned to Capernaum after some days, it was reported that he was at home. And many were gathered together, so that there was no longer room for them, not even about the door; and he was preaching the word to them. And they came, bringing to him a paralytic carried by four men. And when they could not get near him because of the crowd, they removed the roof above him; and when they had made an opening, they let down the pallet on which the paralytic lay. And when Jesus saw their faith, he said to the paralytic, "My son, your sins are forgiven." Now some of the scribes were sitting there, questioning in their hearts. "Why does this man speak thus? It is blasphemy! Who can forgive sins but God alone?" And immediately Jesus, perceiving in his spirit that they thus questioned within themselves, said to them, "Why do you question thus in your hearts? Which is easier, to say to the paralytic, 'Your sins are forgiven,' or to say, 'Rise, take up your pallet and walk'? But that you may know that the Son of man has authority on earth to forgive sins"—he said to the paralytic—"I say to you, rise, take up your pallet and go home." And he rose, and immediately took up the pallet and went out before them all; so that they were all amazed and glorified God, saying, "We never saw anything like this!" (Mark 2:1–12)

As Wolfgang Roth[166] shows, this story of a paralyzed man's friends tearing the thatch off a roof and lowering him to Jesus amid the crowd seems to be based on the Elijah story in 2 Kings 1:2–17a, where King Ahaziah gains his affliction by falling from his roof through the lattice and languishes in bed. Mark's sufferer is already afflicted when he descends through the roof on his bed (pallet). He rises from his bed because whatever sin of his had earned him the divine judgment of paralysis was now pronounced forgiven on account of his friends' faith, though nothing is said of his own. King Ahaziah is pointedly *not* healed of his affliction because of his own pronounced lack of faith in the God of Israel: he had sent to the priests of the Philistine oracle god Baalzebub to inquire as to his prospects. Elijah tells him he is doomed because of unbelief, a dismal situation reversed by Mark, who has Jesus grant forgiveness and salvation because of faith. Mark has preserved the Baalzebub element for use in a later story (3:22).[167]

What would this story look like without the Old Testament "touches," if that's all they are? I suppose something like this.

And when he returned to Capernaum after some days, it was reported that he was at home; and he was preaching the word to them. And they came, bringing to him a paralytic carried by four men. And when Jesus saw their faith, he said to the paralytic, "I say to you, rise, take up your pallet and go home." And he rose, and immediately took up the pallet and went out before them all; so that they were all amazed and glorified God, saying, "We never saw anything like this!" (Mark 2:1–12)

166. Wolfgang Roth, *Hebrew Gospel: Cracking the Code of Mark* (Oak Park: Meyer-Stone Books, 1988), p. 56.

167. These comments are reproduced from my essay, "New Testament Narrative as Old Testament Midrash."

Well, it would still make sense, but the most striking features of the story are gone.

THE INDEPENDENT EXORCIST (MARK 9:38–40)

The man casting out demons outside of Jesus' retinue, intimidating poor John, is based directly on Eldad and Medad, members of the seventy elders who stayed in the camp when the rest followed Moses to the Tent of Meeting to receive prophetic inspiration (Num. 11:24–30). John is a renamed Joshua who protested that "Eldad and Medad are prophesying in the camp," i.e., "not following us" (Mark 9:38). Jesus is depicted as being fully as broad-minded as Moses, happy to acknowledge the work of God where ever he hears of it.[168] Without the Old Testament "coloring" of the Numbers 11 parallel, here's what we've got. "For he that is not against us is for us." The story, such as it is, is just gone.

THE REQUEST OF JAMES AND JOHN (MARK 10:32–40)

The whole episode comes right out of the story of Elisha's request of Elijah just before his ascension, only Mark's version reflects badly on James and John. The structure is exactly the same.[169] As they travel, Jesus announces for the third time his impending death and resurrection, prompting the brothers to venture, "Teacher, we want you to do for us whatever we may ask of you . . . Grant that we may sit in your glory, one at your right, one at your left" (Mark 10:35, 37). This comes from 2 Kings 2:9, "Ask what I shall do for you before I am taken from you." Hearing the request, Elijah reflects, "You have asked a hard thing" (v. 10), just as Jesus warns James and John, "You do not know what you are asking for." The Elijah-Elisha story cements the "apostolic succession"

---

168. John Bowman, *The Gospel of Mark: The New Christian Jewish Passover Haggadah.* Studia Post-Biblica 8 (Leiden: E.J. Brill, 1965), p. 206; Dale Miller and Patricia Miller, *The Gospel of Mark as Midrash on Earlier Jewish and New Testament Literature.* Studies in the Bible and Early Christianity 21. (Lewiston/Queenston/Lampeter: Edwin Mellen Press), p. 242. This paragraph is plagiarized from my own essay, "New Testament Narrative as Old Testament Midrash."

169. Miller and Miller, *Gospel of Mark as Midrash*, p. 253.

from one prophet to the other, whereas Mark's rewrite seems to pass over the two disciples to open the possibility of succession to anyone willing to follow Jesus along the way of martyrdom.[170]

Remove the Old Testament material, and you've got nothing left. Bart, however, would say that the differences rule out any notion of the Mark text having been rewritten from the 2 Kings episode. Look, I'm not saying Mark simply Xeroxed the Elijah/Elisha version. If he had been merely a scribe copying the Old Testament text, he'd have been a mighty poor one. But the whole point is that he used the one story as the basic outline for another. It's not exactly the same; you wouldn't expect that. But when the similarities are so striking, it seems ridiculous to insist they must be independent. Samuel Sandmel once coined the term "parallelomania," referring very specifically to scholars jumping the gun, inferring that a fragmentary text parallel to some other text at some points must have been consistently parallel in the missing portions, too. But evangelical apologists have cast aside this original use and invoked Sandmel's neologism to discount pretty much any appeal to parallels between texts and traditions and so to evade comparisons suggesting Christian dependence on outside sources. I think Bart is, shall we say, "parallelophobic."

THE STILLING OF THE STORM (4:35–41)

Randel Helms[171] demonstrates how this story has been rewritten from Jonah's adventure, with additions from certain of the Psalms. The basis for the story can be recognized in Jonah 1:4–6,

> But the Lord hurled a great wind upon the sea, and there was a mighty tempest on the sea, so that the ship threatened to break up. Then the mariners were afraid, and each cried to his god. . . . But Jonah had gone down into the inner part of the ship and had lain down, and was fast asleep. So the captain came and said to him, "What do you mean, you sleeper? Arise, call upon your god! Perhaps the god will give a thought to us, that we do not perish."

Once Jonah turns out to be the guilty party, they throw him into the maw

---

170. These comments are ripped off from my essay, "New Testament Narrative as Old Testament Midrash."

171. Randel Helms, *Gospel Fictions* (Buffalo: Prometheus Books, 1989), pp. 76, 77.

of the sea, "and the sea ceased from its raging. The men feared [Yahweh] exceedingly" (1:15b-16a). See also Psalm 107:23–29:

> Some went down to the sea in ships, doing business on the great waters; they saw the deeds of [Yahweh], his wondrous works in the deep. For he commanded, and raised the stormy wind, which lifted up the waves of the sea. They mounted up to the heavens, they went down unto the depths; their courage melted away in their evil plight; they reeled and staggered like drunken men, and were at their wits' end. Then they cried to [Yahweh] in their trouble, and he delivered them from their distress; he made the storm be still, and the waves of the sea were hushed.

Without the "coloring" from Jonah, is there a story here at all?

CHOOSING THE TWELVE; EMBASSY OF RELATIVES (3:13–35)

We must imagine that previous to Mark someone had rewritten the story of Moses heeding Jethro's advice to name subordinates, resulting in a scene in which choosing the twelve disciples was the idea of the Holy Family of Jesus. Note the similarities between Mark 3 and Exodus 18. Just as Moses' father-in-law Jethro hears of Moses' successes and brings Moses' wife and sons to him (Exod. 18:1–5), so do the mother and brothers of Jesus hear reports and journey to meet Jesus (Mark 3:21). Moses is constantly surrounded by suppliants (Exod. 18:13–18), just like Jesus (Mark 3:20). Just as Moses' arriving family is announced ("Lo, your father-in-law Jethro is coming to you with your wife and her two sons with her" Exod. 18:6), so is Jesus' ("Behold, your mother and your brothers are outside looking for you," Mark 3:31–32). "Moses went out to meet his father-in-law, and bowed down and kissed him; and they asked each other of their welfare, and went into the tent" (Exod. 18:7). Originally we would have read of Jesus' welcoming his family. And as Jethro voices his concern for the harried Moses, suggesting he share the burden with a number of helpers (Exod. 18:21–22), so we would have read that James or Mary advised the choice of assistants "that they might be with him, and that he might send them out to preach" (Mark 3:14). And Jesus would only then have named the twelve.

Mark, acting in the interest of a church-political agenda, has broken the story into two and reversed its halves so as to bring dishonor on the relatives of

Jesus (representing a contemporary faction claiming their authority) and to take from them the credit for naming the twelve, which is also why he emphasizes that Jesus "summoned those that he *himself* wanted," i.e., it was all his own idea. As the text now reads, Jesus chooses the disciples, and only subsequently do his interfering relatives arrive harboring doubts about his sanity, and he rebuffs them (Mark 3:33–35).

Jesus, however, does not, like Moses, choose seventy (though Luke will restore this number, Luke 10:1), but only twelve, based on the choice of the twelve spies in Deuteronomy 1:23.[172]

It's all too close for comfort, isn't it? Again, ask yourself, if there is a link between the corresponding Old and New Testament texts, can it be adequately accounted for as mere Old Testament "coloring" of a pre-existing Jesus story?

THE PROPHET WHO MAKES THE SIGN OF THE 'Z'

I am very much surprised to see Bart scoffing at the notion of Zoroastrian influence on Judaism. He sets forth this view in the course of dismissing out of hand my suggestion that the story of Jesus' baptism, which strikingly parallels that of Zoroaster at the inauguration of his ministry, may have been based on it. It is certainly my impression that scholars in general have long taken Zoroastrian influence on Judaism for granted.[173] So very much of what eventually became Orthodox Judaism appears to be inheritance from the Persian religion of Zoroaster (Zarathustra). This includes such well-known doctrines as angelology, a virgin-born future savior, the dispensational periodization of history, a Final Judgment, an eschatological resurrection of the dead, the notion of a near-almighty evil anti-God, and the ascription to him of "creeping things" like serpents and scorpions (Luke 10:18–19). The Sadducees rejected these beliefs as unscriptural innovations, as indeed they were. It is no surprise that Judaism should have assimilated many beliefs from the Persian overlords. But the Sadducees were having none of it and dubbed

---

172. Miller and Miller, *Gospel of Mark as Midrash*, p. 117. My comments on this passage come from my essay, "New Testament Narrative as Old Testament Midrash."

173. James Barr, "The Question of Religious Influence: The Case of Zoroastrianism, Judaism, and Christianity." *Journal of the American Academy of Religion* 53, no. 2 (June 1985), pp. 201–235.

the pro-Persian Jews "Pharisees," i.e., Parsees.[174] Some Jews went so far as to identify Zoroaster with Baruch the scribe of Jeremiah.[175] Their theological opponents countered with the claim that Baruch had forsaken Judaism and went on to author the Avesta.[176] I just don't see the difficulty of my suggestion. But again, Bart sides with his former evangelical compatriots in "the scholarly apologetic segregation of early Christian beliefs about Jesus Christ from Greek- and Roman-dominated Mediterranean culture."[177]

MYTHS AND MYSTERIES

Was the resurrection of Jesus derived from the myths of the dying and rising gods? Not bloody likely, saith Bart Ehrman, since there *were* no such myths at the time.[178] Here is the clearest instance of the ex-evangelical Ehrman remaining loyal to the apologetics agenda of his mentor Bruce M. Metzger (and many others). But it is not Metzger whom Bart invokes. Instead, he refers us to the celebrated Jonathan Z. Smith, whose work,[179] along with that of Mark S. Smith, Bart says, has settled the issue and put to rest the notion of dying and rising gods. But it hasn't. Not by a long shot.

Following the two Smiths, Bart seeks to discount the notion of Christians borrowing from the Mystery Religions. First, how do we know that our early Christian writers who set forth these parallels did not *create* them, ascribing to the Mystery Religions their own beliefs about their savior Jesus? As far as I can see, the absurdity of this line of thinking is exceeded only by its perversity.

---

174. Ehrman, *Did Jesus Exist?*, pp. 203–204. T.W. Manson, *The Servant Messiah: A Study of the Public Ministry of Jesus* (Cambridge at the University Press, 1953), pp. 18–20. As often in the Old Testament, the bearers of this heresy-denoting designation redefined and adopted it. "Parsees" became "Perushim," or "Separated Ones."

175. Richard Reitzenstein, *Hellenistic Mystery-Religions: Their Basic Ideas and Significance*. Trans. John E. Steely. Pittsburgh Theological Monograph Series No. 15 (Pittsburgh: Pickwick Press, 1978), p. 58

176. Reitzenstein, *Hellenistic Mystery-Religions*, p. 61.

177. Stanley K. Stowers, cover blurb for M. David Litwa, *Iesus Deus: The Early Christian Depiction of Jesus as a Mediterranean God* (Minneapolis: Fortress Press, 2014).

178. Ehrman, *Did Jesus Exist?*, pp. 222ff.

179. Jonathan Z. Smith, "Dying and Rising Gods" in Mircea Eliade, ed., *Encyclopedia of Religion*. Vol. 4 (New York: Macmillan, 1987), pp. 521–527.

You mean to say the early Christians, for no particular reason, created an unnecessary problem for themselves, undermining their own claims? Tryggve Mettinger[180] rightly disposes of the absurdity, urged by Jonathan Z. Smith and apologists, that Patristic authors who speak of pagan death-and-resurrection rituals are misconstruing some entirely different thing as a copy of their own Easter faith. (If they were so different, where was the point of comparison in the first place?) Picture the ancient apologists first trying to convince pagan hearers that Christianity paralleled paganism (when it actually *didn't*) and then proceeding to discount the parallels or to explain them away!

Second, Bart and the Smiths suggest that the borrowing went in the other direction, that the pagans did not believe in dying and rising gods before Christians came up with it but unfortunately forgot to copyright it. The stake through the heart of this theory is simply this: What about the "Satanic counterfeits" argument?[181]

> You may be sure, Trypho, that the very stories which he who is called the devil deceitfully caused to be told among the Greeks,[182] just as he operated through the wise men of Egypt[183] and the false prophets in the time of Elijah,[184] have confirmed my understanding and faith in the Scriptures. For when they say that Dionysus was born the son of Zeus as a result of his intercourse with Semele, and when they relate that this Dionysus was the inventor of the vine, and that he was torn in pieces and died and rose again and went up to heaven, and when they introduce an ass into his mysteries, can I not recognize that he [i.e., the devil] has imitated the prophecy spoken beforehand by the patriarch Jacob and recorded by Moses [Gen. 49:11–12]? And when they describe Hercules as strong and as journeying through the whole earth and that he was born to Zeus of Alcmena and that he died and went into heaven, do I not recognize an imitation of the passage of Scripture spoken about Christ, *He is strong as a giant to run his course* [Psalm 19:6]? And when he introduces Asclepius raising the dead and curing other human ills

180. Tryggve N.D. Mettinger, *The Riddle of Resurrection: "Dying and Rising Gods" in the Ancient Near East*. Coniectanea Biblica Old Testament Series 50 (Stockholm: Almqvist & Wiksell International, 2001), pp. 136, 153–154, 217.

181. Ehrman, *Did Jesus Exist?*, pp. 214, 229.

182. He refers to Dionysus, Hercules, and Asclepius.

183. He must be thinking of Isis and Osiris.

184. This of course refers to Baal.

am I not to say that he is imitating the prophecies made about Christ on this subject, too?[185] (V.69)

Tertullian says much the same. Is there any possibility that early Christian apologists would have argued this way, claiming that pagan parallels were Satanic counterfeits *in advance*, unless they had to admit the pagan versions were *earlier*?

The idea that Christians started the "dying-and-rising" trend, which pagans then copied for their Brand X saviors, is fully as ridiculous as the claims of Josephus and Philo that Plato borrowed his philosophy from the Pentateuch.

And the notion that there is no pre-Christian evidence, from pagan sources, of belief in resurrecting gods is without factual foundation. J.Z. Smith contends that the pre-Christian versions of the myths of these pagan gods did not depict them as dying and rising. We must review the evidence.

The ancient Hellenistic world abounded in religions based on dying and rising savior deities. At first the rituals of such faiths measured the annual cycle of nature. The death and resurrection imagery stood for the dying of vegetation in Autumn and Winter and its revitalization in Spring and Summer. Alternatively, it stood for the decline of daylight till the Winter Solstice and the increase of the day's length afterward. Yet another closely related variant dramatized planting (i.e., death and burial) the seed and its sprouting (resurrection). One of the oldest of these is the myth of Aleyan (= Elyon) Baal: this god of war and storm strove with the Death monster Mot and suffered bitter defeat. Baal's consort Anath wept and mourned, then resolved to invade the Netherworld to retrieve him. Thus raised up, Baal ascended the throne alongside his father El as Lord ("Baal") of gods and men.

Dumuzi was Baal's Sumerian counterpart, Tammuz his Babylonian alter ego. He, too, died and descended to the Netherworld. His lover Ishtar rescued him, undergoing her own death and resurrection along the way. Both divine couples notoriously received worship in ancient Israel. We know this from the denunciation of their worship by Hosea and Jeremiah. The Song of Songs is most naturally interpreted as the liturgies of Ishtar and Tammuz, though scribes had to suppress the original names to get the book into the canon.[186]

---

185. *Justin Martyr's Dialogue with Trypho*, pp. 42–43.

186. Marvin H. Pope, *Song of Songs: A New Translation with Introduction and Commentary*. Anchor Bible 7C (Garden City: Doubleday, 1977), pp. 145–151. Ishtar Shalmith

Osiris taught agriculture to the Egyptians, but he was betrayed and assassinated by his wicked brother Set (the desert god). Isis his queen bewailed his death and, accompanied by her sister Nephthys, set out to find his missing corpse. The slain Osiris had been dismembered, but Isis put Humpty back together again. Anointing the body, she raised him from the dead, whereupon he impregnated her, and they lived happily ever after. Just not together. Osiris entered into the Netherworld, becoming its supreme judge and ruler. His last fling with Isis? He had fathered upon Isis a son, Harpocrates, his own earthly reincarnation, who grew up to take revenge on the wicked Set.[187]

Attis of Phrygia was either the son or the lover (or both) of the cave goddess Cybele. One day he betrayed her and married a mortal princess. Cybele appeared uninvited at the festivities (just like the witch at Sleeping Beauty's christening) and sent the revelers flying. Attis, too, fled and, filled with self-reproach, castrated himself and bled to death. Cybele was now doubly stricken and managed to raise him from the dead. Adonis betrayed Aphrodite, who sent a vicious boar to gore him to death, but she thought better of it and revived him. On Crete Dionysus suffered the same fate and lived again. In the Orphic myth, Dionysus, in his avatar as Zagreus the Hunter, had been dismembered and devoured by the Titans. Zeus found out and killed the murderers. Then he turned cannibal himself and ate the heart of Zagreus. Thence was Zagreus reborn as the more familiar Dionysus. A sun god, Mithras died on the shortest day of each year but was reborn on the next day.

Originally all these myths were rehearsed yearly in rites intended either simply to commemorate the change of seasons, or actually to effect the change.[188] Later, a new inner significance to the myth was "discovered" by those elite few who found the pantomimes of an agricultural faith to be spiritually inadequate. They had undergone the ritual passage from child to adult, educated in the rituals of their people and qualifying to participate in them.[189] Might one undergo yet a further stage of initiation to a still greater

---

becomes "the Shulamite."

187. Roland Guy Bonnel and Victor Arieh Tobin, "Christ and Osiris: A Comparative Study," in Sarah Israelis-Groll, ed., *Pharaonic Egypt: The Bible and Christianity* (Jerusalem: Avigness Press, 1985), pp. 1–29.

188. Mircea Eliade, *The Sacred and the Profane: The Nature of Religion*. Trans. Willard R. Trask (New York: Harcourt, Brace & World, 1959), pp. 68–115.

189. Arnold van Gennep, *The Rites of Passage*. Trans. Monika B. Visedom and Gabrielle

maturity? Might one somehow participate in the god's death and resurrection, and so share in his immortality? And the Mystery Religions were born.

The Mystery Cult would, then, have been the esoteric core of a traditional religion whose exoteric concern had been the renewal of the fields in the spring. But with the mass social dislocations of the Hellenistic age, great numbers of people found themselves cut off from their rural homelands. In their new urban environments they did their best to maintain an ethnic/cultural identity in a radically pluralistic society. Like Diaspora Jews, who created the synagogue as a magnet for maintaining their heritage, other groups transplanted their religions, too. In a new, urban environment, the original fertility character of their religions was moot. Accordingly, the esoteric, spiritual level assumed newly exclusive prominence. These rituals of mystical transformation were carefully guarded from the prying eyes of outsiders, but outsiders could become insiders. Anyone seeking redemption could find it in their sanctuaries. And, unwilling to take unnecessary risks with their souls, seekers could sign on with more than one Mystery Cult,[190] calculating that the various deities, all seemingly interchangeable, were different aliases for the same savior.

The rituals allowing the initiate to apply to himself the salvific ordeal and triumph of the savior were different in each cult, but most shared this basic element in some form. For instance, the Persian Mithras had wrestled a mighty bull to the death (symbolizing the replacement of Taurus by Perseus in the precession of the Equinox[191]), and the Mithraist initiate stood in a recess below a grate upon which stood a bull whose slit throat rained hot blood down on him (just like Siegfried doused with the blood of the disemboweled dragon Fafnir, gaining invulnerability from it). Brother, have you been washed in the blood?

Attis' devotees staged public Hare Krishna-like displays, featuring ecstatic dances. Idle gawkers would gather, the curiosity of some of them soon succumbing to the drum-throbbing frenzy. Joining in the hypnotic merriment,

---

L. Caffee (Chicago: University of Chicago Press, 1960).

190. Technically, these faiths were "religions" on their home soil and in the culture for which they formed the sacred canopy of norms and values (see Peter L. Berger, *The Sacred Canopy: Elements of a Sociological Theory of Religion* [Garden City: Doubleday Anchor Books, 1969]) but "cults" once transplanted into a new and foreign culture. Sociologically, there is nothing pernicious about the term "cult."

191. David Ulansey, *The Origins of the Mithraic Mysteries: Cosmology and Salvation* (New York: Oxford University Press, 1991).

they found themselves impelled to castrate themselves, tossing their sanguined testicles, like a pair of garlic cloves, into the lap of a silver idol of Cybele. At this point, they were in it for the long haul! "No turning back! No turning back!" There was an annual Spring day of general mourning, both for Attis and for their own lost manhood, culminating in a ritual interment of an crude effigy of Attis crucified to a pine trunk. On the third day his priests would proclaim his resurrection from the dead: "Rejoice, you of the mystery! For your god is saved! And we, too, shall be saved!"[192] They were saved by recapitulating his ordeal and resurrection.

In the same way, burial inscriptions for Osiris' worshippers assure the mourners, "As Osiris died, so has N_ died; and, as Osiris rose, so shall N_ rise." His devotees would partake of a sacramental meal of bread and wine (or beer), symbolizing his body and blood. The Maenads of Dionysus would relive the death of their Lord by entering a frenzied state and ripping live animals limb-from-limb. Hercules' initiates donned lion skins to buy into the victory of Zeus' son over the Nemean Lion. These ancient Holy Rollers joined in Voodoo-like revels as the gathered congregation rejoiced in the unseen presence of their Kyrios (Lord) or Kuria (Lady), e.g., the Lady Isis or the Magna Mater. We possess copies of written invitations to sacramental banquets held in honor of the gods, e.g., "Pray come dine with me today at the table of the Kyrios Serapis." This must be the kind of social event Paul finds so troublesome, when he admits that indeed "there are gods aplenty and *kyrioi* aplenty" (1 Cor. 8:5) but has to remind his Corinthian readers that "for us there is but one God, the Father, who created all things, and one Kyrios, through whom all things were made" (1 Cor. 8:6).

Apologists and their strange bedfellows have to try very hard *not* to see extensive, basic similarities between the Mystery Cults and Christianity. But others can see the elephant in the room. Once John Cuthbert Lawson[193] was touring rural Greece and was present for a local Passion Play. The villager playing the role of Jesus was being carried to the mock-up tomb on Good Friday evening when Lawson was startled to notice an old lady weeping next to him. When he expressed concern, she tearfully exclaimed, "If Christ does

---

192. Firmicus Maternus, *The Error of the Pagan Religions.* Trans. Clarence A. Forbes. Ancient Christian Writers No. 37 (New York: Paulist Press, 1970), p. 93.

193. John Cuthbert Lawson, *Modern Greek Folklore and Ancient Greek Religion: A Study in Survivals* (Cambridge at the University Press, 1910), p. 573.

not rise this Sunday, we shall have no crops this year!" Nobody had to explain James Frazer's theories to her.

Mettinger puts it very well.

> One *sometimes* notes in the research certain evasive strategies designed to avoid the conclusion that the notion of dying and rising deities might be a pre-Christian phenomenon. Ancient Near Eastern gods are freely granted the privilege of rising or returning—as long as they behave like gentlemen and do not do so before Christ.[194]

That's certainly the vibe I'm picking up from Bart Ehrman.

IDOL TYPES

J.Z. Smith's worst error is his failure, as I see it, to grasp the point of an "ideal type," something of a basic text-book definition/description of some phenomenon under study. As Bryan Wilson pointed out, an ideal type is not a box into which all the various instances of a phenomenon must fit snugly. If it were, we would have to either whittle away the rough edges of particular phenomena (in this case redeemer myths) or build our box big enough and shapeless enough to accommodate everything. This would serve no descriptive purpose. An ideal type sets forth a basic skeleton of common features usually present in a group of instances. Any particular example partakes of most of these features while differing in detail. But J.Z. Smith accuses previous scholars of cobbling together disparate features of very different myths in order to construct an artificial synthesis, a chimera which does not resemble any actual myths or gods. He is shocked, *shocked*, to find significant differences between the so-called dying-and-rising god myths and declares the patient dead with no resurrection on the schedule. In other words, if the various myths of Osiris, Attis, Adonis, et. al., do not all conform to type exactly, then they do not fit into the same box, so let's throw out the box. Without everything in common, Smith sees nothing in common. But, again, an ideal type, as Wilson points out, is rather a yardstick abstracted from the admittedly diverse phenomena; it represents a general family resemblance without implying absolute, comprehensive conformity. Indeed, wherever a particular myth does

---

194. Mettinger, *Riddle of Resurrection*, p. 217.

not conform to the type, we have discovered a promising point of departure for understanding its special uniqueness. Why does this one veer off the track at this particular point?

Jonathan Z. Smith[195] makes the same mistake that Raymond E. Brown[196] does when the latter dismisses the truckload of comparative religion parallels to the miraculous conception of Jesus. This one is not strictly speaking a virgin birth, since the mother was a married woman. That one involved physical intercourse with the deity, not overshadowing by the Holy Spirit, etc. But, come on, how close does a parallel have to be to *count* as a parallel? Does the divine mother have to be named Mary? Does the divine child have to be named Jesus? Here is the old "difference without a distinction" fallacy.

J.Z. Smith tries to pry apart the dying-and-rising god mytheme, dissecting it into different, mismatched components. Let's see: there are deities who disappear, then reappear, and there are gods who die but do not rise. Adonis, he says, is never said to have actually kicked the bucket, but only to have undertaken a bicoastal lifestyle, splitting the year between two romantic rivals, Aphrodite and Persephone. To spend the winter with Persephone, he has to head south to Hades. And then he pops up again with the flowers in the Spring, headed for Aphrodite's place. This makes him not dead? What does it mean to say someone has descended to the Netherworld of the dead? Enkidu did not consider it a casual jaunt "to hell and back." He "led me away to the palace of Irkalla, the Queen of Darkness, to the house from which none who enters ever returns, down the road from which there is no coming back." One goes there cuffed by the Grim Reaper. Pausanias relates how Theseus was imprisoned in the Netherworld "until Hercules should bring him back to life" (*Guide to Greece*, I:17:4). Thus, to abide in the Netherworld was to be dead—for as long as you were there!

Aliyan Baal's supposed death and resurrection is not good enough for J.Z. Smith because the surviving text has big holes in it "at the crucial points." Sure, certain mischievous scholars want to patch the holes with the model of the resurrected god, but Smith dismisses it as an argument from silence. Really? Even Smith admits the text actually does say that "Baal is reported to have died" after sinking into the Netherworld. There he is indeed said to be "as

---

195.　Ehrman, *Did Jesus Exist?*, p. 214, falls into the same ditch.

196.　Raymond E. Brown, in *The Birth of the Messiah: A Commentary on the Infancy Narratives in Matthew and Luke* (Garden City: Doubleday, 1977), p. 523.

dead." His consort Anat retrieves the corpse and buries it. Later his father El learns in a dream that Baal lives. After another gap in the text, Baal is shown in battle. What's missing? Smith feels pretty sure that in the missing portion we would have read that Baal was the victim of a premature burial, that the reports of his demise were premature. But does Smith have any particular reason to be sure about this? Who's arguing from silence here? J.Z. Smith is manipulating that hole in the text like a ventriloquist dummy.

The Syrian version of Baal, Baal-Hadad, is even less in danger of death in Smith's reckoning, merely sinking into a bog for seven years. When he reemerges, languishing nature regains its green vigor. Smith concludes, "There is no suggestion of death and resurrection." No hint of ritual reenactment of the myth. What about Zechariah 12:11, where we read of inconsolable ritual mourning for Hadad-Rimmon? What are they mourning? Isn't it usually, ah, *death*?

J.Z. Smith admits that even in very ancient records Osiris is said to have been dismembered, reassembled by Isis like the Frankenstein Monster, and brought back to blood-circulating, breathing physical life. But for Smith, it doesn't count as a resurrection! Why the hell *not*? Well, you see, Osiris did not resume his life on the earthly plane. He reigned henceforth in the realm of the dead. And this is not analogous to Jesus? In case Smith hadn't noticed, the post-Easter Jesus did not take up fly-fishing in Galilee. Instead, he took the celestial omnibus to reign forever at the right hand of God in heaven as the judge of the dead. So, if we go by J.Z. Smith's criteria, not even Jesus would qualify as a dying and rising god. But whatever the heck Osiris is, Jesus is another one.

What about Tammuz, a god so familiar to ancient Israelites that his name graces one month of the Jewish calendar to this day? J.Z. Smith describes how scholars early speculated from the fragmentary Tammuz texts that he had been depicted as dying and rising, though the evidence was touch and go. Subsequently, he grants, more textual evidence turned up, vindicating the old theories. But Smith quibbles even here. Though the new material makes unambiguously clear that Tammuz's lover Ishtar herself also dies and rises, Smith passes this by virtually without remark and picks the nit that Tammuz is "baaled out" of death for only half the year while someone else takes his place. Death, Smith remarks, is inexorable: the most Tammuz could get is a six-month furlough. The case is parallel to that of Adonis, but there Smith denied a half-year return from Hades meant a real death, whereas with Tammuz he says it means no real resurrection.

MEETINGS WITH REMARKABLE METTINGER

Why does J.Z. Smith adopt the program of Christian apologists? I suspect it is part of his root-and-branch campaign to undo the theories of his great predecessor James Frazer. In any case, the viability of the dying-and-rising god mytheme seems to me unimpeached. There was such a myth making the rounds. It is extant in several versions as we have seen.

J.Z. Smith echoes the apologists especially in the case of Attis, where the explicit mentions of his resurrection date from the Christian era (though they are not there mentioned as innovations). But as Maarten J. Vermaseren[197] has shown, we do in fact possess pre-Christian pottery depicting Attis dancing, the traditional posture of his resurrection. J.Z. Smith and others had pointed out that gods like Adonis and Tammuz inspired rituals of mourning for their deaths, but that the sources made no mention of any celebration of their resurrections. But Tryggve Mettinger points out that such a criticism is as futile as those which condemned *Jesus Christ Superstar* for not depicting Jesus' resurrection, failing to recognize it was a Passion, like Bach's *Saint Matthew's Passion*, and was thus meant to cover but one specific segment of the gospel story, available in its entirety elsewhere.

In some cases, though, as Mettinger shows, there were celebrations of a god's resurrection, but they were separated by some months from the mourning rites. This is altogether natural, celebrating each portion of the story at its proper spot on the calendar, waiting till Spring to celebrate the Springtide resurrection. There were others in which the divine death and resurrection were celebrated as a single complex, mere days apart, as in the case of Jesus. (In fact, Mettinger finds vestiges, nothing more, of a possible pattern of third-day resurrections in these myths.) When modern scholars come upon something like Ezekiel 8:14, a ritual of mourning for Tammuz, with no mention of a resurrection celebration, they are inclined to conclude there was no resurrection sequel when there is a good reason for one not being noted in the same reference: it was yet months away.

Richard Reitzenstein[198] and Wilhelm Bousset[199] were two scholars who did

---

197. Maarten J. Vermaseren, *Cybele and Attis: The Myth and the Cult*. Trans. A.M.H. Lemmers (London: Thames and Hudson, 1977), pp. 119–124.

198. Reitzenstein, *Hellenistic Mystery-Religions*, pp. 176 ff.

199. Wilhelm Bousset, *Kyrios Christos: A History of the Belief in Christ from the Beginnings*

manage to grasp the relevance of these ancient faiths for the study of early Christianity. Their conclusion was a simple and seemingly inevitable one: once it reached Hellenistic soil, the story of Jesus attracted to itself a number of mythic motifs that were common to the syncretistic religious mood of the era. Indeed, as people familiar with the other Mystery Religions came to embrace the Christian savior, it would have been practically impossible for them *not* to have clothed him in all the accouterments of his fellow *Kyrioi*. If Jesus was a savior, then he was *ipso facto* to be considered a dying and rising god whose immortality one might share through participatory sacraments.

And we need not only think of the situation as Reitzenstein did, still picturing a process of individuals breaking with their old religion and accepting a new one instead. Since the Mystery Religions made no exclusive claim and begrudged no member his or her simultaneous membership in a parallel Mystery, we must assume that many early Christian "converts" had no thought of abandoning Mithras, Isis, Attis, or Dionysus. Why should they? In the so-called Naassene Liturgy, we have a Christian document from the third century which informs us that the true name of the savior Jesus is Adam or Attis! (Adam and Eve had long been identified with Attis and Cybele, presupposing the ancient version of the Eden myth, echoed in the Nag Hammadi texts, that Eve was a goddess and created Adam.)

"These mystery cults are never mentioned by Paul."[200] Really? What was the danger Paul perceived in the case that one "weaker in faith" should observe another Corinthian partaking in an idol's feast? The "weaker brother," Paul implies, is "weak" precisely for not grasping that Christ is the only real Kyrios. He would take the example of a Christian eating from the communion table of Serapis as confirming his assumption that a Christian might be a Mithraist or anything else he had the funds to pay for. What Paul apparently faced in Corinth in these instances was the practice by Christians of what Max Müller called "kathenotheism," the worship of several gods, but one at a time. With the gates thus open, we would be amazed not to find a free flow of older "pagan" myths and rituals into Christianity. For instance, it is only under the influence of Dionysus (whether in Greece or even in Palestine) that Jesus bequeaths his devotees a sacrament of his body, the body of grain, and his blood, the blood

---

of Christianity to Irenaeus. Trans. John E. Steely (New York: Abingdon Press, 1970), pp. 119–152.

200. Ehrman, *Did Jesus Exist?*, p. 256.

of the grape. Only so is he the True Vine giving vitality to his branches, does he turn water into wine. As Jesus the Corn King whose winnowing fan is in his hand, he is slain while the wood is still green, yields up his life like the planted seed, buried in a garden.

And we need not think that these Corinthians had fallen from some purer version of Christian orthodox truth. No, what we are seeing in the Pauline warnings against syncretic kathenotheism is the beginning of the process to exclude the other faiths as rivals and counterfeits of Christianity. But the barn door was, as usual, shut after the horse had got out (or rather, *in!*).

I Wouldn't Want to Belong to Any Club That Would Want Someone Like Me as a Member

Does it render Mettinger's critiques of the Smiths' case harmless that Mettinger himself exempts the story of Jesus' death and resurrection from the category of the myths of the Mystery saviors?[201] Not when you see why he gives Jesus a break. Mettinger echoes the moot point of Michael Green[202] and other apologists that the resurrection of Jesus is supposed to be a one-time event involving a historical individual, unlike the myths of the Mystery saviors who were cyclically returning figureheads of the harvest. That is beside the point, since the Christ-Myth theory posits a process of historicization through story-telling, by which the initially nonhistorical Jesus was transformed into a supposed figure of history. In precisely the same way, Herodotus sought to fix the dates of mighty Hercules. The Christ-Myth theory rejects Bultmannism, seeing in it an attempt at Euhemerism, the supposition that wholly mythical characters stem from ostensibly historical figures of remote antiquity. On the other hand, the fact that Dr. Mettinger does not espouse the Christ Myth position forbids anyone to dismiss his conclusions about pre-Christian dying and rising saviors as axe-grinding.

Bart warns us not to invoke Mettinger to buttress our case, since he repudiates Mythicism. Similarly, he criticizes Earl Doherty because he "quotes professional scholars at length when their views prove useful for developing

---

201. Ehrman, *Did Jesus Exist?*, pp. 224–225; Mettinger, *Riddle of Resurrection*, p. 220–221.

202. Michael Green, "Jesus in the New Testament." In Green, ed., *The Truth of God Incarnate* (Grand Rapids: Eerdmans, 1977), p. 36.

aspects of his argument but fails to point out that not a single one of these scholars agrees with his overarching thesis."[203] I remember reading pretty much the same contemptuous dismissal in James Barr's great book *Fundamentalism*, where he makes an example of Kenneth G. Howkins's supposedly opportunistic and cosmetic appeal to respected scholars.

> K.G. Howkins' *The Challenge of Religious Studies* (Tyndale Press 1972) is studded with quotations from T.F. Torrance, Alan Richardson, G.W. Anderson, S.C. Neill, H.H. Rowley and others. The book would look a great deal different if, after every case where one of these is quoted with approval, the annotation were added: *The scholar just quoted would, of course, totally repudiate the whole conservative position advocated in this book.* . . . If these various scholars have, as Howkins clearly accepts, valuable insights into the questions he is discussing, then the question has to be asked: how did they come to have these valuable insights when they fully reject the conservative evangelical position the author is trying to support?[204]

I thought the criticism was unfair, because illogical, then, and I feel the same way now. Certainly one can find specific insights to be valuable in an argument which one does not otherwise accept. Arguments are chains of links, some stronger, some weaker, than others. What Howkins did and what Doherty does is in no way hypocritical or inconsistent. I have certainly thought how this or that scholar did not see the rightful or full implications of some solid observation. I'd bet Bart has, too. And if you think someone has good insights, does that mean you have to accept everything else he thinks?

SMOKING GUN CONTROL

Bart states that there is no evidence that Jews in the New Testament period were influenced by Mystery deities.[205] What sort of thing might count as evidence? If what is required is explicit statements to that effect, we might as well ask what evidence there is that Matthew and Luke used Mark. After all, there is no confession in Matthew that, "Verily, brethren, I have undertaken to add new

203. Ehrman, *Did Jesus Exist?*, p. 252.

204. James Barr, *Fundamentalism* (Philadelphia: Westminster Press, 1978), pp. 307–308.

205. Ehrman, *Did Jesus Exist?*, p. 230.

sayings of the Lord Jesus to those that our forefather Mark set down for us." No, it is rather the extensive parallels between Matthew and Mark that count as evidence of dependence. And Bart and I both consider that evidence pretty darn compelling. By the same principle, I should think the numerous parallels between the gospels and contemporary Hellenistic religions are themselves the evidence Bart says we lack.

But in fact, there is explicit evidence of Jewish syncretism in the periods leading up to and following after the New Testament period. Second Maccabees describes the wholesale conversion of Jews to the worship of Dionysus (2 Macc. 6:7). The author would have us believe it was all under-the-gun play-acting, but remember, 1 Maccabees implies it was the widespread, apparently voluntary, apostasy of Jews that led to the fury of Mattathias and his sons (1 Macc. 1:51–52; 2:23–26). Plutarch reports that the Jews worshipped Dionysus (*Symposiacs*, iv, 6), and many non-Jews believed Yahweh and Dionysus were the same. The Epistle of Aristeas, a work of Hellenistic Judaism, equates Yahweh with Zeus (15–16). The cult of Sabazios in Asia Minor conflated the Jewish Yahweh with Dionysus.[206] Reitzenstein comments: "Even in Trajan's time the Roman Jewish community still was not strictly orthodox, but either altogether or in large part worshipped the [Zeus Uranus] and the Phrygian Attis together with Yahweh."[207]

So we have ample evidence that Jews both in the Holy Land and in the Diaspora were susceptible to Hellenistic religious syncretism. It started, at the latest, in the mid-second century BCE and is still evident in the second century CE, after the emergence of what became Rabbinic Judaism, thus in the teeth of the kind of Judaism least likely to tolerate pagan elements. So why should we mark out a magic segment of history[208] in which such elements (e.g., dying and rising gods) were barred from influencing Judaism, like the workers of iniquity banned from the New Jerusalem? The whole notion is obviously a contrivance of Christian apologetics, posited by theologians with a severe distaste for the

---

206. W.O.E. Oesterley, "The Cult of Sabazios," in S.H. Hooke, ed., *The Labyrinth: Further Studies in the Relation between Myth and Ritual in the Ancient World* (London: SPCK, 1935), pp. 113–158.

207. Reitzenstein, *Hellenistic Mystery-Religions*, p. 125.

208. It reminds me of Luke's "Satan-free period" during the ministry of Jesus in Hans Conzelmann, *The Theology of St. Luke*. Trans. Geoffrey Buswell (New York: Harper & Row, 1961).

notion that the pure river of Jehovah's revelation should have been polluted by pagan tributaries. I can only say that I have to suspect that my fellow ex-evangelical[209] Bart Ehrman has retained certain vestiges of that tradition,[210] just as ancient converts to Christianity from the Mystery Religions must have brought with them elements of the faith they thought they had abandoned.

By the way, Bart defies any Mythicist to produce a smoking gun: where is any explicit ancient reference that the Osiris myth was known to ancient Jews or early Christians? See? His assumption is that, in their natural state, everything is hermetically sealed off from everything else. But, in any case, it would be pretty unlikely for Israelites and Jews *not* to have known about Osiris, given that Egypt had ruled Canaan during the third millennium BCE and that in the Hellenistic age the cult of Isis and Osiris/Serapis was widely popular. But whether Jesus was copied form Osiris, like Captain Marvel from Superman, is beside the point anyway. The Mythicist contention is that Jesus and Osiris are phoenixes of a feather. What makes one historical and the other mythical? Plutarch thought Osiris was a historical figure, too, but he wasn't.

SO *DID* JESUS EXIST?

I have suggested that the notion of a purely mythical Jesus Christ is no modern novelty but may have already been familiar to Justin Martyr, Celsus, and the author of 2 Peter. And speaking of pushing back dates, I have contended that it is a vicious circle to argue that a *purely legendary* Jesus could not have developed in the brief time since the death of a *historical* Jesus. The Christ myth was instead the product of an unknown span of mythopoeic percolation. There is no early attestation of a historical Jesus independent of Christian tradition, especially not from the ventriloquist dummy Josephus. The attempt to reconstruct a historical Jesus reduces Jesus to a figure of whom Josephus would have taken no note and who could not have given rise to Christianity.

---

209. Just to be pedantic, I was never an "evangelical preacher" as Bart describes me (*Did Jesus Exist?*, p. 222). My days as a would-be evangelical apologist coincided with my involvement with InterVarsity Christian Fellowship at Montclair State College (1972–1976). I became the pastor of a theologically liberal Baptist congregation some thirteen years later. You may get a taste for my sermons in my collection *Preaching Deconstruction* (Selma: Mindvendor Press, 2014).

210. I still like the hymns; maybe Bart has nostalgia for the apologetics.

No one would buy issues of *Action Comics* if only Clark Kent and not Superman were featured in its pages. On the whole, the epistles speak only of the Man of Steel with no mild-mannered reporter in sight. The few passages that say otherwise have all been suspected by non-Mythicists of being interpolations before Mythicists ever found a use for them. The notion of a crucified messiah was a stumbling block to what we might call "proto-orthodox Judaism," but not to the still-surviving mythology of the Sacred King which survived in the related phenomena of Gnosticism and primitive Christian messianism.

I know better than to hold Mythicism as a dogma. My claim is much more modest: Mythicism commends itself to me as a compelling paradigm, a framework for making the best sense of the data. Maybe there *was* a historical Jesus—who knows?

CHAPTER THREE
WHEN I GET THAT FEELING
I WANT TEXTUAL HEALING

I CAN'T WAIT TO INTERPOLATE!

For a long time textual critics have assured the rest of us that most of the many traceable corruptions in the text of the New Testament were either inadvertent slips of the pen or the eye, or else injudicious attempts to supply or restore what they thought missing, or to smooth out rough readings. And no doubt they are correct. This consensus conclusion Bart Ehrman in his fascinating book *The Orthodox Corruption of Scripture*[1] does not challenge. But he does urge a re-opening of the traditional claim that there were only negligible and sparse attempts to adjust the text to the theological preferences of the scribes. Professor Ehrman spotlights a surprising number (though still, as he admits, proportionately rather small) of corruptions of the text that would make new sense if viewed as the product of an orthodox *Tendenz* to safeguard the holy texts from the possible depredations of various heretical parties including Adoptionists, Docetists,

---

1. Bart D. Ehrman, *The Orthodox Corruption of Scripture: The Effect of Early Christological Controversies on the Text of the New Testament* (New York: Oxford University Press. 1993). Much of this chapter reflects my review of this book in the pages of *The Journal of Higher Criticism* 3/1 (Spring 1996), pp. 146–151.

Patripassians, and Separationists. Separationists (Bart's own helpful neologism, as far as I know) were those who distinguished the human Jesus from the Christ Spirit or Angel who descended upon him at the baptism and departed again at the crucifixion.

Bart sets his inquiry against each variant reading: how might this textual change have served to fend off the supposed text-twisting of the heretics? Many of the textual alterations make surprising sense as anti-heretical paraphrases and rewrites. Previously text critics had been content to dismiss these variants casually as mere harmonizations or meaningless substitutions, e.g., of the title "Christ" for the name "Jesus." But we must ask concerning these readings the same question Freud asked of verbal slips in speech: why just *this* slip and not another? The principle of concrescence in each case may be conscious or unconscious, but either way it is meaningful, not random.

Early on, Bart informs the reader that he is operating within Walter Bauer's paradigm of the study of Christian origins.[2] A helpful sketch of scholarly reactions to and revisions of the Bauer thesis suggests that, if anything, early Christianity was even more diverse than Bauer supposed, that often the lines between so-called heresy and orthodoxy were thin to the vanishing point and were borders often redrawn. He admits, as Bauer did, that the terms "orthodoxy" and "heresy" are anachronistic and loaded terms. Bart, like Bauer, continues to use both terms, however, "under erasure."

Similarly, the word "corruption" Bart retains for the irony of it, since in the cases he discusses, the scribes were trying to improve the text, not to degrade it or confuse it. This insight affords the opportunity for him to explain the utility of contemporary Reader-Response critical categories for his study: every reader upon every reading creates a new textual entity in his mind by construing the signifiers differently, by filling in the blanks differently each time. Every rereading of the text is to some extent a rewriting of the text. And therefore, just as biblical Targums (whether the ancient Onkelos or the modern *Living Bible*) afford a unique insight as to how the paraphraser read his text, so do the variants produced by ancient scribes show us what they thought the text said, i.e., what it really meant. Either they simply assumed they knew what the next words were and substituted the gist according to their own accustomed exegesis, or they actually took the liberty of building a hedge

---

2. Walter Bauer, *Orthodoxy and Heresy in Earliest Christianity.* Robert Kraft and Gerhard Kroedel, eds., Trans. by a team from the Philadelphia Seminar on Christian Origins (Philadelphia: Fortress Press, 1977).

around the Torah, rewriting the text at points so as to preempt the attempts of the heretics to twist the texts to their own destruction. "Sure the scripture says Christ had a phantom body! Just look at passage A . . . Wait a minute, where *is* it?" Heh heh.

When evangelical apologist Timothy Paul Johnson says, "the copyists were more concerned with preserving the words of Scripture than with promoting their own theological agendas,"[3] he is, as apologists so often do, simply asserting as fact what he *wishes* were fact. Bart's *The Orthodox Corruption of Scripture* is 300 pages of refutation of such a claim. Besides, Bart never claims all or most scribes took it upon themselves to "improve" the text in this way.

TEXTUAL CRITICISM AS REDACTION CRITICISM

Much of Bart's study is illuminating simply for the light it throws on otherwise uninteresting minority readings by reconstructing a plausible scribal *Sitz-im-Leben* for them. But there are broader implications which he does not fail to notice. Once he has established the probability that scribes pursued redactional tendencies in producing certain variants that no text critic takes very seriously, he follows the trajectory thus plotted into the debates over certain readings commonly accepted as being the original text. One of these is the reading "the only begotten (or unique) God" instead of "only begotten Son" in John 1:18. Once one recognizes an anti-adoptionist *Tendenz* among scribal corruptions, it is hard not to see this as the single greatest example of it.

The pericope of the bloody sweat in Luke 22:43–44, though just possibly authentic on other grounds, fails the shibboleth test once one notices how it contravenes Luke's larger picture of a mighty Christ who strides confidently to his fate. All that later scribes were likely to notice, however, was that such a portrayal seemed to give aid and comfort to docetic exegesis, where Jesus had nothing to fear, since he would suffer no pain in any case. Hence the interpolation of the bloody sweat: a Jesus is produced who has not only anxiety but sweat and blood, too. For the same reason, some scribe has borrowed the Johannine spear thrust, with its similar emission of blood and water, and inserted it into Matthew 27:49 in some manuscripts. (More about this last in a moment.)

---

3. Timothy Paul Jones, *Misquoting Truth: A Guide to the Fallacies of Bart Ehrman's Misquoting Jesus* (Downers Grove: InterVarsity Press, 2007), p. 43.

Bart dismisses the still-influential attempts of Joachim Jeremias and others to defend the long text of the Lukan Last Supper, containing the Words of Institution, or more to the point, a clear reference to the true flesh of Jesus. Again, he shows how alien such verses would be to Luke in view of his well-known redactional tendency to eliminate a cross-soteriology elsewhere in Luke-Acts. On the same bases, an ill-fit with Lukan theology and style and the sense the texts would make as anti-heretical "corrections," Bart defends Westcott and Hort's preference for the "Western non-interpolations," i.e., the shorter readings, in Luke 24. The longer readings Bart views as non-Western interpolations, Christologically motivated.

Though he considers relevant evidence and factors of every kind, he more than once pauses to note with surprise that text critics do not lend more weight than they do to matters of authorial style and theology, which he judges must be invoked to decide the case where manuscript evidence is inconclusive. Even where manuscript evidence is rather strong, Bart, recognizing the fragmentary nature of the evidence even in such cases, falls back on theological and stylistic criteria. Why are conventional text critics more hesitant to do so? One must suspect that they fear thus to let the camel's nose slip under the tent flap. They do not want to wind up joining William O. Walker and others who seek by similar arguments to pinpoint very early interpolations for which no manuscript evidence at all survives (pro or con, let it be noted).

Bart himself sometimes seems reticent to tread the trail he has blazed. While he recognizes the secondary, tendentious character of the spear-thrust in some copies of Matthew 27:49, he voices no suspicion that the Johannine prototype (John 19:34–35) might itself be an anti-docetic insertion. He notes how Acts 20:28 has accumulated variants: whose blood redeemed the Church? That of "his own," of God, or of the Lord? Here he recognizes wranglings over Patripassianism and docetism, but he leaves intact a posited original reading in which the church was purchased by means of blood, period. Having already noted Luke's seeming distaste for blood-redemption soteriology, Bart must undertake an elaborate argument in order to make the verse seem to say something else. He tries to drive a wedge between the notions of purchasing and redeeming, holding that the text speaks only of the former, not of the latter, as if there were any real distinction. It doesn't seem to wash. Why not instead simply follow Bart's own trajectory a short step further and make the whole phrase an anti-docetic interpolation?

One of the many strengths of this book is that it is able to demonstrate how in case after case we find apparent Christological "corrections" in just the texts over which the Patristic and heresiologist writers are known to have fought. This provides something of an external corroboration for his proposed scribal *Sitz-im-Leben*. One of the most interesting of these is to be found in Tertullian, when he accuses the Valentinians of having corrupted the text of John 1:13 to serve their own blasphemous theology. Actually it appears that Tertullian's foes did have the original text ("who were born"), while his own had been tailored to fit orthodoxy ("who was born," producing a Johannine mention of the Virgin Birth), whether by himself or by a predecessor.

Perhaps historians of the text ought to grow a bit more suspicious of other Patristic claims that their opponents sabotaged the text. Perhaps the shoe ought to go on the other foot in some of those cases, too. Most admit that Augustine was mistaken in making Mark the abridger of Matthew. It would be good to see more scholars taking seriously the compelling arguments of John Knox[4] that neither was Marcion the abridger of Luke that Tertullian and others made him. Unlike many of the scholars on whose work Knox builds, he does not make Marcion's gospel identical to the original Luke. Instead he sees Marcion as having slightly edited an early, shorter "Luke," while many of the Lukan texts Marcion lacked were post-Marcionite and anti-Marcionite redactions and additions. In fact, Knox's careful textual, redactional, and stylistic scrutiny of these passages reminds one of Bart's own weighing of the merits of the Western non-interpolations. Perhaps we will one day recognize a whole set of "Marcionite non-interpolations" in canonical Luke as well. At any rate, should we not drop the Patristic polemical value-judgments and speak of Marcion's texts, as well as the attested readings in the texts of other "heretics," simply as attested variants and then judge them, too, by their own merits?

TEMPESTS IN A TEXTUAL TEAPOT

Though Bart Ehrman is consistently cogent and convincing in his suggestions as to the redactional intentions behind variants, one might take issue with him here and there, or at least suggest other possibilities. For instance, he joins most scholars in rejecting Harnack's suggestion that the Markan cry of dereliction

---

4. John Knox, *Marcion and the New Testament: A Chapter in the Early History of the Canon* (Chicago: University of Chicago Press, 1942).

originally read as we find it in several Western textual witnesses: "My God, my God, why have you reviled me?" But where, pray tell, did this odd and striking variant come from? Bart proposes that it was an orthodox change intended to prevent the text ("My God, my God, why have you forsaken me?") from seeming to abet the Separationist doctrine that Jesus' "God," the Christ-Aion, had abandoned him on the cross as Basilides taught.

But surely "Why have you reviled me?" is a peculiar option if one is trying to render the text theologically innocuous! Instead, may we not suspect that the Western variant is precisely a Gnostic (either docetic or Separationist) alteration in accord with the various Nag Hammadi texts which have the Christ-Spirit standing invisibly at some distance from the cross and laughing in derision at the foolish mortals who believe the crucified form to be his own, perhaps even laughing at the crucified one himself?

Again, when it comes to 1 John 5:6, Bart sides with Schnackenburg and against de Boer in denying that Cerinthian Separationism is in view, since "no Cerinthian would say that 'Jesus Christ' came in water, for this confession would entail a denial of their standard claim that Jesus and Christ were distinct entities."[5] Yet throughout the rest of the book Bart is careful to distinguish what the "heretics" may have actually said from what their detractors attributed to them. He should have been as careful here, for he himself has already quoted Irenaeus as attributing precisely this view to the Gnostics:

> Jesus, by being begotten of a virgin through the agency of God, was wiser, purer, and more righteous than all other human beings. The anointed (Christ) in combination with wisdom (Sophia) descended into him, and thus was made Jesus Christ.

That is, apparently, in context, at the baptism, which is just what Bart cannot imagine any self-respecting Separationist saying. Maybe none would have, but that, again, is not to say that a confused Irenaeus or a careless Johannine Elder might not.

Ehrman rightly sees in 1 John 4:2 a reference to docetic phantom-Christology (as against the quibbling of Raymond E. Brown[6]), but for some

---

5. Ehrman, *Orthodox Corruption*, p. 132.

6. Raymond E. Brown, *The Gospel and Epistles of John: A Concise Commentary* (Collegeville:Liturgical Press, 1988), p. 107.

reason he thinks he must pigeon-hole the Johannine opponents as either consistent docetics or thoroughgoing Separationists. Since he has marked them as the former, then what is he to make of 1 John 2:22, 4:15, etc.? Here we would seem to have warnings against Separationism, condemnations of those who deny that Jesus is the Christ or the Son of God, Jesus being merely the earthly "channeler," as we would say today, of the Christ/Son of God. But for Bart it cannot be so. His eyes must be deceiving him.

> The emphasis of the Johannine homology, then, falls either on the predicate noun, that "the Son of God is Jesus" (the man), or perhaps on the verb itself, that the "Son of God is Jesus" (since in the secessionists' view the Son of God only appears to be the man Jesus).[7]

But is not this the sort of strained exegesis to which one resorts only when in a tight spot? Why must Bart so straightjacket himself and the text? I suspect he is too closely bound to the popular view that in the supposed Johannine schism we are witnessing the beginning of the proto-Gnostic trajectory. In this case we cannot yet have two different and sophisticated Gnosticizing Christological models, only a heretical *tendency* marking a group of dissidents.

But there is nothing to force us to read the text this way. Since the case for reading 1 John 2:22 and 4:15 as anti-Separationist is quite as good as that for reading 4:2 as anti-docetic, should we not rather conclude that the Elder has both heresies in view, and that he writes sufficiently late to be able to do so? 1 John 1:19 need not mean that the writer's own personal colleagues or disciples have broken with him. It need imply no more than that the Separationist and Docetist Gnostics long ago showed their true colors by splitting off from the main Christian body—in short, the classic Eusebian etiology of heresy. Many scholars, one suspects, would like either to date 1 John early for the sake of its supposed "apostolicity" or to date developed Gnostic Christology late so as to maintain some semblance of the Eusebian apologetical paradigm whereby orthodoxy preceded heresy. To be consistent, Bart, elsewhere an adherent of the Bauer thesis, might better reject exegeses which are merely functions of this hidden agenda.

Textual, or "Lower," criticism has often served as a safe haven for those desiring to employ their scholarly gifts in biblical study without venturing into

---

7. Ehrman, *Orthodox Corruption*, p. 133.

the perceived dangers of Higher Criticism. Thus it is no surprise that the strictures of conservative conventionalism have often governed text criticism, even tended toward using text criticism as a form of apologetics assuring us that we have "exactly what the apostles wrote." It is well past time for someone to do what Bart has done so well, to apply both modern literary theory and the Bauer paradigm to textual criticism, in the process blurring much of the line separating Lower Criticism from Higher Criticism.

CALL ME UNRELIABLE

Discussing Bart's book *Misquoting Jesus*, Daniel B. Wallace, a professor at Dallas Theological Seminary (where I suspect Bart would have wound up teaching had he continued on his original path), remarks that the "impression Ehrman sometimes gives throughout the book—and repeats in interviews—is that of wholesale uncertainty about the original wording, a view that is far more radical than he actually embraces."[8] He quotes Bart: "The more I studied the manuscript tradition of the New Testament, the more I realized just how radically the text had been altered over the years at the hands of scribes."[9] But Wallace can appeal to several more quotes in which Bart speaks in considerably more positive terms, admitting that the overwhelming number of textual variants are insignificant, many of them not even noticeable in translation. Jones[10] makes the same observation. So is the text as unreliably corrupt as Bart sometimes contends? Maybe not, but that doesn't mean we have what the original authors wrote. Philosopher John Beversluis points out what should be obvious:

> Since there are thousands of surviving copies, [text critics assure us,] we can study them and thus arrive at a "close approximation" to the originals. However, this seemingly authoritative explanation leaves the most important question unanswered. Since the *autographa* have not survived and nobody has

---

8. Daniel B. Wallace, "The Gospel according to Bart: A Review of Bart D. Ehrman's *Misquoting Jesus: The Story Behind Who Changed the Bible and Why." Journal of the Evangelical Theological Society* 49/2 (June 2006), pp. 331, note 17.

9. Bart D. Ehrman, *Misquoting Jesus: The Story Behind Who Changed the Bible and Why* (San Francisco: HarperSanFrancisco, 2005) p. 207.

10. Jones, *Misquoting Truth*, pp. 46–48.

laid eyes on them for 2,000 years, how could anybody possibly know what was in them—much less, which copies approximate most closely to them? Since there is nothing to which existing manuscripts can be compared, the very ideas of the *original* manuscripts and which manuscripts *approximate most closely* to them are useless ideas and should be abandoned. I can judge that a photo is a good likeness of you if and only if I have seen you and know what you look like. If I have not, then I am the last person on earth to ask. The situation is not improved by assuring me that there are thousands of photos of you. The fact is that I have never seen *you*, so ten million photos would not help.[11]

The unspoken assumption behind the apologists' reassurances is that all our (very similar) manuscripts stem in a direct line from the New Testament writings as they left their authors' hands. But there is another important possibility; perhaps what we are reading are copies made from a standardized edition.

LINE IN THE SAND[12]

Some scholars who exercise critical freedom in studying the New Testament seem to stop on a dime at the point where Higher Criticism gives way to Lower Criticism. They don't mind slicing the pie, but they blanch at the prospect of tampering with its ingredients. Such savants have tried to establish ground rules for scholarly theorizing that would *a priori* rule out arguments in favor of hypothetical interpolations to the New Testament text during that period predating our earliest surviving manuscripts. Two of these prescriptions against heretics are Frederik W. Wisse's "Textual Limits to Redactional Theory in the Pauline Corpus" and Jerome Murphy-O'Connor's "Interpolations in 1 Corinthians."[13] These scholars seem to speak for the majority when they

---

11. John Beversluis, "The Synoptic Gospels" (unpublished manuscript).

12. This section might ring a bell if you've read my article "Apocryphal Apparitions: I Corinthians 15:3–11 as a Post-Pauline Interpolation" *Journal of Higher Criticism* 2/2 (Fall 1995).

13. Frederik W. Wisse, "Textual Limits to Redactional Theory in the Pauline Corpus," in J. E. Goehring et. al., eds., *Gospel Origins and Christian Beginnings: In Honor of James M. Robinson* (Forum Fascicles, 1; Sonoma: Polebridge Press, 1990), pp. 167–178; Jerome Murphy-O'Connor, "Interpolations in 1 Corinthians," *Catholic Biblical Quarterly* 48 (1986), pp. 81–94.

maintain that, short of definitive manuscript evidence, no suggestion of an interpolation in the Pauline epistles need be taken seriously. The texts as they stand are to be judged "innocent until proven guilty,"[14] which in the nature of the case, can never happen. Otherwise, if we had to take seriously interpolation or redaction theories based on internal evidence alone, "the result [would be] a state of uncertainty and diversity of scholarly opinion. Historians and interpreters [in such a case] can no longer be sure whether a text or parts of it represent the views of the author or someone else."[15] The game would be rendered very difficult to play.

I see in such warnings essentially a theological apologetic on behalf of a new Textus Receptus, an apologetic not unlike that offered by fundamentalists on behalf of the Byzantine text underlying the King James Version. Just as the dogmatic theology of the latter group was predicated on particular readings in the Byzantine/King James text and thus required its originality and integrity, so does the "Biblical Theology" of today's Magisterium of consensus scholarship require the apostolic originality of today's Nestle-Aland/UBS text. Herein, perhaps, lies the deeper reason for the tenacious unwillingness of such scholars to consider seriously the possibility of extensive or significant interpolations (or, indeed, any at all).

The issue resolves itself into theological canon-polemics. If the integrity of the "canonical" scholarly text proves dubious in the manner feared by Wisse, the whole text will be seen to slide from the Eusebian category of "acknowledged" texts to that of the "disputed." That is the danger, not that a few particular texts will pass all the way into the "spurious" category and be rendered off limits like the long ending of Mark, but that wherever he steps the New Testament theological exegete will find himself amid a marshy textual bog. The former would actually be preferable to Wisse, since whatever remained could still be considered terra firma. And thus the apologetical strategy is to disallow any argument that cannot fully prove the secondary character of a piece of text. Mere probability results in the dreaded anxiety of uncertainty, so mere probabilities are no good. If we cannot prove the text secondary, we are supposedly entitled to go on regarding it as certainly authentic, "innocent until proven guilty." God forbid the scholarly guild should end up with Winsome Munro's seeming agnosticism:

---

14. Wisse, "Textual Limits," p. 170.

15. Wisse, "Textual Limits," p. 170.

Until such time as the entire epistolary corpus is examined, not merely for isolated interpolations, but to determine its redactional history, most historical, sociological, and theological constructions on the basis of the text as it stands should probably be accepted only tentatively and provisionally, if at all.[16]

William O. Walker Jr., has suggested that, contrary to those opinions just reviewed, "in dealing with any particular letter in the [Pauline] corpus, the burden of proof rests with any argument that the corpus or, indeed any particular letter within the corpus . . . contains no interpolations."[17] Among the reasons advanced by Walker is the fact that

the surviving text of the Pauline letters is the text promoted by the historical winners in the theological and ecclesiastical struggles of the second and third centuries. . . . In short, it appears likely that the emerging Catholic leadership in the churches 'standardized' the text of the Pauline corpus in the light of 'orthodox' views and practices, suppressing and even destroying all deviant texts and manuscripts. Thus it is that we have no manuscripts dating from earlier than the third century; thus it is that all of the extant manuscripts are remarkably similar in most of their significant features; and thus it is that the manuscript evidence can tell us nothing about the state of the Pauline literature prior to the third century.[18]

Bart comments in the same vein:

this study has reinforced the notion that theologically motivated changes of the text are to be anticipated particularly during the early centuries of transmission, when both the texts and the theology of early Christianity were in a state of flux, prior to the development of a recognized creed and an authoritative and (theoretically) inviolable canon of Scripture.[19]

---

16. Winsome Munro, "Interpolation in the Epistles: Weighing Probability," *New Testament Studies* 36 (1990), p. 443.

17. William O. Walker, Jr., "The Burden of Proof in Identifying Interpolations in the Pauline Letters," *New Testament Studies* 33 (1987), p. 615.

18. Walker, "Burden of Proof," p. 614.

19. Ehrman, *Orthodox Corruption*, p. 277. See also pages 55 and 97.

Wisse seems to think it unremarkable that all textual evidence before the third century has mysteriously vanished. But according to Walker, the absence of the crucial textual evidence is no mystery at all. It was a silence created expressly to speak eloquently the apologetics of Wisse and his brethren. Today's apologists for the new Textus Receptus are simply continuing the canon polemics of those who standardized/censored the texts in the first place. But, as Elisabeth Schüssler Fiorenza says in a different context, we must learn to read the silences and hear the echoes of the silenced voices.[20] And that is what Walker and previous interpolation theorists have learned to do.

The only evidence remaining as to a possible earlier state of the text is internal evidence, namely aporias, contradictions, stylistic irregularities, anachronisms, redactional seams. And this is precisely the kind of thing our apologists scorn. As we might expect from an apologetical agenda, the tactic of harmonization of "apparent contradictions" is crucial to their enterprise. Consensus scholarship is no less enamored of the tool than the fundamentalist harmonists of whom their "maximal conservatism" is so reminiscent.[21] Wisse is forthright: the judicious exegete must make sense of the extant text at all costs. "Designating a passage in a text as a redactional interpolation can be at best only a last resort and an admission of one's inability to account for the data in any other way."[22] In other words, any clever connect-the-dots solution is preferable to admitting that the text in question is an interpolation. If "saving the appearances" is the criterion for a good theory, then we will soon be joining Harold Lindsell in ascribing six denials to Peter.[23]

One of the favorite harmonizations used by scholars is the convenient notion that when Paul sounds suddenly and suspiciously Gnostic, for example, it is still Paul, not some sneaky interpolator, but he is using the terminology of his opponents against them.[24] *That's* the ticket! This would seem to be an

---

20. Elisabeth Schüssler Fiorenza, *In Memory of Her: A Feminist Theological Reconstruction of Christian Origins* (New York: Crossroad, 1984), p. 41: "Rather than understand the text as an adequate reflection of the reality about which it speaks, we must search for clues and allusions that indicate the reality about which the text is silent."

21. See James Barr, *Fundamentalism* (Philadelphia: Westminster Press, 1978), pp. 85–87.

22. Wisse, "Textual Limits," p. 170.

23. Harold Lindsell, *The Battle for the Bible* (Grand Rapids: Zondervan, 1976), pp. 174–176.

24. See, for example, Gordon D. Fee, *The First Epistle to the Corinthians* (Grand Rapids:

odd, muddying strategy. But it was no strategy of the apostle Paul, only of our apologists. It commends itself to many, including Murphy-O'Connor: "If Paul, with tongue in cheek, is merely appropriating the formulae of his adversaries, there are no contradictions in substance."[25] Note the talk, familiar from fundamentalist inerrancy apologetics, of merely apparent contradictions. It is implied when Murphy-O'Connor is satisfied with "no contradictions in substance," "no real contradiction."[26]

Wisse even repeats the circularity of apologist C. S. Lewis's argument in the latter's "Modern Theology and Biblical Criticism." Lewis dismisses historical-critical reconstructions, of the historical Jesus, for example, since they are merely a chain of weak links: "[I]f, in a complex reconstruction, you go on . . . super-inducing hypothesis on hypothesis, you will in the end get a complex, in which, though each hypothesis by itself has in a sense a high probability, the whole has almost none."[27] But, we must ask, how is the orthodox apologist's edifice of apologetical bricks any more sturdy? The merely probabilistic character of the critics' position is evident to him; that of his own is not.

And so with Wisse: "since the burden of proof rests on the arguments for redactional interference, the benefit of the doubt rightfully should go to the integrity of the text. If the case of the prosecution is not able to overcome serious doubts, then the text deserves to be acquitted."[28] Again, "This lack of certainty is sometimes obscured by scholars who wishfully refer to certain redactional theories as if they were facts."[29] And yet Wisse seems willing to consider harmonizations as facts, as if they themselves were not just as debatable as the interpolation hypotheses he despises. Because the critical

---

Eerdmans, 1987), p. 102; Ralph P. Martin, *Colossians: The Church's Lord and the Christian's Liberty* (Exeter: Paternoster, 1972), p. 75; Stephen Neill, *Paul to the Colossians* (World Christian Books, Third Series, no. 50; New York: Association Press, 1964), p. 11 ("It is probable that Paul picks up some of the phrases used by the false teachers, and himself uses them sarcastically."); Oscar Cullmann, *The New Testament: An Introduction for the General Reader* (Philadelphia: Westminster Press, 1968), p. 81.

25. Murphy-O'Connor, "Interpolations," p. 83.

26. Murphy-O'Connor, "Interpolations," p. 83.

27. C. S. Lewis, "Modern Theology and Biblical Criticism," in Walter Hooper, ed., *Christian Reflections* (Grand Rapids: Eerdmans, 1967), p. 163.

28. Wisse, "Textual Limits," p. 172.

29. Wisse, "Textual Limits," p. 172.

argument is merely probabilistic and not certain, notwithstanding the similar vulnerability of his own preferred reconstructions (for that is what every harmonization is), Wisse feels as entitled as Lewis did simply to assume the case is closed.

The whole judicial verdict analogy is inappropriate to Wisse's argument anyway. In the one case, we have two choices, to put a man in jail or not. In the other, we have three choices: certainty of an authentic text, certainty of an inauthentic text, and uncertainty. A suggestive argument that nonetheless remains inconclusive should cause us to return the third verdict, but Wisse will not consider it. The logical implication would seem to be textual agnosticism, but Wisse prefers textual fideism instead.

Though Walker and Munro are both willing to set some high hurdles for a proposed interpolation-exegesis to jump,[30] they are not nearly so high as the walls erected by Wisse: one must show manuscript support from that period from which none of any kind survives.[31] And here we are reminded of another inerrantist apologist, Benjamin B. Warfield, who set up a gauntlet he dared any proposed biblical error to run. Any alleged error in scripture must be shown to have occurred in the original autographs, which, luckily, are no longer available. The family resemblance of Wisse's and Warfield's approaches is evident.

Let (1) it be proved that each alleged statement occurred certainly in the original autographa of the sacred book in which it is said to be found. (2) Let it be proved that the interpretation which occasions the apparent discrepancy is the one which the passage was evidently intended to bear. It is not sufficient to show a difficulty, which may spring out of our defective knowledge of the circumstances. The true meaning must be definitely and certainly ascertained, and then shown to be irreconcilable with other known truth. (3) Let it be proved that the true sense of some part of the original autographa is directly and necessarily inconsistent with some certainly known fact of history, or truth of science, or some other statement of Scripture certainly ascertained and interpreted. We believe that it can be shown that this has never yet been

---

30. William O. Walker, Jr., "Text-Critical Evidence for Interpolations in the Letters of Paul," *Catholic Biblical Quarterly* 50 (1988), p. 625; Munro, "Interpolation," pp. 432–439.

31. Wisse, "Textual Limits," p. 173: "Indeed, in view of the heavy burden of proof, it would appear that in practice it is virtually impossible to make a convincing case for any interpolation that lacks manuscript support."

successfully done in the case of one single alleged instance of error in the Word of God.[32]

Warfield sought to safeguard the *factual inerrancy* of the text, while today's consensus scholars want to safeguard the *integrity* of the text, but the basic strategy is the same: like Warfield, Wisse and Murphy-O'Connor have erected a hedge around the Torah.

It is worth noting that the arguments of Wisse and his congeners would seem to mirror precisely those of fundamentalists who dismiss source criticism as groundless and speculative. After all, we don't have any actual manuscripts of J, E, P, or Q, do we? Walker and Munro, it seems to me, are simply extending the analytical tools of the classical source critics into textual criticism. Would Wisse and the others argue, as the Old Princeton apologists once did, that we must uphold Mosaic authorship of the Pentateuch or the unitary authorship of Isaiah until these traditional views are "proven guilty"? I doubt it.

Murphy-O'Connor rejoices at any exegesis "liberating us from speculative interpretations, some with far reaching consequences regarding the authority of Scripture."[33] Here is the heart of the apologetical agenda, but with genuine criticism it has nothing in common. Bart Ehrman evidences just this distaste for interpolation theories.

> For one thing, what is the hard evidence that the words ["But wrath has come upon them at last"] were not in the letter of 1 Thessalonians [2:16] as Paul wrote it? There is none . . . [because] in not a single manuscript is the line (let alone the paragraph) missing. Every surviving manuscript includes it. If the passage was added sometime after the fall of Jerusalem, say, near the end of the first Christian century or even in the second, when Christians started blaming the fall of Jerusalem on the fact that the Jews had killed Jesus, why is it that none of the manuscripts of 1 Thessalonians that were copied before the insertion was made left any trace on the manuscript record? Why were the older copies not copied *at all?* I think there needs to be better evidence of a scribal insertion before we are certain that it happened.[34]

32. A.A. Hodge and B.B. Warfield, "Inspiration," *Presbyterian Review*, April 1881, p. 242.

33. Murphy-O'Connor, "Interpolations," p. 85.

34. Ehrman, *Did Jesus Exist?* pp. 123–124.

This is one of the features of Bart's approach that makes me suspect that, despite his repudiation of evangelicalism, he still to a surprising degree operates within the same basic paradigms. I am no mind reader, but it occurs to me this is because it was not New Testament criticism that sent him packing, but rather the problem of evil in a world supposedly created and supervised by a righteous and loving God.[35] Until this straw broke the camel's back, Bart found it feasible to stretch the edges of evangelical identity, rather like fellow evangelical text critic Gordon D. Fee,[36] who used to say he could sign on to "inerrancy" depending on how many "r's" you spell it with! So I am suggesting Bart leapfrogged some further advancements in critical method. He short-circuited the process by jumping ship over a different issue: theodicy, which has been a rocky reef capable of shipwrecking the faith of so many. Maybe I'm completely off target; it's just a proposal for understanding the contradiction many of his (well-deserved) fans think they see between *Did Jesus Exist?* and his previous, more iconoclastic books.

Inspiration and Preservation

Bart Ehrman departed fundamentalism before he left evangelicalism, a more flexible (or more slippery) position. And what prompted the change? I believe the first crack in the armor was his careful scrutiny of a gospel harmony, one of those coffee table books that run the texts of Matthew, Mark, and Luke in three vertical columns to facilitate the comparison of parallel passages. The layout forces you to realize the small and not so small differences between the three Synoptic versions of the same story or saying. Bart, like most of us, had never noticed the fine print. He was sobered, so to speak, to recognize the devil in the details. Whatever Jesus had originally said, somebody had altered it before the gospel writers put it down in black and white. So much for absolute factual accuracy. If Mark and Luke are correct that Jesus allowed no pretext for divorce but Matthew left one loophole, somebody's not giving the facts. It may seem pretty picky, but I'm afraid inerrantism is all about pickiness. Indeed, that is the whole point.

---

35. Bart D. Ehrman, *God's Problem: How the Bible Fails to Answer Our Most Important Question—Why We Suffer* (New York: HarperOne/HarperCollins, 2009).

36. I am a grateful student of Gordon Fee, though he's probably not too proud of me. Look how I turned out!

It is only the inerrantist who is obliged to lose sleep over the fact that the mustard seed is not in fact, as Jesus says, the smallest of all earthly seeds. For young inerrantist Bart Ehrman this was a bit of a blow. Believe me, I know exactly how he felt.

But that wasn't all. It wasn't just the gospels that disagreed; it was the various manuscripts of each gospel.

> I kept reverting to my basic question: how does it help us to say that the Bible is the inerrant word of God if in fact we don't have the words that God inerrantly inspired, but only the words copied by the scribes—sometimes (many times!) incorrectly?[37]

Wallace does not see the problem. He speaks of the "logical fallacy in denying an inerrant autograph."

> We need to begin by making a careful distinction between verbal inspiration and inerrancy. Inspiration relates to the wording of the Bible, while inerrancy relates to the truth of a statement. American evangelicals generally believe that only the original text is inspired. This is not to say, however, that copies cannot be inerrant. Indeed, statements that bear no relation to Scripture can be inerrant. If I say, "I am married and have four sons, two dogs, and a cat," that is an inerrant statement. It is not inspired, nor at all related to Scripture, but it is true. Similarly, whether Paul says "we have peace" or "let us have peace" in Rom 5:1, both statements are true (though each in a different sense), though only one is inspired. . . . Regardless of what one thinks about the doctrine of inerrancy, the argument against it on the basis of the unknown autographs is logically fallacious. This is so for two reasons. First, we have the text of the NT somewhere in the manuscripts. There is no need for conjecture, except perhaps in one or two places.[38]

To this I have two objections. For one thing, "inerrant" does not merely mean "true," but rather "incapable of being false" *because inspired*. It is ludicrous to affirm that a soup can label is inerrant just because there are no inaccuracies in the ingredient list. Professor Wallace wants to drive a wedge between "inerrancy and infallibility" in the Bible, his goal being to evade Bart's point.

---

37. Ehrman, *Misquoting Jesus*, p. 7.

38. Wallace, "Gospel according to Bart," p. 334.

He wants to defend statements in the Bible as still factually correct (Christ really rose from the dead; the Red Sea parted), thus "inerrant," even if stated in a sentence tarnished by typo-making scribes, thus *not* "infallible." Wallace sacrifices infallible scribal transmission in order to retain mere correctness (his version of "inerrancy"). But this is to throw open Pandora's Box: if you cannot be certain you are reading what the inspired writers originally wrote down (except by the will to believe), how are you to know the statements in the Bible are true? By historical-critical research? I don't think you want to open that door. Timothy Paul Jones[39] does open the door a crack: "the notion of word-for-word agreement is a relatively recent historical development. 'In times of antiquity it was not the practice to give a verbatim repetition every time something was written out.'"

Similarly, Ben Witherington III:

> If you actually bother to read ancient biographies (see e.g. Tacitus's *Life of Agricola*, or Plutarch's famous parallel lives) you will discover that the ancients were not pedants when it comes to the issue of strict chronology as we are today. The ancient biographical or historiographical work operated with the freedom to arrange their material in several different ways, including topically, geographically, chronologically, to mention but three. Yes they had a secondary interest in chronology in broad strokes, but only a secondary interest in that. If one studies the Fourth Gospel in detail and closely in the Greek, comparing it to other ancient biographies what one learns is that it is a highly schematized and edited product, and the sign narratives are arranged theologically not primarily chronologically. And whilst this might cause a modern person some consternation, it is not a reason to say that John contradicts the Synoptics on this Temple cleansing matter.[40]

You've just crossed over into the Tübingen Zone. This is a back-firing strategy. It seems you are disdaining a caricature of your conservative position, but in fact you are allowing the Higher-Critical camel's nose under the apologetical tent flap. If we are to accept ancient standards (which is the fundamental approach of historical criticism), there will be no defense against, e.g., an ancient indifference to fact versus fiction, the didactic, tacit use of

39. Jones, *Misquoting Truth*, p. 31, quoting E.J. Young.

40. Review of Bart Ehrman, *Jesus Interrupted*, http://benwitherington.blogspot.com, April 7, 2009.

myths and legends, the popular embrace of notions or narratives we should consider mutually contradictory.

No, you (think you) can trust all those biblical stories because the inspired texts tell you they happened. In other words, you believe they are inerrant because they are inspired. All the apologetical sophistry of Jones and his brethren is just spin attempting to cover that fact.

For another thing, the notion that the true (original) text survives *some*where among the surviving manuscripts is sheer theological supposition. If Wallace tried to prove that assertion, it would be a necessarily doomed attempt to prove a negative. And wouldn't an evangelical scholar who believed this *ipso facto* be forbidden to espouse the theory, held by many conservatives, that the original ending of Mark's gospel has been lost?

The contention that the needle of the true text is hiding somewhere in the manuscript haystack is comical. Why would the deity who inspired the holy texts subject his people to such a scavenger hunt? The suggestion is a contrived *ad hoc* hypothesis forced upon believers in the doctrine of "preservationism." Bart saw the logic of it quite clearly: if God took the trouble of seeing to it that the very words of the text are precisely as he wanted them, why the heck wouldn't he have seen to it that those performing the sacred task of making copies were superintended in the same way? Of course, "preservationism" is unwittingly the *reduction ad absurdum* of the belief in verbal inspiration. Listen to A.J. Mattill, Jr., another ex-evangelical New Testament scholar.

> We would think that if an omniscient, omnipotent God could inspire 40 different authors over a period of 1,600 years to write 66 books without errors of any kind, then that God could certainly inspire scribes to copy those books with flawless accuracy century after century. But instead of an inerrant Bible once and for all delivered by God to the original writers and reliably transmitted by meticulous scribes, textual criticism reveals to us a long process of textual evolution: the [manuscripts] we have today are the products of change over the centuries.[41]

Preservationists have traditionally advocated the *Textus Receptus*, the Byzantine text form underlying the King James Version, as preserving the

---

41. A.J. Mattill, Jr., *Polluted Texts and Traditional Beliefs* (Gordo, AL: Flatwood Free Press, 1998), p. 3.

original text. This doesn't quite work, however, because there are textual variants even within the Byzantine manuscript family. Once you realize this fact, you realize you have to retreat to the scavenger hunt version. Good luck!

In his debate with Bart Ehrman, Dr. James White[42] rebuked him for setting up a straw man when he insisted that if God had infallibly inspired the text in the first place he must naturally be expected to have infallibly safeguarded its accurate transmission.

What, asks Dr. White, is Bart asking for? Must God have made the scribes into automatic-writing robots? Be realistic! Why not admit that substantially accurate transmission is good enough? Doesn't that qualify as divine providence? Sounds reasonable, except that I cannot imagine Dr. White and his fellow evangelicals allowing the same latitude for the inspiration of the original autographs. Is it good enough to say that what the original authors wrote is substantially but not completely true? Dr. White and company may not believe God literally dictated his Word to passive secretaries, but their (vague) redefinition of inspiration supposedly ensures that the resultant texts are as accurate and true as if they *had* been dictated. As Warfield[43] said, "If God wished to give his people a series of letters like Paul's, he prepared a Paul to write them, and the Paul he brought to the task was a Paul who *spontaneously* would write just such letters." He prepared, through heredity and environment, a writer who would, without overt divine intervention, write exactly what God wanted 1 Corinthians, Galatians, etc., to say. So why couldn't, why *didn't*, God prepare the scribes needed to infallibly copy and transmit them? Dr. White seems okay with a scripture that requires "secular" means and tools to (try to) determine the true text, but I very much doubt he would want to apply historical-critical methodology to the question of the historical accuracy of the original autographs.

The iron curtain between Lower and Higher Criticism, the former being safe for Bible-believers, the latter dangerous, is exactly like the distinction drawn by Creationists between "micro-evolution" and "macro-evolution." Creationists will allow, since they must, that within a species new sub-varieties

---

42. https://www.youtube.com/watch?v=moHlnA9fAsl. Let me be fair: Dr. White generally acquitted himself quite well.

43. Benjamin B. Warfield, *The Inspiration and Authority of the Bible* (Philadelphia: Presbyterian & Reformed, 1948), p. 155, quoted in Clark H. Pinnock, *Biblical Revelation— The Foundation of Christian Theology* (Chicago: Moody Press, 1971), p. 93.

arise, but they deny that one species may give rise to another. But there is no real distinction here after all because interspecies evolution is simply a dotted line traced through the continuous process of accumulation of individual mutations. So-called micro-evolution is the means of macro-evolution. New species are in a sense snap shots taken during the ongoing process. Well, the same is true of textual evolution. Textual criticism is the beginning of historical criticism. As Dewey M. Beegle[44] pointed out many years ago, it is pointless to speak of the inerrancy of the "original autographs," since this presupposes that each biblical writing was produced by one author, maybe at a single sitting. Tradition criticism delineates earlier and later strata, plus redactional alterations, in individual biblical documents. Forget Bart's allegations about the post-publication evolution of the published texts; Beegle appealed to the *pre*-published versions of the texts. Evangelical apologists are not very eager to apply their critical spade in this area. And if they were to be consistent, they would have to.

Does the evangelical doctrine of inspiration (which I am discussing here in order to explore the implications of the supposed analogy between inspiration and preservation) even allow for a biblical writer to have revised or corrected his own work? Was the original inspired draft not quite as inspired as the revised version(s)? I think of Schleiermacher's[45] contrived suggestion that Jesus could not ever have made a mistake in arithmetic, that he did not learn by trial and error, having made no errors. He did not learn from his mistakes since he didn't make any. How *could* he? Same with the inspired writers, right? If God were fully in charge, whether by way of literal dictation or of over-the-shoulder supervision, why would, how *could*, the inspired writers need to rethink anything? Revise anything? Correct anything? If they didn't, because of divine providence, why should it be different with all those copyists? I think Bart is right. The general notion of an inspired text would seem to stand or fall with the falsifiable notion, not hidden from us, of the infallible preservation of scriptures. Did God go to all the trouble preparing scripture, like Noah constructing the Ark, and then launch it, leaving it to luck?

---

44. Dewey M. Beegle, *The Inspiration of Scripture* (Westminster Press, 1963), Chapter 2, "Inspiration and the Autographs," pp. 17–26; Chapter 3, "Transmission, Translation, and Inspiration," pp. 27–40.

45. Friedrich Daniel Ernst Schleiermacher, *The Life of Jesus*. Trans. S. Maclean Gilmour. Lives of Jesus Series (Philadelphia: Fortress Press, 1975), pp. 107–108.

POOF! TEXTS

Are any important doctrines affected or undermined by textual criticism? Bart Ehrman says yes.

> In some instances, the very meaning of the text is at stake, depending on how one resolves a textual problem: Was Jesus an angry man [Mark 1:41]? Was he completely distraught in the face of death [Heb 2:8–9]? Did he tell his disciples that they could drink poison without being harmed [Mark 16:9–20]? Did he let an adulteress off the hook with nothing but a mild warning [John 7:53–8:11]? Is the doctrine of the Trinity explicitly taught in the New Testament [1 John 5:7–8]? Is Jesus actually called "the unique God" there [John 1:18]? Does the New Testament indicate that even the Son of God himself does not know when the end will come [Matt 24:36]? The questions go on and on, and all of them are related to how one resolves difficulties in the manuscript tradition as it has come down to us.[46]

Again, Daniel Wallace disagrees.

> Finally, regarding 1 John 5:7–8, virtually no modern translation of the Bible includes the "Trinitarian formula," since scholars for centuries have recognized it as added later. Only a few very late manuscripts have the verses. One wonders why this passage is even discussed in Ehrman's book. The only reason seems to be to fuel doubts. The passage made its way into our Bibles through political pressure, appearing for the first time in 1522, even though scholars then and now knew that it was not authentic. The early church did not know of this text, yet the Council of Constantinople in ad 381 explicitly affirmed the Trinity! How could they do this without the benefit of a text that did not get into the Greek NT for another millennium? Constantinople's statement was not written in a vacuum: the early church put into a theological formulation what they got out of the NT. A distinction needs to be made here: just because a particular verse does not affirm a cherished doctrine does not mean that that doctrine cannot be found in the NT. In this case, anyone with an understanding of the healthy patristic debates over the Godhead knows that the early church arrived at their understanding from an examination of the data in the NT. The Trinitarian formula found in late manuscripts of 1 John 5:7 only summarized what they found; it did not inform their declarations.[47]

---

46. Ehrman, *Misquoting Jesus*, p. 228.

47. Wallace, "Gospel according to Bart," p. 348.

How interesting, then, that someone still felt the need to secure the Trinity in the text of the Bible. The seeming motive of the interpolator matches the anxiety of modern biblicists who feel uneasy with a supposedly cardinal doctrine that is not clearly taught in the Bible. Professor Wallace may be satisfied with the theo-philosophical deliberations of fourth-century ecclesiastics, but, as an evangelical, should he be? You can see the urgency of the issue in the pathetic but ostensibly satisfactory back-up proof-texts for the Trinity, invariably verses that do not make the point.[48] The Jordan baptism scene features the Father, the Son, and the Spirit, but this says nothing about whatever metaphysical interrelation these characters/entities may possess. If Paul speaks of "the grace of the Lord Jesus Christ and the love of God and the fellowship of the Holy Spirit" (2 Cor. 13:14), is he anywhere near Trinitarianism? These texts would fit as well with Tritheism or Modalism.

Jones contends that you don't really *need* 1 John 5:7–8 to have the Bible "teaching" Trinitarianism, since we can always just flip over a few pages to Matthew 28:19–20, which mandates baptism in the "name" (singular) "of the Father, of the Son, and of the Holy Spirit." See? One name, three persons! Three problems: the "Jesus Only" Pentecostals appeal to the very same verse to justify their Modalist and/or Dynamic Monarchian Christology. And, ironically, this passage, too, is textually doubtful, as Eusebius said he had seen copies that said simply "in my name."

And perhaps the most serious problem with the argument is that it implies that a doctrine requires but a textual toe-hold. It is a game of proof-texting pure and simple. The fundamentalist harmonizes theological contradictions between, e.g., Paul and James by "interpreting the less clear by the more clear," i.e., pretending the verse you *don't* like means the same thing as the one you *do* like. Jones is doing basically the same thing with textual criticism: it's a shell game: this text is dubious? No problem, there's still this one over here. They are fungible. It is only this maneuvering that enables apologists to pretend that no important doctrine is threatened by textual uncertainty.[49]

If 1 John 5:7 were integral to the text, theological apologists wouldn't have to fudge the matter like this. Bart Ehrman is right.

---

48. Jones, *Misquoting Truth*, p. 70.

49. See Jones, *Misquoting Truth*, pp. 75–76 for an even more egregious case of textual criticism as harmonization.

Think, too, of Mark 16:16, where we read that baptism is a prerequisite to salvation. That is, needless to say, a rather important issue. But this verse, which would seem to settle the question, turns out not to be original to Mark's gospel. (And let's not forget the snake-handling.) It is quite revealing that Timothy Paul Jones admits that Mark 16:9–20 "probably weren't in Mark's original Gospel, but they *do* represent an authentic tradition about Jesus' resurrection. When this is taken into consideration, it becomes clear –in the words of Bruce Metzger- 'that the New Testament contains not four but five evangelic accounts subsequent to the Resurrection of Christ.'"[50] In other words, textual criticism is in the end utterly beside the point for this apologist. If a passage is amenable, it doesn't matter if it wasn't actually part of the biblical text. It's like the fundamentalist preacher who exclaims, "It ain't in the Bible, but it oughta be!"

Though Bart is not especially eager to recognize interpolations for (or against) which manuscript evidence does not exist, he by no means denies that there could have been any. He says, rather, that, precisely because there is no way ever to be sure either way, a question mark must always hover like the Sword of Damocles over any doctrinal or historical appeal to the New Testament text as we have it. The problem is the same as that pertaining to the historical Jesus question: there can only ever be the most tentative, provisional confidence in our evidence. Was Jesus an apocalyptic preacher? Maybe. Does the Bible teach Predestination? Maybe. And maybes are not sufficient if one wants to dogmatize, as Bible readers have traditionally done. Martin Kähler depicted the plight of a would-be Christian believer secretly tormented by the fear that tomorrow some shocking archaeological discovery might debunk the gospel story. "I cannot find sure footing in probabilities or in a shifting mass of details the reliability of which is constantly changing."[51] In just the same way, should not scholarly believers live in fear that some astonishing New Testament manuscript might come to light, upsetting the Edenic apple cart of knowledge?

I take this to be the real point of Bart Ehrman's "destructive" appeal to

---

50. Jones, *Misquoting Truth*, p. 64.

51. Martin Kähler, *The So-called Historical Jesus and the Historic Biblical Christ.* Trans. Carl E. Braaten. Seminar Editions (Philadelphia: Fortress Press, 1964), p. 111. There is a whole subgenre of mystery novels embodying this very premise, novels in which someone unearths the body of Jesus or an authentic gospel which gives the lie to the canonical four. See Robert M. Price, *Secret Scrolls: Revelations from the Lost Gospel Novels* (Eugene: Wipf & Stock, 2011).

textual corruption. Not that we can demonstrate that there was hopeless and thorough corruption, but that we cannot be so all-fired sure, as apologists would like us to believe, that there *wasn't*.[52] I think the most hardcore fundamentalists, deep down, understand this. Even the most seemingly insignificant correction of the Greek text threatens their confidence in biblical authority. They're right: there's no telling where it will end. There's *really* and *literally* no end to it in view of the lack of original autograph manuscripts. There will never be a way of corroborating textual authenticity.

Of course, many fundamentalists *embrace* the Lower Criticism precisely because of their belief in verbal inspiration: if God inspired the wording, we damn well better try to pin down the right words. They are to be commended. But I think that ultra-fundamentalists who advocate the "King James Only" position reveal the real motivation that also lurks behind the urgency to minimize the dangers of textual criticism: they are clinging to "the Bible" they grew up with, the one they heard authoritatively quoted in sermons, like a cherished Teddy Bear. To claim, in extreme cases, that the KJV, *in English*, is uniquely authoritative is to try to stave off the cancer of uncertainty. Even to grant that different translations of the biblical text are possible is to make the biblical bugle produce an uncertain sound (1 Cor. 14:8).

---

52. Of course, this is exactly my own position when it comes to finding authentic sayings of Jesus. Those sayings that pass the criteria of dissimilarity, multiple attestation, embarrassment, etc., may yet be inauthentic. It shouldn't seem unlikely given the evidence of mass fabrication. You still have to wonder.

CHAPTER FOUR
BLESSED ARE THE CHEESE MAKERS

All Workers in Dairy Products

In his excellent book, *Jesus Before the Gospels*, Bart Ehrman utterly and definitively demolishes the hackneyed argument for gospel accuracy: the stories and sayings ascribed to Jesus are eyewitness reports and transcriptions preserved with verbatim accuracy over several decades of oral tradition/transmission. This result need not be miraculous but presupposes only the supposedly razor-sharp (virtually phonographic) memory of Non-Western oral cultures. I'm delighted to see this moldy vampire staked, not because I giggle with glee over the prospect of debunking the Christian faith, but because I despise humbug and hokum. And by that I mean, not Christianity, but bogus, axe-grinding arguments. There is much in the Christian tradition to love, and I do love it, but that definitely does not include what Albert Schweitzer called "the crooked and fragile thinking of Christian apologetics."[1]

Professor Ehrman has dived deep into the fields of memory studies, oral tradition, and collective social memory, areas of study highly relevant to New Testament scholarship but often neglected—or abused.[2] He shows how

1. Albert Schweitzer, *Out of my Life and Thought: An Autobiography* (New York: Mentor Books/New American Library, 1953), p. 186.

2. Paul Rhodes Eddy and Greg Boyd, *The Jesus Legend: A Case for the Historical Reliability*

experiments of various sorts map the surprisingly narrow limits of memory. When exposed to staged, striking, and dramatic events, people cannot recover much of what they saw but did not expect and could not readily construe. The mind resists bafflement and at once begins to fill in gaps and connect dots with "stock footage" drawn from our memory "files." We have the same tendencies even with common, everyday recollections. We often think we have vivid memories of important events, only to discover we got it very wrong. This is because there are lacunae in the memories we summon, and, at lightning speed, we try to enhance the sketch with details from other memories of similar events. It's like the movie *Jurassic Park*, when scientists have only fragmentary dinosaur DNA to work with and borrow genetic material from roughly similar frogs.

Bart admits he is not the first New Testament scholar to consider the research of Milman Parry[3] and Albert Lord,[4] but he reconsiders the application of its results to the doctrine of "accurate" transmission in oral cultures. Parry and Lord, classicists and anthropologists, were interested in finding a "control" to test theories of Homeric criticism. Could the *Iliad* and the *Odyssey*, hugely long, possibly have been composed in one big gulp by a single bard? Or were they compilations of originally separate works? These intrepid scholars decided to get off their butts, leave the ivy-covered towers of rarified speculation, and go find some modern bards who made their living by public recitals of exceedingly long poetic ballads. No script, no teleprompter.[5] The scholars tape-recorded various performances of (ostensibly) the same

of the Synoptic Jesus Tradition (Grand Rapids: Baker Academic, 2007). See my critique, "Jesus: Myth and Method." In John W. Loftus, ed., *The Christian Delusion: Why Faith Fails* (Amherst: Prometheus Books, 2010), pp. 273–290.

3. Milman Parry, *The Making of Homeric Verse: The Collected Papers of Milman Parry* (New York: Oxford University, 1987).

4. Albert Bates Lord, *The Singer of Tales*. Harvard Studies in Comparative Literature 24 (Cambridge: Harvard University Press, 1960); Lord, *Epic Singers and Oral Tradition*. Myth and Poetics (Ithaca: Cornell University Press, 1991); John Miles Foley, *The Singer of Tales in Performance* (Bloomington and Indianapolis: Indiana University Press, 1995).

5. Unlike the time a parishioner told me it was the centennial of Poe's *The Raven*, whereupon I strode into the Borders bookstore where my wife Carol worked and demanded a PA system so I could do a reading of Poe's masterpiece to the nonplussed coffee drinkers! So I guess I qualify as something of a coffee house bard myself! Did I recite the poem from memory? Are you kidding?

work. Though the bards insisted the recitations were "the same," they actually varied significantly, one performance omitting significant material prominent in the one before it and/or added new stuff. Wording varied. The "fidelity" appropriate to their appointed task consisted in ringing new changes. This is what Russian Formalist critic Viktor Shklovsky[6] called "defamiliarization" to break through the wall of over-familiarity that prevents us from seeing a text afresh. Bart appeals to other studies, e.g., of African tribal societies where the main entertainment was to hear campfire performances of elaborate creation epics. The reciters insisted on the identity between all recited versions despite pretty big omissions, additions, and variations. Apologists would like to believe that oral traditions in oral cultures would be carefully policed by the audience or by tribal authorities to ensure accuracy, but these studies showed that, when someone did challenge the reciter ("Hey! You left out the part where the High God sneezed the world into existence!"), it was a rival reciter arguing on behalf of *his*, quite different, version! *Ahem!*

As long as I have been acquainted with the Parry/Lord research, I have been astonished to read evangelical apologists appealing to this work to buttress their claims about the gospels. Did they even *read* it? If they embrace *this* standard of "accuracy," they are giving up the game, though they don't seem to realize it. Hel-*lo!*

But memory is not simply individual. We inherit mores, values, assumptions, biases, and beliefs, all of which define us. Among our society's bequests will be certain historical narratives, or in other words, social memory. Bart offers the example of the way the War Between the States is "remembered" depending on whether you find yourself in the North or the South. Yankees think of it as "the Civil War," a bit of intra-national turbulence analogous to a coup attempt. Southerners "remember" it as "the War of Northern Aggression," like England trying to drag the American Colonies back into the Empire. The

---

6. This is the term as rendered from the Russian by Lee T. Lemon and Marion J. Reis in their translation of Shklovsky's "Art as Technique" in Lemon and Reis, eds. and trans., *Russian Formalist Criticism: Four Essays*. Regents Critics Series. Bison Books (Lincoln: University of Nebraska Press, 1965), p. 13. Personally, I prefer this translation to that of Benjamin Sher as "estrangement" in Shklovsky, *Theory of Prose* (Elmwood Park, IL: Dalkey Archive, 1990), Chapter 1, "Art as Device," p. 6. Not that I know Russian or anything; I guess I just like "defamiliarizing" because it reminds me of Bultmann's "demythologizing."

change in the weather was starkly evident to Bart as soon as he moved from New Jersey to North Carolina. I can empathize with him: when I was a lad of ten, my family moved from Mississippi to New Jersey. The day we arrived, my folks went into our new home to wrap up some details, leaving my brother and me waiting in the car. We were shooting the breeze, and somehow the Civil War came up, I guess because we were newly-minted Yankees. To my complete amazement, Byron (three years my senior and not stupid like me) broke the news that the South had *lost* the Civil War! No one had ever told me one way or the other before now. I had simply been left to draw my own inferences from the fact that "we" had won every war, e.g., against King George, Kaiser Bill, and the Nazis. We used to watch *Major Mosby* on TV; he was the hero who always triumphed, and he was a Confederate! We went to football games to see the Ole Miss Rebels play. You get the picture. That day (February 5, 1965), I got dragged kicking and screaming into a very different social memory—darn it! In junior high history class, I wrote a paper titled "Why the South Was Justified in Seceding from the Union." My teacher, Richard Faller, commented in red: "I wish they'd succeeded!"

Social memories shape and serve the needs of particular communities, and they may or may not have any basis in fact. A contemporary example would be the Black Lives Matter movement which is predicated on the false report that street thug Michael Brown had been murdered by a police officer who shot him while he was surrendering, hands held aloft. Despite the sound debunking of this claim, the momentum keeps the movement and the false "memory" alive and kicking. Social memory is like that. Similarly, the political Left has a very different "memory" of America from that "remembered" by the Right. Christians remember history very differently from Muslims and Jews. And you know where this is all headed: the "memories" of Jesus enshrined in the gospels and, even more, the "memory" of Jesus in the post-Chalcedonian church, while they serve and inspire Christians, may have little or no basis in fact.

As he did in *Jesus: Apocalyptic Prophet of the New Millennium*, Bart Ehrman accepts the axiom that the gospel tradition goes back, by hook or by crook, to the eyewitnesses of Jesus. Very much of it has probably been distorted beyond recognition, some of it invented out of whole cloth. And I want to re-emphasize that, even granting an eyewitness origin, Bart has shown the complete futility of the traditional apologist argument. At the same time, from my perspective, perhaps he is granting too much. I will suggest that the eyewitness origin business is itself a piece of dubious apologetics.

The Community College of Apostles[7]

I believe the eyewitness origin notion is circular to a degree seldom envisioned by either scholars or apologists. They don't even seem to realize the need to deal with the relevant point: do we even know there *was* an original "college of apostles" from whom the tradition might have stemmed? It is a live question as to whether there was such an apostolic band, or whether, as Walter Schmithals,[8] Günter Klein,[9] and Robert Eisenman have all suspected, this list of characters is a fiction. It might be that the list of "the twelve" represents a reading back into the ministry of Jesus of a group only subsequently constituted as such by a shared resurrection vision (an appearance or an hallucination, I leave to you to decide). These men may have actually been among the associates of Jesus even though he had never chosen a circle of twelve.

Or they may not have been associates of Jesus at all, owing their leadership role to other factors entirely. For instance, they may have been chosen as leaders of a Jewish-Christian faction, standing for the number of the twelve tribes, just as the Qumran sect had a council of twelve. And then, at some later time, they may have been fictively retrojected into the time of Jesus to increase their clout. (The early Catholic appeal to eyewitnesses was itself a function of the system of apostolic succession, positing recent historical founders to authorize the position of the institutional hierarchy.)

Or, a la Eisenman,[10] the twelve apostles may be fictional replications (more than one of each) of the earlier leadership group who survive alongside them in Galatians and to some extent in Acts, the Pillars or the Heirs (*Desposunoi*), the brethren of the Lord. These, in turn, were eventually understood to be literal, fleshly siblings of Jesus, but they were also understood in Gnostic (and maybe other) circles as spiritual brethren of Jesus. Eisenman opts for a

---

7. The next three sections are based on the first half of Chapter 2, "How Secure Is the New Testament Tradition?" of my book *Jesus Is Dead* (Cranford: American Atheist Press, 2007), pp. 11–34.

8. Walter Schmithals, *The Office of Apostle in the Early Church.* Trans. John E. Steely (New York: Abingdon Press, 1969), pp. Part Four, IV, 4, "Emergence of the Twelve-Apostles Tradition," p. 261–265, and V, "The 'Twelve Apostles,'" pp. 265–272.

9. Günter Klein, *Die zwölf Apostel: Ursprung und Gehalt einer Idee* (Göttingen: Vandenhoeck & Ruprecht, 1961).

10. Robert Eisenman, *James the Brother of Jesus: The Key to Unlocking the Secrets of Early Christianity and the Dead Sea Scrolls* (New York: Viking Penguin, 1996), pp. 807–816.

physical, dynastic understanding. At any rate, their ranks included James the Just (also represented as Salih, "the Just," in the Koran, as well as, I would add, Silas in Acts), Judas Thomas, Simeon bar-Cleophas, and Joses.[11] On Eisenman's theory (though some of the details are my inferences), *James bar Zebedee* and *James "of Alphaeus"* (meaning "the substitute," "the caliph") are both transformations of James the Just, brother of the Lord. *Simon Peter* and *Simon Zelotes* would be versions of Simeon-bar-Cleophas, the brother of Jesus who succeeded James as bishop (*mebaqqr*) of Jerusalem. *Judas Thomas* became *Judas Iscariot* ("the False One," reflecting later doctrinal disputes), *"Judas not Iscariot," Bar-Tholomew, Thaddaeus*/Addai, as well as Thamoud and Hud in the Koran. *Andrew* the brother of Simon Peter reflects the Son of Man (*aner, andros*), brother of Simon bar-Cleophas. *Matthew* is a broad pun on *mathetes*, "disciple." *Lebbaeus* is another form of Oblias, "the Bulwark," a title of James the Just. *Philip* has been misplaced from the list of seven Deacons. *John bar Zebedee* represents the Pillar John, Jesus' brother instead of the misplaced Joses.[12]

The scarcity of information about the twelve in the New Testament is startling and more than a little suggestive of the possibility that they represent an artificial construction. Every single instance of Peter, James, or John taking the stage looks like one of the Buddhist tales of Ananda where the disciple is simply a straight man for the Master. Plus the fact that when one of them momentarily surfaces to volunteer something, he is merely an artificial mouthpiece for the group. And notice, it is always only James, John, and Peter (Mark 8:29; 9:5, 38; 10:28, 35; 11:21; 13:3; 14:29, 66–72; Matt. 14:28–31; 5:15; 17:4, 24–27; 18:21; 26:35; Luke 5:5–8; 8:45; 9:54; 12:41; 22:8, 31–33; John 6:68; 13:6–9, 24, 36; 18:10; 20:6; 21:15–21),[13] the same names, though supposedly not entirely the same characters, as the Pillars of Galatians 2:9, implying these have been chosen for fifteen minutes of fame on account of the lingering memory of their original identity as Jesus' brethren.

Thus we have no reason at all to believe there would have been a group

---

11. I think his presence in Mark 6:3 is a scribal slip or alteration, misplacing the name of Jesus' father Joseph and replacing a fourth brother named John (reflected in the Catholic belief that James and John bar Zebedee were Jesus' "cousins" and in Luke's nativity story that makes Jesus the cousin of another John, the Baptist.).

12. See previous note.

13. John gives bit parts to Philip (6:7; 12:22; 14:8), Andrew (6:8; 12:22), Thomas (11:16; 14:5; 20:24–28), and Judas not Iscariot (14:22).

of apostolic censors whose job was to ride herd on early Christians, keeping them straight about what Jesus said and did. Indeed, in view of the competing factionalism existing between leadership groups (what other way can we explain the trouncing the twelve and the Heirs take in Mark, a la Marcion?), I should expect the opposite: the wholesale fabrication of ostensible Jesus sayings such as Matthew 16:17–19 (pro-Peter); Mark 10:35–40 (against James and John); Mark 3:20–21, 25, 31–35 (against the Heirs), Mark 10:38–40 (pro-Paul), Matthew 5:17–19 (against Paul).

The notion of the apostles carefully policing the circulation of Jesus stories and sayings ascribed to him is obviously a case of wishful thinking on the part of apologists. They are really talking about what they *wish* the imagined apostles had done, what the apologists themselves would have done if they had been there. It reminds me of what Albert Schweitzer said about the historical Jesus scholars of Protestant Liberalism: they recreated Jesus in their own image. That's what the apologists are doing. But, on the other hand, one might view the gospel form critics as actually taking on themselves the task imagined for the apostles, namely, weeding out bogus sayings and stories.

I have expressed the opinion, however, that the fundamental principle of form criticism thoroughly vitiates the use of the criterion of dissimilarity (as well as the criterion of embarrassment, which amounts to another version of the same thing). How? On the one hand, the criterion of dissimilarity proposes that any saying attributed to Jesus is probably authentic if it belies the practice or doctrine of "the early church." Christians then cannot have created it. Any story about Jesus that embarrassed early Christians must be factual since Christians wouldn't have created trouble for themselves by fabricating such tales. The problem with this is that there was no single, monolithic "early church." What embarrassed some Christians was embraced enthusiastically by others, as Bart Ehrman himself explains so well in his *Lost Christianities*.[14]

On the other hand, form criticism posits that nothing was preserved in tradition that had not served some purpose (ethical, liturgical, doctrinal) for

---

14. Not to be confused with another very fascinating book, Jacob Needleman's *Lost Christianity*. And see Bart D. Ehrman, *How Jesus Became God: The Exaltation of a Jewish Preacher from Galilee* (New York: HarperOne/ HarperCollins, 2014), p. 295: "Of course, every group representing every view of early Christianity claimed that its views were the original teachings of Jesus and his earthly followers." Also p. 237: "Different Christians in different churches in different regions had different views of Jesus, almost from the get-go."

early Christians. "Every detail of the apostolic recollection of Jesus can be shown to have been preserved for the sake of its religious significance." [15] Thus, if we are reading it, it must have been amenable to *someone* in early Christianity. And if a unit of tradition served Christian interests we can by no means be sure it wasn't made up for the purpose *by* Christians.

Bart discounts my suggestion this way:

> it is a misuse of the criterion of dissimilarity to use it to show what did *not* happen in the life of Jesus. The criterion is designed to be used as a positive guide to what Jesus really said and did and experienced, not as a negative criterion to show what he did not. . . . And there are a number of traditions about Jesus that easily pass the criterion of dissimilarity, making their historicity more probable than their non-historicity. [16]

But even if a gospel unit passes the gauntlet of the criteria of dissimilarity, multiple attestation, etc., all one can rightly say is that it has not been debunked *yet*. So far, so good. I don't see how anyone can build on such a foundation of drifting sand. Yes, of course the criterion of dissimilarity is intended to differentiate the gold from the pyrite. But it cannot do the job. "We undertake, when we apply it, to believe everything our informant tells us so long as it satisfies the merely negative criterion of being possible. . . . The critical attitude has not been achieved." [17] "For the positive conclusion is in effect that . . . the statement itself bears upon it no recognizable marks of being untrue. But it may be untrue for all that." [18]

COPYRIGHTED CHRIST

Second, what exactly are the twelve supposed to have to do with the four gospels? There are two claims often made. One is that advanced by Harald

---

15. Martin Kähler, *The So-called Historical Jesus and the Historic Biblical Christ*. Trans. Carl E. Braaten. Seminar Editions (Philadelphia: Fortress Press, 1964), p. 93.

16. Ehrman, *Did Jesus Exist?*, p. 187.

17. R.G. Collingwood, *The Idea of History* (New York: Oxford University Press, 1946), p. 239. Collingwood is talking about the criterion of the analogy to present-day experience, but I think his words apply just as well here.

18. Collingwood, *Idea of History*, p. 261.

Riesenfeld[19] and Birger Gerhardsson[20] that, since the gospels stem from the circle of twelve disciples, they must be accurate because these men must have followed the rabbinical practices of strict memorization and transmission of their Master's sayings. This, again, is hopelessly circular, even if for the sake of argument we were to grant that there was such a circle of close disciples. For we just do not know where the gospel materials came from. *If* they stem from a circle of stenographer disciples who memorized everything for posterity, then, fine, the gospels can be trusted. But that is a big if! That is precisely what we do not know! And this is where internal evidence, the phenomena of the texts themselves, comes in. There are so many variations and contradictions between sayings, not to mention stories, of Jesus that surely the most natural explanation is that of the form critics: Jesus traditions arose as needed in this and that quarter of the early church, the coinages of anonymous prophets and catechists. Did Jesus prohibit preaching to Samaritans and Gentiles or not? Did he say no longer to fast, temporarily to leave off fasting, or to fast? Was there one pretext for divorce or none? Is the kingdom of God to be heralded by apocalyptic signs or not? Did he proclaim his messiahship or keep it a secret? As reporter Harry Reasoner once commented, at the end of a Christmas edition of *Sixty Minutes*: "It seems that, like beauty, Jesus Christ is in the eye of the beholder." If the texts are anything to go by, no one held the copyright on Jesus.

CHARACTER WITNESSES—OR JUST CHARACTERS?

Appeal is also made to various persons whose testimonies allegedly underlie the gospels. These individuals seem to sit so close to the narrated events that, *provided the events happened at all, and that these characters were the source of the narrator's "knowledge" of these events*, we would have good grounds for confidence in the narratives. I have just indicated the multiple difficulties besetting this grossly circular claim. Do we have any reason to believe there were such people and

19. Harald Riesenfeld, "The Gospel Tradition and Its Beginnings," in Riesenfeld, *The Gospel Tradition*. Trans. Margaret Rowley and Robert Kraft (Philadelphia: Fortress Press, 1970), pp. 1–30.

20. Birger Gerhardsson, *Memory and Manuscript, Oral Transmission in Rabbinic Judaism and Early Christianity*. Trans. Eric J. Sharpe (Uppsala: Almqvist & Wiksells, 1961).

that, if there were, they reported their experiences to the gospel authors?

For instance, the women who discovered the empty tomb: are we sure there even *were* such women? It is not at all implausible that Jesus, like all gurus ancient and modern, attracted a circle of smitten, usually middle-aged, female admirers. But then, on the other hand, the only actual stories we possess starring these women characters bear a striking resemblance to the passion, burial, and resurrection narratives of other Hellenistic redeemer gods. Mary Magdalene, Salome, Joanna, et. al., look a lot like Isis and Nephthys who mourn for the betrayed and slain Osiris, search for his body, and anoint it, raising him from the dead. They bear more than a passing likeness, too, to Cybele who discovered the body of her beloved Attis and resurrected him. And let's not forget Ishtar Shalmith ("the Shulammite") who, as the Song of Solomon knew, had descended into Sheol to recover the slain Tammuz. And there was Athena who found the remains of Dionysus Zagreus and besought Zeus on his behalf, occasioning his rebirth. Aphrodite similarly found the gored corpse of Adonis and raised him to new life. Not to mention Anath who sought Baal, found his death site, the field of blood, and rescued him from the Netherworld.

Let's take an inventory, shall we? The *only* story in the gospels that features the women is the one in which they seek the tomb of the slain savior, leading to his resurrection. (Luke 8:2–3 merely prepares for Luke's Easter story.) And this story exactly parallels the stories of women devotees seeking the body of the other slain saviors who rise from the dead. I'd say it is at best a toss-up whether these women ever existed as anything but Christian counterparts to the women characters of the resurrection myths of neighboring religions, whence they were likely derived. And if we cannot even make it look all that likely that they *existed*, it is obviously moot to appeal to them as sources of information. One might as well appeal to the testimony of Cybele to argue that Attis rose from the dead.

The Emmaus disciples might be called to the stand as witnesses of the risen Christ—except for two damning criticisms. First, the story looks an awful lot like biblical and classical myths in which gods travel among mortals incognito as a kind of *Candid Camera* stunt, to test their reactions. Yahweh's angels visit Sodom, after visiting Abraham for the same reason. Zeus and Hermes visit palaces and hovels to determine whether mankind deserves destruction in a flood. They appear to the pious old couple Baucis and Philemon, whose generosity allows them to be spared and made into pillars of Zeus's temple upon death. But the Emmaus story most resembles a fourth-century BCE story, repeated long afterwards, in which a couple has journeyed far to the healing shrine of Asclepius, son of Apollo. Like other suppliants, they had expected a dream-appearance of the god who would relieve the woman of a prolonged pregnancy. But he had not appeared, and they are headed home depressed—until a mysterious stranger joins them and asks why they are so glum. Hearing their sad tale, he tells them to set down her stretcher, whereupon he heals her of what turns out to be tapeworms, not a pregnancy at all. Then he disappears. Sound familiar? What are the chances the Asclepius version is but a myth, while the Jesus version is true fact reported by eyewitnesses?

But suppose we *do* take the story as a record of a strange encounter on the lonely Emmaus road. What kind of evidence for the resurrection does it provide? Very ambiguous evidence, if that, for the simple reason that the pair of disciples travels with Jesus for hours *without recognizing him*! Oh, you can just cover up the problematical nature of this feature as Luke does, by simple authorial fiat: "They were prevented from recognizing him," but then you're just dealing with a literary composition, not reporting. Imagine if you read such a detail in a newspaper. What would you think? Funny business! The fundamentalist apologist is willing to swallow the problem only because he already wants to believe the text is inspired and inerrant. He is only interested in historical plausibility insofar as he needs it as an argument to rope you in. Where it is lacking he does not miss it.

No, if they spent all that time with the famous Jesus of Nazareth and only decided *after he was gone* that it had been he, then what we have is a case of wistful mistaken identity. Hugh J. Schonfield saw this, and he was right. The story practically invites disbelief, as does the similar one in John 20:1–18, where Mary Magdalene does not recognize Jesus either. So does Matthew 28:17, which actually says, "And when they saw him, they worshipped him, but they doubted."

But let's go the second mile. Suppose the story does stem from the breathless testimony of the Emmaus disciples, and suppose it is fairly represented in Luke 24, so that you are sure you have the authentic report of what they told the eleven. Should you believe it? Would you believe such a thing if your friend told you he had seen a mutual friend, known to be dead, alive again? I think you would not. You would suddenly transform into David Hume. You would ask yourself, "Which is more probable? That Bill is alive again? Or that Stan is lying, or hallucinating, or deceived?" You would automatically assume Stan is not to be believed, though you cannot imagine he is consciously lying. And this is only if you are quite sure Bill is dead.

Once a parishioner told me that Alan Duke, our church's almost-resident street bum, had died during the harsh winter. A couple of weeks later, someone else told me he had seen Alan, alive if not well. It was easy to conclude that my first informant had been the victim of a false rumor, perhaps a case of mistaken identity. Another time, my friend Ralph was sitting outside a convenience store, growing increasingly feverish. He spotted his roommate and hailed him, but he received no acknowledgement. When my friend returned home, his roommate denied having been there at the store. Well, it turned out that Ralph was suffering hallucinations from a ruptured gall bladder poisoning his pancreas! He was rushed to the hospital and came out fine some weeks later. My mother was in the hospital under heavy drugs. She told me she had seen my father and my uncle Douglas, both long dead, come walking through her hospital room, wordlessly waving to her! Were my dad and my uncle raised from the dead? Or was it no coincidence she was drugged at the time? In short, if you heard your friend report that another was resurrected from the dead, you would not automatically believe him, and probably not at all. You would know that some neglected factor must be making the difference. These informants were all eyewitnesses. So what?

The Eyewitness Apologetic

Let's try a thought experiment, taking as historically accurate, as the apologists want us to do, the gospel statements about who witnessed what events and sayings of Jesus in the gospels. Form-criticism, though it bids us infer audience from content, assumes each pericope was passed down by itself with no commentary on such matters as who heard what originally. Redaction criticism bids us notice how different evangelists make different audiences hear the same saying, implying fictive ascription. Soon we will see why.

Assuming that the materials have reached us from these various audiences, what scale of reliability can we infer for the various units? This is important in view of the claim that the Jesus materials stem from a well-defined "official" circle of ordained disciples who orally Xeroxed what they were taught, repeating the process with their own disciples until the material was transcribed into the gospels. Who do the gospels themselves say witnessed Jesus' deeds and received Jesus' teachings? We may discover unintended consequences of the apologetical arguments.

Reports stemming from *the circle of disciples* would presumably be most accurate. Those in which only *isolated individuals who played no significant role in the church* as far as we know, would be less reliable. We might wonder if these individuals are rather literary characters supplied in a fictive scene. If only *crowds* are said to have heard or seen something, hence to have reported it, we may be dealing with rumor because the disciples could not have been in the position to correct, affirm, or deny it. If the disciples are present but there is said to have been crowd acclamation, we may wonder (in accord with Noth's redundancy principle[21]) if the crowd is the real source, though the disciples may have okayed it. But then, if it is legitimate, why do we not hear it from the disciples?

Keeping in mind the apologetic argument that *critics of Jesus* would have hastened to correct any fabrication or exaggeration, let us notice when critics are said to have been on the scene. If they are not, then that leaves us with material not susceptible to such criticism or verification. And doesn't the implicit assumption that Jesus' enemies' corrections ought to be accepted if available mean that their versions of events are to be preferred for the sake of argument? Otherwise, what's the point of the apologetic?

If only an *inner circle* of disciples are said to have been the witnesses, we may suspect we have a later bit of material, being read back into the tradition in the manner of the Gnostics.

If there were *no* witnesses, how do we know of the "event" at all? We have to assume it is fiction.

We must also note instances where it says Jesus himself tried to prevent the circulation of stories. Could this mean they were untrue? Perhaps the narrator's assertion that this or that miracle was nonetheless true, despite Jesus trying to hush it up, reflects Christian propagation of these stories even though Jesus

---

21. Martin Noth, *A History of Pentateuchal Traditions*. Trans. Bernhard W. Anderson (Englewood Cliffs: Prentice-Hall, 1972), p. 162. Noth's suggestion is that, when we see characters on stage who play no real role, standing silently alongside the central character, chances are they were the heroes in the original version. Their superfluous presence in the extant version looks like a vestige retained by the reviser who shoved them aside when he inserted the new hero. Had that character occupied center stage from the start, the others wouldn't be there taking up space.

would have denied them. So now bear with me as we categorize a number of gospel passages according to the degree of eyewitness origin the evangelists claim for each.

No Witnesses

Who might have witnessed the descent of the dove and the voice from heaven (Mark 1:9–11; Matt. 3:13–17; Luke 3:21–22)? Mark makes Jesus himself the only immediate witness of the voice and of the sight of the sky parting and the dove descending, nor does Jesus tell anyone. Luke omits "he saw," objectifying the descent of the dove, but he still has the voice speak only to Jesus, implying there were no eyewitnesses but Jesus. Matthew omits "he saw" and has the voice speak of Jesus in the third person, therefore presumably to the crowd, making them at least partial eyewitnesses. But of course this is a redactional rewrite, positing on-site witnesses unhinted in his source. In later versions there is also a fire on the surface of the Jordan, as well as theologically loaded exchanges between John and Jesus.

What about Jesus' encounter with Satan (Mark 1:12–13; Matt. 4:1–11; Luke. 4:1–13)? To this remarkable scene there are no eyewitnesses but Jesus, who is having a series, as far as we can tell, of visions, of which he is said to tell no one. Note that Matthew and Luke have much more elaborate versions, depicting a Daniel Webster-style dialogue between Jesus and Satan, unlike Mark.

When Jesus transforms water into wine (John 2:1–11), the disciples and Mary are on hand, but they only *infer* that a miracle has taken place. Suppose the steward of the feast actually *had* reserved the best for last? I know this sounds ridiculous, but this sort of old-time Rationalist quibble is inevitable when one posits that the story must be based on eyewitness testimony, which is, I am of course suggesting, a big indication that the approach is totally wrong-headed.

Who witnesses Jesus' Gethsemane prayer? Mark has carefully removed all potential witnesses from the scene as Jesus leaves eight disciples on the outer margin, then distances himself from the inner circle of three. Who could have heard anything he said? Similarly, how does Mark know what the young man at the tomb said to the holy women—since Mark tells us "they said nothing to anyone" (16:8)? What sort of connection can any of this material have with eyewitnesses? Not even the gospel writers suggest any.

WITNESSED BY DISCIPLES

There must have been plenty of witnesses to the Sermon on the Mount/Plain (Matt. 5–7; Luke 6:20–23; 11:2–4, 9–13; 12:22–36; 13:23–24; 16:13, etc.). Jesus' disciples (not limited to the twelve) form the audience. But the sermon vehicle (and thus the scene) is artificial, as it is obvious how Matthew and Luke have arranged the same material in different ways. It cannot have been a single sermon, for no one could possibly memorize it from just hearing it once.[22] Some of it sounds as if originally addressed to committed disciples, warning them of trials to come, while other sayings might be imagined as directed to interested outsiders or just a religious public in general.

The Mission Charge (Mark 6:7–11; Matt. 10:5–23; Luke 9:1–6; 10:2–12) is ostensibly addressed to the twelve and, in Luke's doublet, the seventy, anticipating the Gentile Mission.

The disciples are the audience for various sayings including the exhortation to fearless confession (Matt. 10:26–33; Luke 12:2–9) and the warning about divided households (Matt. 10:34–36; Luke 12:51–53), though this one is really a quote from Amos, here treated as a saying of Jesus.

Who heard Jesus say that one must esteem him more highly than one's own family (Matt. 10:37–39; Luke 14:26–27)? Presumably potential recruits. No disciples are explicitly said to have been present, but it seems assumed.

In his woes on unrepentant towns (Matt. 11:20–24; Luke 10:13–15), Jesus is giving apostrophic address to Bethsaida, Capernaum, and Chorazin. He is not necessarily in any of them at the moment. So we are not to number their populations as witnesses who might one day have repeated the sayings to others. Here we readers are reduced to receiving hearsay once removed, as Jesus' wasted miracles are merely alluded to, not shown onstage.

When Jesus thanks his Father, really a blessing on those around him (Matt. 11:25–27; Luke 10:21–22), it must have been a prayer in the hearing of the crowds, as it concerns them.

I suppose the disciples would have been hanging around when (Matt. 12:42; Luke 6:43–45) Jesus rebuked . . . whom? The scribes? The crowds? Somebody had trouble with the concept of good fruit implying good trees and bad fruit denoting bad ones. But would the objects of his rebuke have carefully

---

22. Bart Ehrman, *Jesus Before the Gospels: How the Earliest Christians Remembered, Changed, and Invented their Stories of the Savior* (New York: HarperOne/HarperCollins, 2016), pp. 196–197.

passed it down? Not likely, huh?

In Mark chapter 4, Matthew chapter 13, and Luke 8:4–8; 10:23–24; 13:11–21, Jesus is explicitly said to speak his parables to the crowds, but to interpret them in private to the twelve and those around them, the larger orbit of disciples. Has anyone suggested that the Synoptic versions stem from the inner circle, who were thus able to preserve both the parables and the interpretations, while those in the Gospel of Thomas, which lack (or skip) the interpretations, stem from the mystified crowds? I hope not, but it would not be too surprising.

There are three major Passion predictions, the first in Mark 8:31; Matthew 16:21; and Luke. 9:22; the second in Mark 9:30–32; Matthew 17:22–23; and Luke 9:43b-45; and the third in Mark 10:32–34; Matthew 20:17–19; and Luke 18:31–34. As they are spoken only to the disciples, you might think these sayings have a secure origin among Jesus' immediate associates. But it's not so simple. First, despite the blow-by-blow clarity, the disciples utterly fail to grasp what Jesus is telling them, implying the Passion predictions are a classic case of rhetoric aimed by the author over the heads of the characters, as an aside straight to the reader.[23] Second, is it possible to imagine anyone who passed these on by word of mouth being able to keep straight the differences in detail between the three predictions so as to maintain the original wording of each?[24]

In the exchanges over ritual defilement (Mark 7:1–23; Matt.15:1–20) Jesus replies to Jerusalem scribes (whose presence in Galilee seems anachronistic), then to the crowds, who are thus assumed to be listening to the exchange, and lastly to the disciples who express surprise at what he has said publicly. So there is a pretty wide selection of eyewitnesses on the imagined scene. But, as he is quoting the Greek Septuagint translation of Isaiah to a crowd of Palestinian Jews, the whole thing cannot be historical. It also attributes uniquely Diaspora Jewish customs to Palestinian Jews. So wherever this episode originated, it wasn't with any of these characters.

---

23. Robert M. Fowler, *Let the Reader Understand: Reader-Response Criticism and the Gospel of Mark* (Minneapolis: Fortress Press, 1991), pp. 138, 199, 249,

24. Erhardt Güttgemanns, *Candid Questions Concerning Gospel Form Criticism: A Methodological Sketch of the Fundamental Problematics of Form and Redaction Criticism.* Trans. William G. Doty. Pittsburgh Theological Monographs Series # 26 (Pittsburgh: Pickwick Press, 1979), p. 327.

The teaching about true greatness (Mark 9:33–37; Matt. 18:1–5; Luke 9:46–48) is of course directed to the disciples, so they might well have repeated it to others.

The Lost Sheep parable has two different points depending on which gospel one reads. In Matthew18:12–14 the parable tells Christian pastors to seek out straying congregation members and to persuade them to return to the fellowship. But in Luke 15:1–10 the identical story defends Jesus' association with irreligious Jews, risking his reputation as a holy man.[25] One might suggest that Jesus spoke the parable on two different occasions. But source criticism rules that out. If Matthew and Luke both took the same parable from the Q source, then the different audiences (disciples in Matthew, blue-nosed critics in Luke) must both be redactional in origin. The parable raises two related questions.

First, though it is seldom noticed, there is a gross inconsistency between the acceptance of the Mark/Q source-critical theory and the belief in an accurate, virtually verbatim preservation of the material in oral transmission. All theories of Synoptic interrelations are predicated on the understanding that the Synoptic gospels could not agree so well with one another if each were an independent collection of oral tradition. Such agreement requires literary dependence. So evangelical apologists, believing in complete accuracy, need not waste their time with things like Q. But insofar as they accept any theory of Synoptic relations, they have no business defending wholesale gospel accuracy.

Second, the sheer absurdity in the parable's description of a shepherd's behavior, leaving ninety-nine defenseless sheep to fend for themselves while he scours the hillsides for *one* single sheep, implies both that the parable was created by someone unfamiliar with the art of shepherding in Palestine and thus not living there, *and* that the transmission of Jesus material did not in fact have to run the gauntlet of unfriendly critics (which common psychology should tell us anyway). If non-Christian critics' skeptical disapproval carried enough weight to debunk and squelch any particular unit of tradition, this scoff-engendering parable should not have survived. Of course, the Christian

---

25. Joachim Jeremias, *The Parables of Jesus.* Trans. S.H. Hooke (New York: Scribners, 1972), pp. 38–41. "Details about the audience belong to the setting of the parables, and were therefore liable to be more freely handled than the parables themselves. Hence they require a specially careful analysis, a view which is borne out by the fact that the Gospels are occasionally inconsistent with one another in such details" (pp. 40–41).

response to outsider scoffing has always been to laugh it off, an attitude on display in 2 Peter 3:3–5, etc.

The Dishonest Steward parable seems to be addressed to sympathetic hearers, since Jesus refers to them as "sons of light" rather than "sons of this age." But they were apparently not yet fully committed to his itinerant band, as he is urging them to make the sacrifice of their possessions as a wise investment in view of the eschatological stakes. It seems most likely that these new recruits would have been the ones to remember this parable and to pass it on. It implicitly enhanced their reputations since they had accepted Jesus' challenge.[26] Surely no one who had sidestepped Jesus' summons would have been eager to do anything but forget it as quickly as possible!

The saying about faith like a mustard seed is, in Matthew 17:20, addressed to the disciples (implicitly to the nine disciples who were not on hand for the Transfiguration, though in the hearing of them all, since Peter, James, and John now have returned with Jesus). But in Luke 17:56 it is a completely different situation, and Jesus is replying to the disciples' request for "more faith." Again, the redactors have supplied the identity of the hearers.

In Mark 10:35–45 and Matthew 20:20–28 Jesus speaks to James and John, answering their question, but in the presence of the other disciples, or else how do they hear about it subsequently, as the text says they did?

When Jesus gives the parable of the Talents in Matthew 25:14–30 (or Minas in Luke 19:11–27) he is speaking only to Peter, Andrew, James and John, since Matthew tacks it onto the Olivet Discourse. In Luke Jesus says it to dampen the enthusiasm of hot-heads in the crowd. Each evangelist has substantially reworked the Q parable, and each has assigned a different group of hearers. Q obviously did not stipulate any particular audience.

Whatever Jesus said at the Last Supper, he said it to the twelve, but look at the four gospel accounts! Wherever they came from, it plainly cannot have been via a group of vigilant guardians of gospel accuracy.

---

26. Gerd Theissen, *Sociology of Early Palestinian Christianity*. Trans. John Bowden (Philadelphia: Fortress Press, 1978), Chapter II, "The Role of the Wandering Charismatics," pp. 9, 15. In a strange way, I think, the same issue is presupposed in Paul's dispute with his itinerant charismatic opponents in 2 Corinthians. See Dieter Georgi, *The Opponents of Paul in Second Corinthians*. Trans. Harold Attridge, Isabel and Thomas Best, Bernadette Brooten, Ron Cameron, Frank Fallon, Stephen Gero, Renate Rose, Herman Waitjen, and Michael Williams (Philadelphia: Fortress Press, 1986), p. 238–241.

We hear that the boat was filled with eyewitnesses both times when Jesus stilled the squall (Mark 4:35–41; Matt. 8:23–27; Luke. 8:22–25) and defied gravity on the Lake of Galilee. One wonders if, when apologists triumphantly point to eyewitness testimony, they have forgotten they are putting walking on the water under the same umbrella. Don't look now, but those people standing next to you claim to be UFO abductees.

Jesus made his remark on the widow's mite (Mark 12:41–44; Luke 21:1–4) to the twelve, though apparently Pat Robertson was there, too, and already scheming.

In the story of the woman with the blood flow (Mark 5:24b–33; Matt. 9:20–22; Luke 8:43–48) both the disciples and the members of the crowd closest to Jesus are rendered first-hand receivers of hearsay by her report, but the healed woman herself merely infers what has happened, based on her expectation. Interestingly, Jesus and the narrator are at odds as to what happened. Mark thinks Jesus felt an expenditure of power, while Jesus says the woman healed herself. The story has already become confused by the first time we read it.

The Nain resurrection (Luke 7:11–17) features as eyewitnesses the widowed mother, the disciples, the pallbearers, and the mourners. Many hearsay "witnesses" are implied by the acclamation of the crowd, since they would have spread the news to others back in town. I guess we would have to say the same for a nearly identical miracle performed by Apollonius of Tyana.

The exciting story of the Gerasene Demoniac (Mark 5:1–20; Matt. 8:28–34; Luke 8:26–39) casts the disciples as eyewitnesses. Local herders are at least partial eyewitnesses, since they see the ex-demoniac dressed in duds he got from somewhere. The townspeople are second-hand hearsay receivers. Presumably Jesus or the ex-demoniac will have told the story to the pig herders, who then blabbed it to the villagers who swarm onto the scene like Tyrolian peasants in a Frankenstein movie. But the story is confused: shouldn't the fearful townspeople have appeared earlier, while the monster was still roaming the countryside? Not after Jesus has tamed him? Besides, if this tale is based on the testimony of the disciples, shouldn't we ascribe the *Odyssey*'s episodes of the Cyclops and Circe the sorceress to Odysseus' soldiers whom she had turned into swine?

At the feeding of the five thousand (Mark 6:30–44; Matt. 14:13–21; Luke. 9:10–17; John 6:1–14), those present are not said to be aware of the miracle. Nor are we told what anyone saw Jesus doing. The miracle is *inferred* from the amount of the food. Ditto with feeding the four thousand (Mark 6:30–44; Matt. 14:13–21; Luke 9:10–17). And the fact that the disciples are equally baffled both times when Jesus suggests they feed the crowd with a single can of tuna and a packet of Lance crackers makes it plain that we have two versions of the same story. How obtuse can the disciples have been? Some apostle in charge of weeding out mistakes must have been nodding off, and a whole extra miracle is the result.

In the episode of the epileptic deaf-mute demoniac (Mark 9:14–29; Matt. 17:14–21; Luke 9:37–43), the disciples, the boy, and his father are eyewitnesses. The narrative is unclear as to whether the people in the crowd are eyewitnesses or partial eyewitnesses, as the crowd is said to be there at the start, but later we read that a crowd is *beginning* to form, prompting Jesus to act before witnesses are in place. Did the ever-vigilant approval board miss ironing out a kink in the narrative?

As for the lone exorcist (Mark 9:38–41; Luke 9:49–50 *vs.* Matt. 7:22–23), we are told John and some other disciple(s) saw unauthorized exorcisms, but they happen (if they do) offstage, so we readers are reduced to hearsay witnesses.

When Jesus, in a fit of pique, blasts the fig tree (Mark 11:12–14, 20–25) the disciples see the curse and the next day *infer* Jesus has destroyed the tree. In Matthew's version (Matt. 21:18–22), they *see* the tree wither at his word. The story, unlike the poor fig tree, has grown in the telling, despite the efforts of the board of censors.

When Jesus glued the guy's severed ear back on (Luke 22:51), did anyone see it—*including Jesus?* At the same point in the story Matthew 26:52 has Jesus say, "Put *your sword* back into its place." John 18:11 has him say, "Put *your sword* into its sheath." The healing seems to be an *inference* based on Luke's misinterpretation of an original which must have said, "Let *it* be restored to its place." Matthew and John rightly took "it" to mean the *sword*, while Luke took it to refer to the severed *ear*.[27] So there were a number of eyewitnesses—but to *what?*

When the resurrected Jesus appears behind closed doors (Luke 24:36–49; John 20:19–23), John says the doors were closed, implying a miraculous "beaming down" or a ghostly passage through solid wood, which seems to undermine the subsequent demonstration of his physical solidity. The

---

27. G.A. Wells, *The Jesus of the Early Christians: A Study in Christian Origins* (London: Pemberton Books, 1971), p. 197.

confusion implies a fiction. The story in John clearly implies there are eleven eyewitnesses, as it includes the impartation of the Spirit to the apostles for their ministry. But the very next episode in John (20:24–29) says, "Wait a second! Thomas wasn't there after all!" This scene retroactively reduces the number of eyewitnesses in the previous scene by one. The fact that the scene ends with a stage whisper to John's intended readers marks it as confessedly artificial.

TWELVE DISCIPLES IMPLIED AS SECONDARY AUDIENCE

When Jesus urges would-be disciples to think twice, who is he talking to? In Luke 9:57–60, the interlocutors are anonymous. In Matthew 8:18–22, they are "a scribe" and "another disciple." The latter betrays Matthew's notion of disciples as "scribes trained for the kingdom of heaven" (13:51). He has added the identification to the Q original.

"Take up the cross and follow me" (Mark 8:34–35; Matt. 16:20–25; Luke 9:23–24). Mark says he said it to the larger "multitude of his disciples." The reference is obviously to the crucifixion of Jesus, which, however, had not happened yet. Was Jesus even in hot water at this point? I doubt the multitude would have taken care to pass on a saying of which they could make no sense. But they didn't. Because they didn't hear him say it, because he didn't say it. If there was ever a channeled revelation from the ascended Jesus (something still common today in Charismatic and Pentecostal circles), this is it.

The sign of Jonah passage is quite interesting for our purposes because of both the stipulated audience and the growth of the saying from one gospel to another, indicating that "faithfulness" in transmission certainly in no way guaranteed unvarnished accuracy. The earliest version is found in Mark 8:11–12, where Jesus rebuffs his critics' request for an authenticating miracle ("a sign from heaven," i.e., from God). He says, simply, "no sign shall be given to this generation." Nothing yet about Jonah. But wait a minute! Did Jesus just say he will not do any miracles for that generation? Doesn't that imply all the miracle stories of the gospel must be subsequent fabrications? No one wants to hear *that*, even today. So it comes as no surprise that the saying got embellished. The Q version (Matt. 16:1–4; Luke 11:29–32) reads, "An evil and adulterous generation seeks for a sign, but no sign shall be given to it except the sign of (the prophet [so Matthew]) Jonah. You see what's happening, right? Jesus' "Sorry, no miracles from me" is qualified: there *will* be a "sign," that of the half-digested prophet Jonah. What, pray tell, does *that* mean? I suspect the point is not what it *does* mean but what it *doesn't*. That is, the supplement serves as a distraction from the theologically dangerous dismissal of miracles. It is in that respect like Jesus' ambiguous reply to the reluctant John the Baptist: "Let it be so now, for thus it is fitting for us to fulfill all righteousness" (Matt. 4:15). Huh? Again, the point is not whatever the reply may mean, but rather that, whatever's going on, Jesus is *not* getting baptized to be absolved of any sins.

Matthew 12:38–42 adds an important extension seeking to explain the Jonah reference. It must be that Jonah's metaphorical (but almost literal!) death and resurrection by becoming fish food, then a fish cathartic, prefigures the impending crucifixion and resurrection of Jesus. That's quite a big item for Mark (and Q) to have left out! But of course he didn't. Q already added new material to the original version as attested in Mark, but this Matthean addition is a real whopper! You can't tell me that these texts attest a faithfully accurate passing along of a saying of Jesus by officially sanctioned tradition bearers. On the contrary, it is clear proof that whoever passed on the Jesus tradition felt completely at liberty to amplify and fabricate as they saw fit.

And to whom is Jesus depicted as speaking these words? He is answering scribal critics who want to paint him into a corner from which he cannot return with reputation intact. And here is the real reason for the Matthean addition. He thus creates an unprecedented public prediction by Jesus that he would rise from the dead. Matthew needs to set the stage for the Sanhedrin's approach to Pilate asking him to post guards at the tomb in order to fend off a resurrection hoax. How did the Jewish leaders know to expect this? Because Jesus told them they could not keep him in the grave.[28]

OTHER WITNESSES, WITH NO DISCIPLES MENTIONED

Jesus' eulogy of John the Baptist (Matt. 11:2–19; Luke 7:18–35) addresses crowds of John's disciples and admirers who might indeed have remembered his words and passed them down in their circles, eventually to be used by Baptist polemicists to undermine Christian claims as we see them doing in the

---

28. Ironically, the Sanhedrinists might be seen here as performing the role assigned to the apostles by our apologists, as zealous control freaks trying to prevent falsification of the Jesus story.

Pseudo-Clementines. But the clause, "yet he who is least in the kingdom of heaven is greater than he," must have been added by Christians in response to the Baptist apologetic.

When the Jewish leaders demand that Jesus justify his disruptive actions at the Temple (Mark 11:27–33; Matt. 21:23–27; Luke 20:1–8), he responds to them in the hearing of the crowd. Thus both groups would be witnesses, though we cannot easily imagine the former caring to preserve the holy words.

The Bartimaeus incident (Mark 10:46–52; Matt. 20:29–34; Luke 18:35–43) implies a crowd of eyewitnesses at the beginning, but where is Jesus when they bring the blind man to him? In private as with some other healings?

When Jesus rebukes those who cannot reckon the signs of the times (Luke 12:54–56; Matt. 16:1–3) whom is he addressing? In Matthew he speaks to the Pharisees and Sadducees, but in Luke it is the multitude—*all* "hypocrites"? Matthew has extra spite for these particular villains and more than once inserts them where his source lacked them. He has done that here. Again we see how the identity of Jesus' supposed hearers is not original to the story, a factor that undermines the claim of a brokered tradition under the supervision of authorized eyewitnesses.

Jesus' late-night dialogue with Nicodemus (John chapter 3), which might as well be the sole contents of the Bible for some people, seems restricted to the ears of the two partners. Nicodemus seems to have made a nocturnal visit in order to keep his dealings with Jesus secret from his colleagues, so it would be natural to suppose that Jesus' disciples were similarly asnooze, as in Mark 14:37, 40–41. Sure, Nicodemus might have remembered Jesus' words, though it seems unlikely if he went away puzzled. One wonders if he noticed the seamless stylistic continuity between Jesus' words and those of the narrator.

The dialogue with the Samaritan woman (John chapter 4) occurred while the disciples were away at the local supermarket, hence they could not have heard it. The woman, however, is said to have reported her conversation to her compatriots back in town. Or did she? The narrator tells us only that she said Jesus had told her, like a telephone psychic, "all I ever did." This does not even quite square with the dialogue as narrated. It certainly leaves out the best parts.

OTHER WITNESSES, WITH DISCIPLES PRESENT

Luke has grouped the material in his Central Section (9:51–18:14) according to the topical outline of Deuteronomy,[29] something apparent only to the reader, not in the imagined situation, where no group of hearers would hear enough of it to get the point. But it depicts him speaking to local crowds of the curious or the sympathetic as he makes his way to Jerusalem (over a much longer time than it would actually have taken to get there). See Luke 13:22: "You taught in our streets."

The twelve witness the congenitally blind man's washing and recovery of sight in John chapter 9. Many eyewitnesses afterward come forth to attest the man's former blindness, though they were not on hand for the cure. The parents and Pharisees hear of it, becoming receivers of first-hand hearsay when the healed man makes the claim in their hearing.

THE INNER CIRCLE

When Jesus asks Peter if he really thought through his answer to the collector of the Temple tax (Matt. 17:24–27) he is speaking to an audience of one. And presumably not even Jesus sees him reel in the magic fish! Too bad the Big Fisherman didn't pass on an explanation of how a coin could have remained in the fish's mouth while he opened it to take the hook.

In the Olivet Discourse Jesus is speaking only to Peter, John, James, and Andrew (Mark 13; Matt. 24–25), implying, as we might otherwise guess, that it is a later text no one had previously heard of, just like the Gnostic revelations of Nag Hammadi: "No wonder you folks never heard this until now! It was, ah, delivered only to a select few!" Luke 17:21 omits the mountaintop setting and changes the audience to an unspecified "some."

In an implicitly humorous episode, Peter's mother-in-law (let's call her Estelle) is too sick to fix supper for Jesus and his men. She is lucky to be treated better than the fig tree of Mark 11:12–14, 20–21, which also frustrated Jesus' hunger. He heals her so she can get up and get back into the kitchen (Mark 1:29–31; Matt. 8:14–15; Luke 4:38–39). Mark has four disciples as eyewitnesses.

---

29. C.F. Evans, "The Central Section of St. Luke's Gospel." In D.E. Nineham (ed.), *Studies in the Gospels: Essays in Memory of R.H. Lightfoot* (Oxford: Basil Blackwell, 1967), pp. 37–53.

Matthew suggests Peter may have seen it. Luke implies family members saw it. There is nothing about anyone spreading the news.

Jesus raises Jairus' daughter (Mark 5:21–24a, 35–43; Matt. 9:18–19, 23–26; Luke 8:40–42, 49–58) from the dead or out of a coma. For Matthew, there are no eyewitnesses at all. For Mark eyewitnesses are restricted to Peter, Andrew, James, and John, plus Mr. and Mrs. Jairus. Jesus forbids creating hearsay receivers, even though such secrecy is scarcely possible, given that the house is surrounded by mourners!

Only the inner circle of Peter, James, and John witness the Transfiguration (Mark 9:2–8; Matt. 17:14–21; Luke 9:28–36), not the rest of the disciples. And the three eyewitnesses are told not to create hearsay receivers until later, implying the lateness and fictional character of the story, as skeptics contended even back then (2 Peter 1:16–18).

ONLY SCRIBES AND CRITICS

The story of the Nazareth synagogue sermon (Luke 4:16–30; Mark 6:4; Matt. 13:57) has Jesus speaking to *hostile* villagers, no disciples being present yet. Who would have passed this on? Nor are any disciples mentioned when Jesus defends his association with tax collectors and sinners (Mark 2:17; Matt. 9:12–13; Luke 5:31–32). We are told only that Jesus replied to Pharisaic scribes.

To whom does Jesus speak when asked why his disciples do not fast (Mark 2:18–22; Matt. 9:14–17; Luke 5:33–39)? Matthew has Jesus talking with John's disciples, while Mark has Jesus talking to "people," apparently curious outsiders. Luke is indefinite. Nobody knew.

Jesus goes into a tirade against the Pharisees. In Luke11:37–52 Jesus addresses Pharisees face to face, without the twelve present. Luke 14:7–11 has Jesus speaking to one of his fellow dinner guests at another supper hosted by a Pharisee. No disciples are said to be present.

In the same context Jesus tells the parable of the Great Supper (Luke 14:15–24), but Matthew 22:1–10 has him address it to a public crowd. Obviously Q did not specify the audience. The evangelists have supplied them for the sake of the narrative. Luke 18:9–14 says Jesus addressed the parable of the Pharisee and the Publican "to some who trusted in themselves that they were righteous." I'm guessing these people would not have been eager to pass on this parable to posterity.

Did the Roman soldiers who mocked and abused the thorn-crowned Jesus carefully commit an accurate account of their brutal horseplay to eager Christian hearers? Because no one else is said to be present to see it. Or did Pontius Pilate have a stenographer transcribe his interrogation of Jesus? Did Christians buy a copy off of eBay? Because they couldn't have heard it for themselves. Ditto for the Sanhedrin trial.

SCRIBES AND CRITICS WITH OTHERS PRESENT

In the Beelzebul controversy (Mark 3:22–27; Matt. 12:22–30; Luke 11:14–23) Mark's dialogue refers to recent exorcisms but relates none on the spot, unlike Matthew and Luke. The scribes and the crowds are thus either eyewitnesses or hearsay receivers. In any case, they make a different *inference*, that Jesus is a sorcerer. This shows how much *interpretation* is involved in "witnessing" what one regards as miracles performed by one's savior or as a sorcerer trafficking with infernal powers. What are you actually beholding?

OTHER INDIVIDUALS ONLY

Mary and Martha play host to Jesus (Luke 10:38–42), seemingly *only* to Jesus. Thus he speaks only to the two women, and, though he teaches something to Mary, the content is not related, only his rebuke to Martha, which is the punch line of the story. Was the rebuke more memorable than the teaching?

The annunciation to Joseph (Matt. 1:20–21) has a single witness. A man has a dream addressing a stressful subject, and it helps him come to terms with it. He *infers* it is a message from God. Does he tell others? The text does not say so, so we cannot assume there are any hearsay witnesses. Joseph is not likely to report it to others since the explanation would only raise the very suspicions about Mary that he was trying to avoid. Nor can we say he *must* have told others or we would not be hearing about it. That begs the question whether this is a report or a piece of fiction.

Do we owe the tale of the Wise Men (Matt. 2:2, 9–10) to eyewitness testimony? Charting a star involves no miracle. A moving star, hovering close to the ground, would be a genuine wonder, but the story presupposes an ancient view of stars as small and moving. Hence it is a fiction. Any further significance of the star, determining that Jesus is the child of prophecy, is a matter of their *inference*. It was, in the nature of the case, not something even onlookers could have *seen*. How could the Magi themselves have decided which hovel in Bethlehem was directly below a star in the sky?[30]

Joseph's prescient dream of Herod's slaughter of the innocents (Matt. 2:13) leaves him as the sole "witness" of the dream. Imagine him subsequently telling people about it, inviting the response, "Why the hell didn't you bother telling your neighbors to get out of town, too?"

Only Zechariah sees the vision in Luke 1:11–17, though he does try to communicate it to others. Rendered a deaf-mute, he pantomimes the news, hence may not have communicated it correctly. Plenty of room for garbling if you're trying to decipher a game of charades.

The Temple theologians are the immediate hearers of the boy Jesus' surprising erudition (Luke 2:41–52). Mary and Joseph, uncomprehending and coming in on the tail end of the meeting, are but partial eyewitnesses. Presumably we are to imagine they told the others in the caravan, making them first-hand hearsay receivers. But what sense could Jesus' block-headed parents have passed on? The narrator knows more than they did.

To the healing of a leper (Mark 1:40–45; Matt. 8:1–4; Luke 5:12–16), Matthew implies the presence of many eyewitnesses, while Mark and Luke lack these but do imply many first- and second-hand hearsay receivers. The twelve are not mentioned.

Jesus heals the centurion's son (Matt. 8:5–13; Luke 7:1–10; cf., John 4:46–54). Since the sick son is not on the scene, and we as readers are mere first-hand hearsay receivers, there are no eyewitnesses of the actual healing. How did our narrator know it actually happened? Did it?

Of the Syro-Phoenician woman's demon-possessed daughter (Mark 7:24–30; Matt.15:21–28) the woman is the only eyewitness. Everyone else is at best a partial eyewitness, since the healing happens by remote control. The miracle must be *inferred* by the characters from the coincidence in time, to which the evangelist draws attention.

The Bethsaida blind man (Mark 8:22–26) is the only possible eyewitness. All others are excluded from the scene. Jesus told him not to return to his village, so he couldn't have told anyone there. It seems uncertain whether he

---

30. The scenario is fully as ludicrous as that in one of my favorite flicks, *Omen III: The Final Conflict*, when a bunch of Catholic monks visit an observatory to watch three stars *visibly converging* in the sky to herald the rebirth of Christ.

would have told anyone in a new village, who had not previously known him. Contrast this with the spread of the news of a blind man's healing among those who knew him in John chapter 9.

The ten lepers (Luke 17:11–19) were their own eyewitnesses. No disciples are said to be present.

When Jesus healed the lame man at the Bethzatha Portico (John 5:11–18) there may have been other eyewitnesses among the suppliants at the pool, but we do not hear this. The healed man tells others, who would qualify as first-hand hearsay receivers. The Pharisees hear it first- or second-hand. They are not likely to have passed down this "tradition," and Jesus finds the man and threatens him with divine punishment if he doesn't shut the hell up. So did the story proceed any further?

When Peter spews out his repudiations of Jesus he is speaking to different eyewitnesses in each gospel. Notoriously, fundamentalists have proposed that Peter denied Jesus at least six times in order to juggle all of the different versions. Yet Jesus predicts there will be *three* denials. So once again, the supposed hearers seem to be fictive, interchangeable "extras" on stage. It seems unlikely that Peter himself recounted the tale for the simple reason that it is a story of rank *apostasy*. Peter does that which Jesus warns will result in eschatological damnation (Mark 8:38). No doubt the story began as a polemical slur by anti-Petrine Christians.[31]

To the darkness at noon (Mark 15:33; Matt. 27:45; Luke 23:44) everyone on the scene is inevitably an eyewitness, but there is no suggestion in any of the canonical narratives that any of the bystanders took any notice of the prodigy, unlike the Gospel of Peter, where people panic, thinking the sun has already set, stumbling in the dark and lighting lamps. Obviously, in the canonical accounts, this sign from heaven is for the reader, since it is exclusively a narrative event, not a historical one.

Who witnessed the earthquake at the crucifixion (Matt. 27:51)? Had it really happened, obviously there must have been plenty of witnesses. But only Matthew has it, and he mentions only the centurion on duty witnessing it. The coincident resurrection of the entombed pious (Matt. 27:52–53) is only more, even worse, gospel-to-gospel embellishment. Though Matthew does not say who, if anyone, saw the *Tales from the Crypt*-like emergence of the revenants,

31. Alfred Loisy, *The Birth of the Christian Religion*. Trans. L.P. Jacks (London: George Allen & Unwin, 1948), p. 102.

he does tell us there were subsequently many (no doubt terrified!) eyewitnesses in Jerusalem, flabbergasted at the appearance of their deceased loved ones, in scenes right out of Stephen King's *Pet Sematary*. If some apologist wants to maintain that this story was passed down by these witnesses, he is stuck with admitting that Jesus' Easter appearances were only part of a mass wave of hallucinations in Jerusalem that weekend.

Who attested the man or men or angel or angels at Jesus' tomb (Mark 16:5–7; Matt. 28:2–10; Luke 24:2–7; John 20:11–13)? In all four gospels women disciples are eyewitnesses of *something*. Mark mentions a "young man," whom the reader may infer to have been an angel. John doubles the man. Luke infers that the two (did he get them from John?) are angels. Matthew divides Mark's young man into an angel (who is now actually observed descending from heaven and shouldering aside the stone) and into the risen Christ, having him only repeat the angel's charge. In John, the women as a group see nothing and no one at the tomb, but the returning Mary Magdalene sees the angels and, again, a man, whom she first assumes is the gardener, then *infers* to be Jesus. According to Matthew and Luke, the women create first-hand hearsay receivers by telling the eleven disciples, whereas in Mark they tell no one, leaving the reader to guess how Mark found out. As it lacks any possible chain of transmission, we have to conclude the story is a fiction, not a report.

No eyewitnesses saw the disciples steal Jesus' body (Matt. 28:11–17) since it didn't happen, but lying witnesses created many generations of hearsay receivers. The report was still circulating in the evangelist's day. Why could the same thing not have happened in the cases of the various miracle stories, even if they, too, were mere rumors, since Matthew himself admits it worked pretty well with a rival story he himself dismisses as groundless?

POPULAR REPORTAGE

Contrary to the eyewitness origin theory (or claim, depending on whom you're reading), a surprisingly large number of gospel episodes are said *in the text* itself to be bottled messages afloat on a pitching ocean of popular reportage, i.e., rumor. This is the case with Zechariah's recovery of speech (Luke 1:65), the angelophany to the shepherds (Luke 2:17–18), Simeon's recognition (Luke 2:38), the Capernaum synagogue exorcism (Luke 4:37; Mark 1:28), the cleansing of the leper (Luke 5:15; Mark 1:45), the healing of the stretcher-bound paralytic

(Luke 5:26; Mark 2:12), the Nain resurrection (Luke 7:17), Jesus' true family (Mark 3:20–21, 31–35; Luke 8:19–21), the Gadarene Demoniac (Luke 8:36, 39; Mark 5:14, 20; Matt. 8:28–34), the resurrection of the Baptist and return of Elijah (Luke 9:7–8, 18–19; Mark 6:14–29), the healing of the Decapolis deaf-mute (Mark 7:35–37), the deaf-mute epileptic exorcism (Luke 9:37–38, 43), the Beelzebul controversy (Luke 11:15), the woman with the bent spine (Luke 13:17), Bartimaeus (Luke 18:39, 43), Zacchaeus (Luke 19:7), the Triumphal Entry, and Barabbas' release.

For example, who witnessed the resurrection of Lazarus (John chapter 11)? Jesus' disciples and a crowd of eyewitnesses who *infer* that Lazarus has been raised, after *inferring* that he is decomposing, *assuming* he was really dead. Often such ancient stories are about a wise man rescuing someone prematurely buried, mistakenly thought to be dead. At any rate, there are many eyewitnesses, if you can call them that, who generate many first- and second-hand hearsay receivers. Presumably, some of these witnesses were unsympathetic to Jesus. Keep in mind, though, that, as with all these gospel stories, the presence of witnesses is itself part of the story and not external attestation of it.

Besides, the story looks like it is based on the parable in Luke 16:19–31. There, too, we read of a man named Lazarus who dies, and of someone requesting that Lazarus be sent back among the living. And in both cases we are told this would not create faith among those who do not already have it.

Popular rumor lies at the root of all these units *according to the texts themselves*. So much for a proto-rabbinical magisterium stingy with the awarded imprimaturs. Had anyone in authority actually attempted to control the propagation of Jesus stories, would they have been able to suppress any they didn't like? The whole idea is absurd. Try to imagine such an enterprise in the real world. The closest analogy to what apologists envision (fantasize) is the later attempt to prosecute heresies. And how did *that* work out? Of course these inquisitors managed only to create their own competitors, since, once excommunicated, the "heretics" set up their own rival churches, hanging out their own shingles.

But the greatest irony is this: according to the gospels themselves, *even Jesus could not close down the rumor mill*. He warns the ex-leper not to tell anyone how he was cleansed, but the big-mouth cannot contain himself (Luke 5:14–15; Mark 1:44–45). Jesus visits Tyre and Sidon (Mark 7:24) incognito, but the sun glasses don't fool anyone. He heals a deaf-mute in the Decapolis (Mark 7:36) and tells him to keep his newly functional mouth shut, but the guy can't resist the temptation. Jesus heals two blind men (clones of Bartimaeus) in Matthew 9:27–31. No eyewitnesses are present because Jesus seeks indoors seclusion. Despite his command, the once-blind men go and spread the news.

Do the gospel stories sound like anyone's memories?[32] I think not.[33] The best argument for their being units of oral tradition is their spare compactness and their conformity to stereotypical outlines. Ironically, this also makes it impossible to show they stem from eyewitness recollections. They *might* have begun with eyewitnesses, but once set adrift, like baby Moses, on the flowing river of oral tradition, they get smoothed out, simplified, condensed, and you can no longer tell. F.F. Bruce says,

> there are occasions on which a stereotyped style is insisted upon even in modern life. When, for example, a police officer gives evidence in court, he does not adorn his narrative with the graces of oratory, but adheres as closely he can to a prescribed and stereotyped 'form.' . . . What his narrative lacks in artistic finish, it gains in accuracy.[34]

In other words, even if the story originated in witnessed fact, the stereotyping process would make it impossible to tell any longer.

It would be a little bit better if the gospel episodes were framed as "table talk." "I remember how one time some scribes approached Jesus as he was about to pray. They asked him why he wasn't wearing a yarmulke, whereupon he answered, saying, 'Verily, they haven't been invented yet, *bubula*.'" Something like that. Interestingly, whoever wrote the Apocryphal Acts of John understood this. In the section called the Preaching of John, the son of Zebedee is depicted as sharing memories of Jesus in exactly this form. But then again, the Acts of John are fiction, aren't they? So that wouldn't prove an eyewitness origin either.

We have seen that many gospel scenes are populated with witnesses, both disciples and bystanders. We've also seen how Matthew and Luke have

---

32. Ehrman, *Jesus Before the Gospels*, p. 225.

33. D.E. Nineham, *Explorations in Theology I* (London: SCM Press, 1977), Chapter 2, "Eye-witness Testimony and the Gospel Tradition I," pp. 24–37; Chapter 2, "Eye-witness Testimony and the Gospel Tradition II," pp. 38–48; "Eye-witness Testimony and the Gospel Tradition III," pp. 49–60.

34. Bruce, *New Testament Documents*, p. 32.

gratuitously supplied hearers when their common Q original must have had none. Furthermore, not even these episodes make a claim that they were derived from any of those characters. But even if that were implied, wouldn't that mean the whole notion of an eyewitness origin of the gospel materials is really an *intra-diegetic* feature? A part of the story rather than documentation for the story? Is it in principle any different from using parts of the Easter narrative (e.g., the empty tomb) as evidence for the factual character of the narrative?

And this consideration applies not only to evangelical apologetics but equally to the notion, advanced by Bart Ehrman, that, even allowing for massive distortion and embellishment, the gospel tradition originated among the eyewitnesses of a historical Jesus. But, you ask, where else could the tradition have originated?

THE PEN IS MIGHTIER THAN THE MOUTH

I wonder if the gospel tradition is not social memory *all the way back*, pure *Gemeindetheologie*, the product of the "creative community" posited by the form critics. We are still working out the implications (really reverberations) of Burton L. Mack's[35] proposal that, while the resurrection is commonly thought to have been the "Big Bang" from which Christianity spread out in many directions, it was more likely only one of several memory-constructions appropriate to and produced by the particular needs and self-understandings of various Jesus movements and Christ cults.[36]

---

35. Burton L. Mack, *A Myth of Innocence: Mark and Christian Origins* (Philadelphia: Fortress Press, 1991), pp. 7–9,

36. Mack, *Myth of Innocence*, p. 13: "Each of the several movements stemming from Jesus had worked out a rationalization for its distinctiveness in which Jesus played a founder's role by inaugurating just those features of the new social unit that set it apart." Page 112: "It should now be clear that the idea of the resurrection of Jesus was not a commonly shared datum among all forms of the Jesus movements. It was an idea limited to the Christ cult and derived from the Christ myth." Similarly, see Maurice Casey, *From Jewish Prophet to Gentile God: The Origins and Development of New Testament Christology*. The Edward Cadbury Lectures at the University of Birmingham, 1985–85 (Louisville: Westminster John Knox Press, 1991), p. 92: "these developments [divine vindication, ascension into heaven, supernatural transformation, etc.] . . . were caused by the needs of the community. The nature of the development of these Jewish figures [Enoch, Moses, Wisdom, the Logos, etc.] should lead us to expect that the figure

As Hans Jonas[37] and Rudolf Bultmann[38] explained, the myths cherished by any society embody in narrative form the self-understanding of that community. It should be no surprise that different groups of Christians had different self-understandings reflected in very different Christian myths. Jonas ascribed the cosmic alienation posited by Gnostics to their own alienation as intellectuals in the larger society. Bultmann, of course, explained faith in Jesus Christ's death and resurrection as the mythopoeic statement of Christians' feelings of liberation and authentic existence. Mack pointed to the variety of different Attis cult myths scattered in various places as a parallel. The normative version of the Jesus story familiar to us represents a convergence of some of the different Jesus and Christ myths and the suppression and/or fading away of others.

Even if Mack is correct, as I believe he is, this would not really affect the possibility of the gospel traditions going back to eyewitnesses of Jesus. But I would suggest that we move the line back a notch: perhaps the very notion of a "historical Jesus" was the (fictive) Big Bang. The various Jesus movements and Christ cults had various origins, none of them necessarily starting with a historical Jesus. Of course, the gospels may still be based on oral traditions, just not stemming from eyewitnesses of a historical Jesus.

Bart treats inter-gospel differences as the sort of alterations that occur in oral transmission (as Albert Lord himself did). This treatment accords with two different possibilities. First, if, as Bultmann thought,[39] there is a seamless continuity between oral tradition and literary redaction, that would legitimate

---

of Jesus would be developed in accordance with the needs of the early Christian community."

37. Hans Jonas, *The Gnostic Religion: The Message of the Alien God and the Beginnings of Christianity* (Boston: Beacon Press, 1963), Chapter 13, "Epilogue: Gnosticism, Existentialism, and Nihilism," pp. 320–340.

38. Rudolf Bultmann, "New Testament and Mythology," in Hans-Werner Bartch, ed., *Kerygma and Myth*. Trans. Reginald H. Fuller. Harper Torchbooks Cloister Library (New York: Harper & Row, 1961), pp. 10–11.

39. Gerd Theissen, *The Miracle Stories of the Early Christian Tradition*. Trans. Francis McDonagh (Philadelphia: Fortress Press, 1983), p. 189. Güttgemanns sums up the same tenet of the form critics: The "redaction and composition of the materials in the gospels ... were understood as having been completed according to the same laws as the tradition in the individual units, since form criticism denied a *major* differentiation between the oral and the written transmission" (p. 96).

Bart's approach. Second, if oral and written alterations of oral and written sources respectively are quite different in nature,[40] Bart's approach may run into trouble. This is because he accepts Synoptic interdependence, implying that their differences are the product of the literary redaction of written sources, but then he gives inter-gospel differences as examples of oral-traditional mutations as if all four gospels were merely deposits of individual streams of oral tradition, freeze-framed at different stages.

What if the gospels (as Philip R. Davies[41] posits for the Old Testament) began as literary, scribal products, written *by* scribes *for* scribes? They must have been! Who else would even be in a position to study them and thus to appreciate, hell, even to *notice*, their revisions and nuances? And what if all these scribes got their material from the Old Testament? Two possibilities exist. The fact that the gospel episodes make so much sense as Thomas L. Brodie, et. al.,[42] map them out seems to tilt toward the redactional character of the gospel episodes as scribal adaptations of Old Testament tales. Are we going to say that these patterns deserve to be ignored as Richard Bauckham and Kenneth Bailey

---

40. Theissen, *Miracle Stories*, p. 190: "Even in the observable process of the written transmission of oral tradition, we can detect only typical processes of change which point in various directions. To trace them back into the previous oral history of a text is an uncertain operation, even when we assume that the same tendencies existed in the process of oral transmission."

41. Philip R. Davies, *In Search of 'Ancient Israel.'* Journal for the Study of the Old Testament Supplement Series 148 (Sheffield: Sheffield Academic Press, 1992), p. 104: "The readers of this literature, like the writers, must also be *professionally literate.* The literature is not written for the rural peasantry, for these can neither read, nor if they could do that, could afford to obtain scrolls to read, nor if they could do that, would have the time (during daylight hours?) nor, if they had the time, would have the energy or the inclination. The literature is not for a whole society, as supposed by many biblical scholars. It is written largely for self-consumption." Similarly, Mack observes that Mark's "gospel is not . . . the product of 'collecting' and 'passing on' early traditions about Jesus. . . . It is, instead, a highly conscious scholarly effort in fabricating a new text by taking up strands from textual patterns that belonged to the multifaceted cultural fabric of his times" (*Myth of Innocence*, p. 323, note 3).

42. Thomas L. Brodie, "Luke the Literary Interpreter, Luke-Acts as a Systematic Rewriting and Updating of the Elijah-Elisha Narrative in 1 and 2 Kings." Ph.D. diss., Pontifical University of St. Thomas Aquinas, 1981; Randel Helms, *Gospel Fictions* (Buffalo: Prometheus Books, 1989); Robert M. Price, "New Testament Narrative as Old Testament Midrash" in Jacob Neusner and Alan J. Avery-Peck (eds.), *Encyclopaedia of Midrash: Biblical Interpretation in Formative Judaism* (E.J. Brill, 2005), Vol. One, pp. 534–573.

want to ignore the pronounced redactional patterns Hans Conzelmann and his colleagues[43] have delineated in the gospels?[44] If the gospels were sophisticated pastiches of the Old Testament (Septuagint version), this would make a lot of sense of the late appearance of the gospels. Schmithals[45] speaks of "the 'Synoptic deficiency,' of the 'apocryphal' character of this oral tradition," and of the "fact that the synoptic tradition ranked as 'apocryphal' right up to Justin."[46] Bart rightly suggests that the canonical four were not denominated as "according to Matthew, Mark, Luke, and John" before Irenaeus in the late second century. I think the gospels were not even written till about that time.

Remember, Strauss observed that there existed a Jewish predisposition to expect the messiah to replicate or to exceed the feats of the Old Testament heroes, so that their stories would automatically be applied to anyone thought to be the messiah. This is all we'd need to explain the repurposing/rewriting

---

43. Hans Conzelmann, *The Theology of St Luke*. Trans. Geoffrey Buswell (New York: Harper & Row, 1961); Willi Marxsen, *Mark the Evangelist: Studies on the Redaction History of the Gospel*. Trans. James Boyce, Donald Juel, William Poehlmann, and Roy A. Harrisville (New York: Abingdon Press, 1969); Günther Bornkamm, Gerhard Barth, and Hans Joachim Held. *Tradition and Interpretation in Matthew*. Trans. Percy Scott. New Testament Library (Philadelphia: Westminster Press, 1963); Joachim Rohde, *Rediscovering the Teaching of the Evangelists*. Trans. Dorothea Barton. New Testament Library (Philadelphia: Westminster Press, 1968); Norman Perrin, *What Is Redaction Criticism?* Guides to Biblical Scholarship. New Testament Series (Philadelphia: Fortress Press, 1969).

44. Theodore J. Weeden, "Kenneth Bailey's Theory of Oral Tradition: A Theory Contested by Its Evidence." *Journal for the Study of the Historical Jesus* 7 (2009), pp. 3–43; Weeden, "Polemics as a Case for Dissent: A Response to Richard Bauckham's *Jesus and the Eyewitnesses*." *Journal for the Study of the Historical Jesus* 6/2 (2008), pp. 211–224. "Also the precise conceptual and at the same time refined stylistic distinction assumed by Conzelmann could be credited only to a reflective theologian and be expected to be found in his school, but not in this case in the effectively diffuse and broadly diversified church tradition." Walter Schmithals, *The Theology of the First Christians*. Trans. O.C. Dean, Jr. (Louisville: Westminster John Knox Press, 1997), p. 37.

45. Schmithals, *Theology of the First Christians*, pp. 19, 312: "Only with the formation of the canon do the Gospels enter the broad Christian consciousness and the stage of general knowledge and use. In the first three or four generations of the Christian church, the Gospels received little attention, and their importance for the development of early Christian theology tends to be nil."

46. Walter Schmithals, *Paul and James*. Trans. Dorothea M. Barton. Studies in Biblical Theology No. 46 (Naperville: Alec R. Allenson, 1965), p. 117.

of so many Old Testament stories. Add to this the well-known law of oral transmission (noted by Bart[47]) of names to be substituted. Thus, the gospel stories' marks of oral transmission do not denote these tales' own oral origin; instead these marks have simply been inherited from their copied Old Testament prototypes, themselves the products of oral tradition.

There is another possible reason for all these Old Testament materials to have been Christianized. Marcionites rejected the Old Testament but may have wanted to preserve what elements of it they liked by switching them over to Jesus instead of their original heroes. Catholic scribes may have countered with some of their own rewrites.

Bart Ehrman has expertly dismantled the tiresome apologetical argument that the chasm between the historical Jesus and the gospel narratives can be bridged by eyewitness testimony and communal memory. It is hard to see how conservatives can continue to maintain their talking points with a straight face. It is now more evident than ever that their schema, while posing as evidential *support* for faith, actually turns out to be no less an *object* of faith than that for which it is offered. It is just absurd to think that the gospel "records" accurately depict what happened and what Jesus "actually" said, that specific wording "spoken" between characters in dramatic scenes can have been accurately remembered over decades.[48] You can't get here from there. But I would go further still. It seems to me that even the critical enterprise of sifting an "oral tradition" to distill a historical Jesus who gave rise to it is just an exercise in modern Euhemerism. "Oral tradition" is a bridge to nowhere, or rather to a quite different destination. A more realistic approach to oral transmission and community memory such as Bart offers, while valuable in itself, is actually beside the point, as it still assumes it can break a path back to a historical Jesus. I think the gospel stories are most naturally explained as transformations of Old Testament materials, and this applies all the more to the numerous marks of

---

47. Ehrman, *Jesus Before the Gospels*, p. 138.

48. In the same vein, Gunkel pointed out the absurdity of imagining that the Genesis writer could have had access to the words exchanged between Abraham and Sarah, e.g., as they bickered over what to do about Hagar. See Hermann Gunkel, *Genesis Translated and Interpreted*. Trans. Mark E. Biddle. Mercer Library of Biblical Studies (Macon: Mercer University Press, 1997), pp. viii-ix. Come on, snap out of it! If you want to shift ground and suggest that someone could have remembered "the gist" of what Abraham or Jesus said, you are only pulling your finger out of the dyke. Thar she blows!

orality in the gospel pericopes, as these were demonstrably present in the Old Testament passages on which they were based and have simply been inherited.

Have I proven my case? To put it in those terms is anachronistic. That is the language and conceptuality left over from apologetics which "demands a verdict." We ought to know by now that it is all a question of alternative paradigms, hypothetical frameworks for construing the data, connecting the dots. New Testament scholarship is a multi-pronged and ongoing research project in which scholars pursue a number of models and in which the critiques of one model on behalf of another serve to sharpen each and to further the forever open-ended process. That is how I hope you will understand my contrast of Bart Ehrman's approach with my own. That is how I view it.

CHAPTER FIVE

NO TALK OF GOD THEN, WE CALLED YOU A MAN

HOW BART EHRMAN'S JESUS BECAME GOD

Where did ancient Christians get the idea that Jesus was the incarnation of God? The traditional, orthodox answer was that "Jesus claimed to be God" at least implicitly if not explicitly, and that his apostles taught this truth to their converts. Of course, it is admitted, there were various other, dissenting opinions, but these were later heresies whispered into the ears of troublemakers by Satan. Try to envision the implied scenario: Jesus was known to have announced himself to be God on earth, but some imagined they knew better! It is easy to picture the opponents of Jesus or of his apostles denying the belief, but why would those who deemed themselves Jesus' followers reject his teachings on this point? If you knew he'd made such claims but you didn't buy it, you'd just write him off as a kook, wouldn't you? The whole thing doesn't make sense. Obviously it is much more likely that Jesus left his status unaddressed, and that, after his death, his hero-worshipping devotees advanced all sorts of honorific estimates of his significance.

Some esteemed Jesus a righteous mortal rewarded with immortality. On the opposite end of the spectrum, others believed he had not been a genuine human being at all, but rather a kind of holographic epiphany like the angelic visitations of the Old Testament. As time went by, much more complex models

205

of Christology appeared as debates led to ever more hair-splitting: Did the Incarnate Christ have a full divine nature but only two-thirds of a human nature? If he had both a complete human and a complete divine nature, were the two mingled and mixed, or did they remain distinct? If the latter, were they united, or was Christ to be divided into two cohabiting Persons? If the two natures were inseparable in a single Person, did that Person stem from the divine or from the human side? Had Jesus actually taught any of these doctrines, where would the others have come from?

Bart Ehrman is a critical scholar not obliged to toe any doctrinal party line. In his book, *How Jesus Became God*,[1] Bart traces what he sees as the trajectory of Christological evolution. As with many aspects of New Testament scholarship, he is well within the mainstream. Similar treatments are available in Reginald H. Fuller's *The Foundations of New Testament Christology*[2] and Maurice Casey's *From Jewish Prophet to Gentile God*.[3] But orthodoxy has its stubborn defenders, its institutional spin doctors. They have been alarmed by the popular accessibility of Bart's work to an intelligent lay public. So they feel they cannot allow his "heresies" to go unchallenged. A team of these guardians of traditional faith got together to issue a symposium cleverly titled *How God Became Jesus*.[4] In its pages we find, not surprisingly, what amounts to simple proof-texting like you expect to find in dogmatics manuals. Posturing as critical scholars, these apologists seem never to have met a gospel saying they didn't think authentic.

Michael F. Bird holds it against Bart that "he thinks that we cannot take the Gospels at face value as historically reliable accounts of the things Jesus said and did" and regards "the Gospels as faith-documents that should render us historically suspicious of their accounts of Jesus."[5] Yet he goes on to say,

---

1. Bart D. Ehrman, *How Jesus Became God: The Exaltation of a Jewish Preacher from Galilee* (New York: HarperOne, 2014).

2. Reginald H. Fuller, *The Foundations of New Testament Christology* (New York: Scribners, 1965).

3. Maurice Casey, *From Jewish Prophet to Gentile God: The Origin and Development of New Testament Christology*. Edward Cadbury Lectures at the University of Birmingham, 1985–86 (Cambridge: James Clarke / Louisville: Westminster/John Knox Press, 1991).

4. Michael F. Bird, ed., *How God Became Jesus: The Real Origins of Belief in Jesus' Divine Nature—A Response to Bart D. Ehrman* (Grand Rapids: Zondervan, 2014).

5. Michael F. Bird, "Did Jesus Think He Was God?." In Bird, ed., *How God Became Jesus*, p. 48.

trying to sort out the authentic traditions from the inauthentic traditions is not really that easy, for the simple fact that the history of Jesus has been welded together with the early church's proclamation of Jesus at every point. Trying to separate the history from theology in the Gospels is a bit like trying to separate blue from red in the color purple.[6]

Again, "we cannot hope to penetrate the impregnable bedrock of the church's interpretation and proclamation of Jesus found in the Gospels and discover a deeper layer of historically accurate data laid beneath."[7] Uh . . . has Dr. Jekyll suddenly turned into Mr. Hyde in mid-sentence? For it would seem he *agrees* with Bart Ehrman after all. What is going on here?

> Ehrman is dependent on the use of several 'criteria' to establish the authenticity of stories about Jesus in the Gospels . . . [but] many of the criteria have been critically examined and found to be inadequate as a way of establishing the historical or unhistorical nature of any given unit in the Gospels.[8]

So what's the alternative? Why, just to accept everything in the gospels as historically true! As so often in apologetics, a train of thought that leads naturally to agnosticism suddenly jumps the rails and heads for fideism.

Similarly, Larry Hurtado's approach[9] seems to be, at bottom, one more piece of evangelical apologetics: the belief in Jesus' godhood must go back to Jesus himself. He thus seeks to avoid the anxiety over whether Christology is a (possibly fallible) development by Christians rather than a revelation from the Son of God himself—which shows the question-begging character of the whole enterprise.

Clearly, I side with Bart in this matter. Yet, once again, I personally find Bart himself to be way too generous when it comes to vetting gospel sayings as genuinely authentic. And my greater skepticism is no mere function of my preference for Christ Mythicism. I do not begin with some axiom that no historical Jesus existed. No, in evaluating ostensible Jesus sayings I always

---

6. Bird, "Did Jesus Think He Was God?" pp. 49–50.

7. Bird, "Did Jesus Think He Was God?" p. 51.

8. Bird, "Did Jesus Think He Was God?" pp. 49, 50.

9. Larry W. Hurtado, *One God One Lord: Early Christian Devotion and Ancient Jewish Monotheism* (Philadelphia: Fortress Press, 1988).

start from a conventional picture of a first-century itinerant preacher and faith healer. Measured by that yardstick, does this or that saying presuppose anachronistic circumstances? Can a historical Jesus really have been debating the need for circumcision as per Thomas saying 5? Doesn't the "Take up your cross" saying (Mark 8:34) presuppose the hearer (actually, the reader) knows the crucifixion has already taken place? And so on.

Like his orthodox critics, Bart does ground his account of Christological origins in the (supposed) teaching of Jesus, but he reckons that teaching as more modest, "merely" that he was the prophesied messiah. Nothing about divine nature or incarnation. But what is the evidence that Jesus so taught? If he had so indoctrinated his men, why does he have to ask their opinions on his identity (Mark 8:29)? Was he giving them a pop quiz on material he had covered in class? If you take the Confession of Peter as historical, it looks like Peter is boldly venturing his *inference* that Jesus is the Christ. If Jesus *had* been teaching the disciples that he was the messiah, would the story read as it does? Peter's reply would read more like: "Uh . . . , you're the *Christ*, . . . right?"

Interestingly, Bart points to Acts 2:36; 13:33 and Romans 1:3–4 as evidence of early adoptionism, that Jesus was entirely mortal and was at some point awarded messiahship. But he does not see the implication highlighted by Rudolf Bultmann,[10] namely that such a belief can never have arisen in the first place had Jesus declared himself to be the Christ during the pre-Easter period. I don't see how you get around this.

Probably the strongest argument for Jesus having claimed to be the Christ is the inscription on the cross "Jesus of Nazareth, King of the Jews." Mustn't this mean he was getting executed for having made such a claim? "The man who would be king." But given the fact that the same story, in all four gospels, asserts that the whole thing was a frame-up, I'm not sure how strong this "evidence" is. Presumably the seditious "King of the Jews" claim was part of the "false witness" against him.

It is surely relevant that nowhere in the gospels does Jesus ever make the assertion that he is the messiah. At most, he acquiesces when someone else says it about him. At his trial he is asked point-blank whether (he thinks) he is the Christ. How does he reply? Most manuscripts of Mark 14:62 have him confess forthrightly, "I am." Some few give his answer as "You say," which

---

10. Rudolf Bultmann, *Theology of the New Testament*. Trans. Kendrick Grobel. Scribner Studies in Contemporary Theology (New York: Scribners, 1951), Vol. I, p. 27.

is pretty much what Matthew 26:64 and Luke 22:70 have him say. It seems obvious to me that Matthew and Luke must have been using a copy of Mark that had Jesus answer evasively. It is nigh-inconceivable that a later evangelist, much less two of them independently, would have read Mark's "I am" and decided to make a bold, clear reply into an equivocal one. (Apologists assure us that "You say I am" really means "You bet I am," but that sounds spurious to me.) But it's really moot since the whole narrative is plainly unhistorical. A Sanhedrin session on Passover Eve? Not likely! Was Joseph of Arimathea the court reporter? Was it blasphemous, as Caiaphas is made to call it, for a man to claim to be God's messiah? Nope.

Does Jesus tell the Samaritan Woman that he is the messiah? Not exactly. She mentions the expected messiah and suggests they put off theological debates till Mr. Know It All shows up to answer all questions. Then Jesus tells her she doesn't have long to wait, because *he* is the messiah. But all he actually *says* is, "I who speak to you am he" (John 4:26). Even here, for what it's worth, he doesn't say, "I'm the messiah, you know!" But it's pretty close. Two problems, though. One, the story is unhistorical as denoted by the narrator's goof in having the woman at the well speak of the "messiah," when in fact Samaritans repudiated the Jewish expectation of the messiah, a king from the Davidic (i.e., Judean) dynasty. Instead, Samaritans looked forward to the advent of the Taheb ("the Restorer"), a prophet like Moses.

Second, the relevant saying is ambiguous. The traditional translation is entirely fine, but there is another, equally valid as far as I can see, and that is, "I am the one who is speaking to you." Translated this way, the statement, with the whole scene, would exactly parallel Thomas saying 52, "His disciples say to him, 'Twenty-four prophets spoke in Israel, and all of them testified of you!' And Jesus says to them, 'You ignore the Living One who is before you and prattle on about the dead.'" The only real difference is that, in John, Jesus' interlocutor defers to a future authority ("the messiah") rather than, in Thomas, to one in the past ("twenty-four prophets"). Who knows which is intended? But that's just my point. It is hazardous to build a case on the saying being read one way rather than the other.

At this point, apologists resort to the contention that Jesus fostered an "implicit Christology" by virtue of his presumption of forgiving sins, overruling the Sabbath, and daring to set aside the Torah with his own replacement commandments.[11] All of these arguments are pathetic. Surely the logic of Jesus' words in Mark 2:10, "So you may know that God has given the son of man authority *on earth* to forgive sins . . .," is exactly parallel to that in Matthew 16:19 and John 20:23. God has delegated to his earthly agents the task of absolving sinners as he himself does up in heaven. The parallel is drawn between human beings (the generic "son of man") and God as forgivers, each in the appropriate venue. Matthew understood Mark this way: "They glorified God who had given such authority to *men*" (Matt. 9:8), i.e., not just to Jesus.

Did Jesus go around saying, "It's the Sabbath, you say? Big deal! I'm sick and tired of the damn Sabbath! Okay, from now on, it's cancelled!" Of course not. It's not even Paulinism. In all such passages, Jesus is shown disputing with scribal colleagues over how strict Sabbath observance had to be. It was legal casuistry, not libertinism or Lutheranism.

In the so-called Matthean Antitheses (Matt. 5:21–48), Jesus contrasts the literal observance of various Torah commands with his own extensions of them to cover internal motivations, not just outward actions. It is a development well known in rabbinical ethics. Making anger tantamount to murder, ogling to adultery, etc., is by no means to supplant the biblical commandments but rather to safeguard them. The rabbis called this approach "building a fence around the Torah."[12] To forbid rage and lust is to cut off the path to committing murder and adultery. There is nothing here to imply Jesus thought himself either a new Moses or a new God.

If Jesus had wanted people to recognize him as the promised messiah, why would he have played theological charades? What's with all the hints (if that's even what they are)? When he declared the paralytic forgiven, did he give a wink to the audience? ("If you know what I *mean*!") Celsus describes Syrian prophets proclaiming, "I am God, or the Son of God, or a Divine Spirit," etc. What's wrong with that, if you really thought you were? Was it too "forward"? Too gauche? Jehovah, after all, had no hesitation about declaring, "I am Yahweh! There is no other; besides me there is no God!" (Isa. 45:5). Was that immodest? Should he have been more cagey? Should Jesus?

Bart's major textual argument is that Jesus implied he was the messiah in the twelve thrones saying: "In the regeneration, when the Son of Man

---

11. Bird, "Did Jesus Think He Was God?" pp. 57–58.

12. Solomon Schechter, *Some Aspects of Rabbinic Theology* (New York: Macmillan, 1910), pp. 210–214.

sits on his glorious throne, you who have followed me will also sit on twelve thrones judging the twelve tribes of Israel" (Matt. 19:28). Luke 22:28–30 reads a little differently: "You are those who have continued with me in my trials; and I assign to you, as my Father assigned to me, a kingdom, that you may eat and drink at my table in my kingdom, and sit on thrones judging the twelve tribes of Israel." But there are more versions still. It also occurs in 1 Corinthians 6:2–3; 2 Timothy 2:12; Revelation 2:26–27, with no hint that it was a Jesus quote. I think it most likely that the saying was secondarily ascribed to Jesus and restricted to the twelve. But Bart takes the saying as genuine and as implying that Jesus considered himself the messianic king with the twelve as his lieutenants.

Walter Schmithals[13] makes a powerful case that there *was* no college of the twelve in the days of Jesus but that the group was constituted only afterwards, when a random collection of twelve disciples happened to share a resurrection epiphany which they felt qualified them to occupy a special position of apostolic authority. But when other Jesus followers began to make similar claims on similar grounds, the authority of the twelve was reinforced by the claim (made by them or by their successors or followers) that they had been an elite circle of apprentices of Jesus while he was still on earth. We see the same sort of debate in the Pseudo-Clementines (based on a second-century Ebionite Acts) when Simon Magus (a cipher for Paul) claims unique apostolic authority based on a resurrection vision of Jesus, only to be opposed by Simon Peter who affirms the superior authority of himself and his colleagues who had been trained by Jesus in person, during his ministry on earth. The twelve thrones saying would make sense as part of this retrospective polemical agenda. Thus the implicit point of this Q saying, once it got reapplied to the twelve, was to reinforce the rule of the twelve, i.e., their latter-day successors, over against rival leadership factions.

Once we recognize that the saying is not really from Jesus, we can descend from the magical realm of an apocalyptic messiah to the mundane realm of church politics which, however depressing, is at least terra firma. If we insist on pulling the apocalyptic Jesus down into our sub-lunar world as a deluded lunatic parceling out fiefdoms to his buddies, we will find this "historical Jesus"

---

13. Walter Schmithals, *The Office of Apostle in the Early Church*. Trans. John E. Steely (New York: Abingdon Press, 1969), Part Two, IV, 2. "The Circle of the Twelve Emerges After Easter," pp. 68–71.

every bit the embarrassment Albert Schweitzer[14]said he would be for moderns. In his description of the eschatological messiah, it appears to me that perhaps Bart has not gotten his evangelical "suspension of disbelief" completely out of his system. Remaining under the charm of the wonderful gospel fictions, one creates what Niels Peter Lemche[15] calls "a rationalistic paraphrase" of the biblical saga.

Going a step further, Bart seems to use the apologetical stand-by that we can't explain the rise (or at least the ignition and launch) of Christianity without the resurrection *visions* of the disciples. In all this not only is Bart way too optimistic about the New Testament evidence for anybody having had such visions, but is also, ironically, assuming the Big Bang model of Christian origins,[16] something seemingly at odds with his own approach in *Lost Christianities*.[17]

Bart's rationalism is evident in his explaining the Easter visions in psychological terms, a la Gerd Lüdemann.[18] It is a return to the Protestant Rationalists of the eighteenth century who, e.g., tried to retain the superficially factual character of the Pillar of Fire in Exodus by identifying it with the volcanic eruption of Thera. He gives a similarly rationalistic account of the doubts of the disciples when faced with the risen Jesus. But surely a better explanation is a purely literary one: the common motif of skepticism in miracle stories.[19] The disciples jeer at Jesus as the waves fill the boat, little suspecting

---

14. Albert Schweitzer, *The Quest of the Historical Jesus: A Critical Study of its Progress from Reimarus to Wrede*. Trans. W. Montgomery (New York: Macmillan, 1968), p. 401.

15. Niels Peter Lemche, *The Israelites in History and Tradition*. Library of Ancient Israel (London: SPCK / Louisville: Westminster John Knox Press, 1998), pp. 148–156.

16. Burton L. Mack, *A Myth of Innocence: Mark and Christian Origins* (Philadelphia: Fortress Press, 1988), pp. 8–9. What Mack means is that even critical scholars seem unable to see through the theological fiction of some dramatic "Easter Event" from which Christianity exploded like a nova. Even the "skeptical" Bultmann thought everything began with the Easter morning experience of the original disciples. Mack sees the whole Easter business as a mythicizing creation of one of the many proto-Christian sects. It is the fruit, not the root.

17. Bart D. Ehrman, *Lost Christianities: The Battles for Scripture and the Faiths We Never Knew* (New York: Oxford University Press, 2003).

18. Gerd Lüdemann, *The Resurrection of Jesus: History, Experience, Theology*. Trans. John Bowden (Minneapolis: Fortress Press, 1995), "Excursus: A Retrospective Survey of the Vision Hypothesis in the Nineteenth Century," pp. 54–108.

19. Rudolf Bultmann, *The History of the Synoptic Tradition*. Trans. John Marsh (New York:

that their Master can still the storm with a word (Mark 4:38). When Jesus reassures Jairus' neighbors that Jairus' daughter will soon return to life, they jeer at him, thinking it outrageous showmanship (Mark 5:40). Pressed by a crowd of fans, Jesus feels a charge of healing power escaping him and asks whose touch sparked it. His disciples are indignant: "What do you mean, 'Who touched me?' Who *didn't?*" (Mark 5:31). When Jesus comments that his huge audience looks hungry, the disciples retort, "Well, what do you expect *us* to do about it?" (Mark 6:37). And so on. You see it on TV all the time, as on *The X-Files* when, no matter how many times Mulder's zany theories have been vindicated, Scully is incredulous whenever Mulder proposes a new one. The skepticism serves to magnify the miracle once it happens against the odds.

Why does Bart strive for a historical core to the Easter visions? (He doesn't contend that these visions prove the resurrection happened, just that the disciples had the visions.) So he can use them as the cause for early Christian belief in Jesus' sudden divine exaltation. Bart says[20] that Jesus must have taught his disciples he was the messiah if for no other reason than that his disciples *believed* he was, after experiencing resurrection visions. No one expected the messiah to die and rise, so even if Jesus did rise, that would not have suggested he was the messiah unless the resurrection were understood as a vindication of a claim Jesus had already made. Isn't this really another version of the old "What changed the disciples?" apologetic, only pushed back a notch? Instead of "He must have risen!" The aim is to show "He must have claimed messiahship, or we wouldn't have the early Christians proclaiming it!"

I find the links in Bart's chain to be fatally weak in that there is insufficient reason to believe either that Jesus made claims to messiahship or that the resurrection appearances of the New Testament, whether in the gospels or in 1 Corinthians, are anything but literary creations.

OSCILLATING CHRISTOLOGY

As I have said, the mainstream critical view of the evolution of New Testament Christology posits a development beginning with adoptionism (still attested in

---

Harper & Row, 1972), p. 221; Gerd Theissen, *The Miracle Stories of the Early Christian Tradition*. Trans. Francis McDonagh (Philadelphia: Fortress Press, 1983), chapter II, A, 14, "Scepticism and Mockery," p. 56.

20. Ehrman, *How Jesus Became God*, p. 119.

Romans 1:3–4,[21] Acts 2:36, and Mark 1:11), then passing to the notion of Jesus as a demigod hero via a miraculous conception (Matthew and Luke), to a belief in Jesus as a divine incarnation of some sort, whether of a created Logos, or an archangel, or God Almighty. This reflects the likely order of gospel composition: Mark, then Luke and Matthew, then John. The later the gospel, the higher the Christology. The monkey wrench in the works, though, is the Pauline Corpus, which, on the conventional view, dates earlier than any gospel. Christ Mythicists observe that, while the Pauline epistles already presuppose a high Christology of a pre-mundane celestial Christ, they offer no clear picture of an earthly historical Jesus. From this Mythicists infer that the purely heavenly Christ was the starting point and that, by the time of the evangelists, Christians were well into the process of transforming the object of their worship into a historical founder-figure.

It would have been a bid to trump those who claimed the authority of (competing) revelations from a heavenly Christ-deity. Since these supposed bulletins from out of the blue often contradicted one another (or seemed obvious ploys to manipulate), someone got the bright idea of "canonizing" their own favorite Christ-oracles as a body of teachings ostensibly imparted by a recently active teacher and miracle-worker.[22] This is an only slight variant of the polemical device noted above, namely the creation of an authoritative college of "the twelve" who were eyewitnesses of Jesus and could authenticate his teachings as opposed to heresies attributed to him via supposed revelations claimed by rival Christian sectarians. (The untenability of the whole notion is, ironically, demonstrated by the continued use of the gimmick by modern conservative apologists who never really come to grips with the real-world ramifications: could the apostles have possibly had either the time or the means to operate some sort of Snopes.com rumor-squelching operation? Absurd.)

By the way, how did docetism arise? This was, of course, the belief that Jesus did *seem* to appear on earth among men, but that it was an optical illusion. When Catholics decided to turn Jesus into a recent historical founder in order

---

21. Could Romans 1:3–4 be a conflated, compromise creed, combining a "born messiah" Christology with a "resurrected Son of God" Christology? See Ehrman, *How Jesus Became God*, p. 221.

22. Charles H. Talbert, *Luke and the Gnostics: An Examination of the Lucan Purpose* (New York: Abingdon Press, 1966), Chapter I, "The Authentic Witness," pp. 17–32.

to claim copyright over against the contradictory, subjective visions of the Gnostics, the Gnostics decided to return the favor, making their own claims of apostolic succession from various disciples. This of course entailed their own historicization of Jesus. But some split the difference, positing that Jesus did indeed appear on earth but not really: he was a divine hologram.

If all of this is true, Mythicists must still explain the growth of low-to-high Christology though the gospels. But it seems to me pretty easy to explain. Here I want to propose an analogy to William Wrede's Messianic Secret theory.[23] Wrede posited that a predecessor of the evangelist Mark had sought to reconcile two current Christologies, one supposing Jesus became the Christ only as of his resurrection, the other imagining him becoming Christ at the Jordan baptism. His solution was to suggest that Jesus' Messiahship had indeed begun at the baptism, but that the belief in his Easter Messiahship had been a natural inference since he (must have!) kept it a secret till the resurrection.

Wrede noted certain inconsistencies in Mark's presentation implying that, while he preserved the Secret motif largely intact, he no longer understood it. The post-Markan evangelists were even more distant from the Secret and the disputes that had occasioned it. Hence their portrayals of Jesus allow the messiahship of Jesus to appear onstage more and more openly during the public ministry.

In a similar manner, I propose a model whereby Mark presupposes the historicization of a heavenly, never-incarnated Christ. By the time he writes, the historicization is far enough behind him that he is not aware it happened. He presents a human Jesus, and we can recognize only inadvertent glimpses of the original Christ-concept that is more clearly manifest in the Pauline epistles. And just as the evangelists following Mark, oblivious of the Messianic Secret, portray Jesus in increasingly messianic, even divine, glory, so, on my proposed schema, post-Markan evangelists gradually undid the humanization of Jesus, redivinizing him until docetism very nearly reversed the original historicization with the doctrine that, though the Christ did seem to come to earth, he never really did. And all this time, the original Christology survived in Gnosticism and Paulinism alongside the gospel evolution. As Wrede envisioned a manifest messiahship fictively suppressed in secrecy, a secrecy gradually dispelled in subsequent gospels, so I propose an original belief in a heavenly Christ-*aion*,

23. William Wrede, *The Messianic Secret*. Trans. J.C.G. Greig. Library of Theological Translations (Cambridge: James Clarke, 1971).

reconceived as a historical mortal, a "demotion" did not last either, being gradually reversed in a deification, then docetization of Christ, pretty much restoring the original notion. One might say that New Testament Christological evolution goes from Paul down to Mark, then ascends though Matthew and Luke to John, who reconnects with Paul.

So I am taking Wrede a step farther: instead of saying retroactively that the historical advent of Jesus was (reinterpreted as) messianic in light of the delay of his second (but first *messianic*) advent, I would suggest that Jews avidly hoping for the coming of the messiah (a la the Sacred King myth) eventually decided he had come already without being recognized, then "discovered" what he had done by sniffing out "prophecies" of that coming.

ANGELOMORPHIC CHRISTOLOGY AND ITS IMPLICATIONS

"We know that some Jews thought it was right to worship angels in no small part because a number of our surviving texts insist that it *not* be done. You don't get laws prohibiting activities that are never performed."[24] Bart is responding to, e.g., Larry Hurtado who denies that angel-worship occurred before Christianity because he wants both to make room for some influence on early Christian belief from the Jewish tradition of the exaltation of Jewish patriarchs to heavenly, angelic status, and to make the same notion as applied to the ascended Jesus distinctive.[25] None of these angelic patriarchs ever actually got worshipped, but Jesus did, so Christianity is still qualitatively different. I side with Bart.

Whence angel worship? First, keep in mind that angels were identified with stars, "the heavenly hosts." Under Assyrian influence, the hosts of heaven were worshipped in the Temple. In the Song of Deborah, the stars are invoked to fight on Israel's behalf (Judges 5:20), implying warrior angels. Second, remember that the Priestly creation account says the celestial bodies were created to "rule" the night and the day. Consider in light of this the archaic poem in Deuteronomy 32, where the ultimate God, El Elyon, apportions a

---

24. Ehrman, *How Jesus Became God*, pp. 54–55

25. This is an example of what I like to call "dissimilarity apologetics." How tiresome: pathetic special pleading. See Price, Review of Jonathan Z. Smith, *Drudgery Divine: On the Comparison of Early Christianities and the Religions of Late Antiquities. Journal of Higher Criticism* 3/1 (Spring, 1996), pp. 137–145.

nation apiece to the (implicitly) seventy Sons of God, including Yahweh who chose Israel as his protégés. Each nation, then, properly worships its godling, *including Israel*. This means that, as in Galatians 4:19 and Colossians 2:8, both Israel and the Gentiles worshipped the elemental spirits (the angels presiding over weather, etc.). Thus the worship of angels (Col. 2:18).

This is perhaps why we read of "the Angel of Yahweh," i.e., the Angel Yahweh, the Lesser Yahweh ("My name is in him"). Despite the Deuteronomic attempt to fuse Yahweh with El Elyon,[26] not everyone got on board, Gnostics included. They clearly regarded Yahweh (Ialdabaoth) as a self-aggrandizing godling, the god of Israel, far inferior to the ultimate deity (El Elyon). Via the traditional (re)use of the Sons of God/Daughters of men story (Gen. 6:1–4), the gods/angels of the nations became the sinister Archons. Since (as in Galatians 3:19) it was the angels/Archons who gave the Law, not the Ultimate God, those who kept the Law were worshipping the true authors of their religion, the angels (as were all the pagans!).This is what is referred to in Galatians and Colossians as the worship/serving of the angels/elemental spirits. This is not to say these worshippers realized they were merely worshipping angels. After all, the fact that they were is the Gnosis that they lacked! Once you accepted the Gnostic view of things, you would drop your devotion to these beings like a hot potato.

Margaret Barker argues that early Christians thought Jesus was the Old Testament Angel of Yahweh. In short, Jesus was Yahweh, appearing on earth as he had several times in ancient Israel. When he spoke of his Father in heaven, he was referring to El Elyon. All this was part and parcel of a Jewish belief that had not been displaced by Deuteronomic monotheism which had mandated that henceforth Yahweh and El Elyon should be regarded as one and the same. One crucial bit of evidence for this is that never in the New Testament is Jesus called "the son of the Lord," i.e., the son of Yahweh. Because he *was* Yahweh! He was instead "the Son of *God*" (i.e., Elyon). This possibility again raises the question of docetism since, as in Tobit 12:19, angels appearing on earth were not composed of material flesh.

The situation is parallel to that of an ostensibly historical Buddha versus the twenty-four Buddhas previous to Prince Siddhartha, like Dipankara,

---

26. Margaret Barker, *The Great Angel: A Study of Israel's Second God* (Louisville: Westminster / John Knox Press, 1992), Chapter two, "The Evidence of the Exile," pp. 12–27.

Amitabha, Manjushri, and others. All these characters are devoutly believed historical by pious Buddhists, but Western scholars of Buddhism write them off as mythical retrojections of the (more or less) historical Gautama into the remote past. But Gautama might as well be just as mythical, the latest instantiation of the old mythic pattern.[27] Buddhists haven't retrojected the pattern of the Siddhartha legend into the past; rather, the repeating legend was fictional every time, and the latest instance was that of Siddhartha. It's as if Western scholars decided that the most recent (mythic) appearance of Hercules was historical. So with Jesus, the latest instance of angelophanies or theophanies, regarded as, finally, a real one. Patristic apologists, seeking to find Jesus already in the Old Testament, used to claim the appearances of the Angel of the Lord were pre-Christian Christophanies, but what if the truth were the reverse, if the gospel Jesus were one more (fictive) angelophany?

Bart argues that Galatians 4:14 proves that Paul understood the pre-existent Christ not as God but as an angel (as did Justin Martyr and some other early Christians[28]). The idea is that when it says, "You welcomed me as an angel of God, as Jesus Christ himself," it means not "not only as an angel, but more than that, even as Jesus Christ himself," but rather "as an angel, and not just any angel but Jesus Christ in particular." This exegesis is quite plausible, though still debatable,[29] but the point is really moot once you look into some utterly fascinating research Bart cites on Jewish angelology and the exaltation

27. Robert M. Price, "Of Myth and Men: A Closer Look at the Originators of the Major Religions—What Did They *Really* Say and Do?" *Free Inquiry* (20/1) Winter 1999–2000; Acharya S (D.M. Murdock), *Suns of God* (Kempton, IL: Adventures Unlimited Press, 2004), Chapter 10, "Life of Buddha," pp. 290–333; Chapter 11, "Buddha, Light of the World," pp. 334–371.

28. Aloys Grillmeier, *Christ in the Christian Tradition: From the Apostolic Age to Chalcedon (451)*. Trans. J.W. Bowden (New York: Sheed & Ward, 1965), pp. 52–53; Jean Daniélou, *The Theology of Jewish Christianity*. The Development of Christian Doctrine Before the Council of Nicaea Volume I. Trans. John A. Baker (London: Darton, Longman & Todd / Chicago: Henry Regnery, 1964), Chapter 4, "The Trinity and Angelology," pp. 117–146; Richard N. Longenecker, *The Christology of Early Jewish Christianity*. Studies in Biblical Theology Second Series 17 (Naperville: Alec R. Allenson, 1970), pp. 26–31; Loren T. Stuckenbruck, *Angel Veneration and Christology: A Study in Early Judaism and in the Christology of the Apocalypse of John*. Wissenschaftliche Untersuchungen zum Neuen Testament 2. Reihe 70 (Tübingen: J.C.B. Mohr (Paul Siebeck), 1995), p. 138, note 238.

29. Gordon D. Fee, *Pauline Christology: An Exegetical-Theological Study* (Grand Rapids: Baker Academic, 2007), pp. 229–231.

of certain biblical patriarchs. He distinguishes between ancient Jewish beliefs in immortals who temporarily became mortals on the one hand and mortals exalted to immortality on the other. The first group (e.g., Eve, Abel, Seth,[30] Jacob, and Joseph) were earthly avatars of pre-existent heavenly/divine beings, archangels, etc., who resumed their celestial existence once their earthly tasks were completed. Sometimes such a being was even identified as the very Angel of the Lord or even as a "Lesser Yahweh" (a survival of the earlier ditheistic belief in Yahweh as Elyon's Son). The second group (overlapping the first) included Adam, Abel,[31] Enoch, and Moses. These attained heavenly glory and power as a well-deserved reward for heroism and holiness.

The whole schema no doubt stems from the ancient Sacred King mythology.[32] In the course of the New Year festival, whether in Jerusalem or in Babylon, the king would renew his royal mandate by ritually play-acting the primordial victory of the storm god over the Chaos Dragon, which proved his merit to become the new king of gods. His crown restored, the king would enter the temple where, behind closed doors, his subjects believed, he should ascend to heaven (of which the temple was the earthly effigy) and there be shown as much of the Tablets of Destiny as "precorded" the events of the coming year. The king, now briefed with the information needed to anticipate crises and deal with them wisely, would henceforth function as Yahweh's or Marduk's vicar, his counterpart on earth, wielding divine authority, even bearing divine nature. It sounds just like Enoch, Moses—and Jesus.

Adam was an angel, though soon to be a fallen one. "I commanded my wisdom to create man . . . And on the earth I assigned him to be a second angel, honored and great and glorious." (2 Enoch 30:8–11, first century CE)[33]

---

30. E.S. Drower, *The Secret Adam: A Study of Nasorean Gnosis* (Oxford at the Clarendon Press, 1930), chapter IV. "Adam and his Sons," pp. 34–38. The Apocalypse of Sethel, preserved by the Manicheans, has Seth born a man but transformed into an angel.

31. See Phillip B. Munroe III, *Four Powers in Heaven: The Interpretation of Daniel 7 in the Testament of Abraham.* Journal for the Study of the Pseudepigrapha Supplement Series 28 (Sheffield: Sheffield Academic Press, 1998).

32. Geo Widengren, *The Ascension of the Apostle and the Heavenly Book.* King and Saviour III. Uppsala Universitets Arsskrift 1950: 7 (Uppsala: A.B. Lundequistska Bokhandeln, 1950), p. 33.

33. "2 (Slavonic Apocalypse of) Enoch." Trans. F.I. Andersen. In Charlesworth, ed., *Old Testament Pseudepigrapha.* Vol. I, *Apocalyptic Literature and Testaments* (Garden City: Doubleday, 1983), 151–152.

With the archangel Michael as guide, Abraham beholds the following.

So Michael turned the [cherub-borne] chariot and brought Abraham to the east, to the first gate of heaven; and Abraham saw two ways, the one narrow and contracted, the other broad and spacious, and there he saw two gates, the one broad on the broad way, and the other narrow on the narrow way. And outside the two gates there he saw a man sitting upon a gilded throne, and the appearance of that man was terrible, as of the Lord. And they saw many souls driven by angels and led in through the broad gate, and other souls, few in number, that were taken by the angels through the narrow gate. And when the wonderful one who sat upon the golden throne saw few entering through the narrow gate, and many entering through the broad one, straightway that wonderful one tore the hairs of his head and the sides of his beard, and threw himself on the ground from his throne, weeping and lamenting. But when he saw many souls entering through the narrow gate, then he arose from the ground and sat upon his throne in great joy, rejoicing and exulting. And Abraham asked the chief-captain, "My Lord chief-captain, who is this most marvelous man, adorned with such glory, and sometimes he weeps and laments, and sometimes he rejoices and exults?" The incorporeal one said: "This is the first-created Adam who is in such glory, and he looks upon the world because all are born from him, and when he sees many souls going through the narrow gate, then he arises and sits upon his throne rejoicing and exulting in joy, because this narrow gate is that of the just, that leads to life, and they that enter through it go into Paradise. For this, then, the first-created Adam rejoices, because he sees the souls being saved. But when he sees many souls entering through the broad gate, then he pulls out the hairs of his head, and casts himself on the ground weeping and lamenting bitterly, for the broad gate is that of sinners, which leads to destruction and eternal punishment. And for this the first-formed Adam falls from his throne weeping and lamenting for the destruction of sinners, for they are many that are lost, and they are few that are saved, for in seven thousand there is scarcely found one soul saved, being righteous and undefiled."

While he was yet saying these things to me, behold two angels, fiery in aspect, and pitiless in mind, and severe in look, and they drove on thousands of souls, pitilessly lashing them with fiery thongs. The angel laid hold of one soul, and they drove all the souls in at the broad gate to destruction. So we also went along with the angels, and came within that broad gate, and between the two gates stood a throne terrible of aspect, of terrible crystal, gleaming as fire, and upon it sat a wondrous man bright as the sun, like to the Son of God. Before him stood a table like crystal, all of gold and fine linen, and upon the table there was lying a book, the thickness of it six cubits, and the breadth of it ten cubits, and on the right and left of it stood two angels holding paper and ink and pen. Before the table sat an angel of light, holding in his hand a balance, and on his left sat an angel all fiery, pitiless, and severe, holding in his hand a trumpet, having within it all-consuming fire with which to try the sinners. The wondrous man who sat upon the throne himself judged and sentenced the souls, and the two angels on the right and on the left wrote down, the one on the right the righteousness and the one on the left the wickedness. The one before the table, who held the balance, weighed the souls, and the fiery angel, who held the fire, tried the souls.

And Abraham asked the chief-captain Michael, "What is this that we behold?" And the chief-captain said, "These things that you see, holy Abraham, are the judgment and recompense." And behold the angel holding the soul in his hand, and he brought it before the judge, and the judge said to one of the angels that served him, "Open me this book, and find me the sins of this soul." And opening the book he found its sins and its righteousness equally balanced, and he neither gave it to the tormentors, nor to those that were saved, but set it in the midst.

And Abraham said, "My Lord chief-captain, who is this most wondrous judge? And who are the angels that write down? And who is the angel like the sun, holding the balance? And who is the fiery angel holding the fire?" The chief-captain said, "Do you see, most holy Abraham, the terrible man sitting upon the throne? This is the son of the first created Adam, who is called Abel, whom the wicked Cain killed, and he sits thus to judge all creation, and examines righteous men and sinners. For God has said, 'I shall not judge you, but every man born of man shall be judged.' Therefore he has given to him judgment, to judge the world until his great and glorious coming, and then, O righteous Abraham, is the perfect judgment and recompense, eternal and unchangeable, which no one can alter. For every man has come from the first-created, and therefore they are first judged here by his son, and at the second coming they shall be judged by the twelve tribes of Israel, every breath and every creature. But the third time they shall be judged by the Lord God of all, and then, indeed, the end of that judgment is near, and the sentence terrible, and there is none to deliver. And now by three tribunals the judgment of the world and the recompense is made, and for this reason a matter is not finally confirmed by one or two witnesses, but by three witnesses shall everything be established. The two angels on the right hand and on the left, these are they that write down the sins and the righteousness, the one on the right hand writes down the righteousness, and the one on the left the sins. The angel like the sun, holding the balance in his hand, is the archangel, Dokiel the just weigher, and he weighs the righteousnesses and sins with the righteousness of God. The fiery and pitiless angel, holding the fire in his hand, is the archangel Puruel, who has power over fire, and tries the works of men through fire, and if the fire consume the work of any man, the angel of judgment immediately seizes him, and carries him away to the place of sinners, a most bitter place of punishment. But if the fire approves the work of anyone, and does not seize upon it, that man is justified, and the angel of righteousness takes him and carries him up to be saved in the lot of the just. And thus, most righteous Abraham, all things in all men are tried by fire and the balance." (Testament of Abraham CE, 11–13, first century)[34]

An Uthra was called forth from the side of that Lord of Greatness and was sent out, whose name is Hibil [i.e., Abel]-Ziwa and who is called 'Gabriel the Messenger.' . . . When the sublime King of Light willed it, he called me forth from the radiance and light in which he stands . . . and spoke to him: 'Set off, go to the World of Darkness . . .' He said to him: 'Go, trample down the darkness and the inhabitants which were fashioned from it. Solidify the earth, span out the firmament, and make stars in it.' (Right Ginza I, first–third century CE)[35]

Mother Eve vivifies the torpid Adam, the oven-fresh creation of the evil Archons, and winds up creating an earthly counterpart of herself as a decoy to divert the lustful angels.

And the spirit-endowed woman came to him and spoke with him, saying, "Arise, Adam." And when he saw her, he said, "It is you who have given me life; you will be called 'mother of the living'.—For it is she who is my mother. It is she who is the physician, and the woman, and she who has given birth." Then the authorities came up to their Adam. And when they saw his female counterpart speaking with him, they became agitated with great agitation; and they became enamored of her. They said to one another, "Come, let us sow our seed in her," and they pursued her. And she laughed at them for their witlessness and their blindness; and in their clutches she became a tree, and

---

34. Trans. W.A. Craigie http://www.newadvent.org/fathers/1007.htm.

35. Trans. Peter W. Coxon. In Werner Foerster, ed., *Gnosis: A Selection of Gnostic Texts II. Coptic and Mandean Sources.* (Oxford at the Clarendon Press, 1974), pp. 182–183.

left before them her shadowy reflection resembling herself; and they defiled it foully.—And they defiled the stamp of her voice, so that by the form they had modeled, together with their (own) image, they made themselves liable to condemnation. Then the female spiritual principle came in the snake, the instructor; and it taught them, saying, "What did he say to you? Was it, 'From every tree in the garden shall you eat; yet—from the tree of recognizing good and evil do not eat'?" The carnal woman said, "Not only did he say 'Do not eat', but even 'Do not touch it; for the day you eat from it, with death you are going to die.'" (Hypostasis of the Archons, third century CE)[36]

Scholars have quite naturally understood the Kenosis Hymn in Philippians 2:6–11 as describing the incarnation of Jesus Christ. James D.G. Dunn,[37] for example, sees in these verses a contrast between Adam's fatal misstep of seeking equality with God and Jesus' disdain for such self-aggrandizement. I think this is not quite right. In my view the Kenosis Hymn not only *reflects* the story of Adam; it *is* the story of Adam, an alternative version analogous to that in Ezekiel 28.[38] "Being in the form of God, he did not think equality with God a thing to be seized but emptied himself, taking the form of a servant, etc." This sounds to me like an express repudiation of the Genesis version, asserting not that Christ refused to make the same mistake that Adam had made, but rather that *Adam* did not make the mistake some *said*[39] he made. He did indeed depart from his original heavenly state to assume the burdens of earthly existence, but this was not a punishment as some believed. Rather it was voluntary (perhaps in order "to learn obedience" as in Hebrews 5:8). Originally the text lacked the phrase "even death on a cross"[40] but referred only to death, mortality in general, the human lot. God then exalted Adam to heavenly glory, the state in

36. Trans. Bentley Layton. http://www.gnosis.org/naghamm/hypostas.html.

37. James D.G. Dunn, *Christology in the Making: An Inquiry into the Origins of the Doctrine of the Incarnation* (London: SCM Press, Second edition 1989), pp. xviii–xix, 113–121.

38. Cf., Margaret Barker, *The Gate of Heaven: The History and Symbolism of the Temple in Jerusalem* (London: SPCK, 1991), pp. 70–75.

39. James A. Charlesworth, "The Portrayal of the Righteous as an Angel." In George W.E. Nickelsburg and John J. Collins, eds., *Ideal Figures in Ancient Judaism: Profiles and Paradigms.* Septuagint and Cognate Studies 12 (Chico: Scholars Press, 1980), p. 138.

40. Ralph P. Martin, *Carmen Christi: Philippians ii.5–11 in Recent Interpretation and in the Setting of Early Christian Worship.* Society for New Testament Studies Monograph Series 4 (Cambridge at the University Press, 1967), pp. 220–222.

which we see him in the Testament of Abraham, investing him with the divine Name, "Yahweh Is Salvation." Just like Moses and Metatron and the angel Yahoel.[41] Philippians 2:6–11 obviously applies the story to Jesus, but it is not about Jesus of Nazareth. "Jesus" ("Yahweh Is Salvation") in the hymn referred to the Great Angel receiving the divine Name, just like Yahoel and the Lesser Yahweh. I suspect this is the theo-mythical background for the Ebionites' and the Naassenes' identification of Jesus with Adam.

Enoch recounts how he was transfigured into the angel Metatron:

> The Holy One, blessed be he, laid his hand on me and blessed me with 1,365,000 blessings. I was enlarged and increased in size till I matched the world in length and breadth. He made to grow on me 72 wings, 36 on one side and 36 on the other, and each single wing covered the entire world. He fixed in me 365,000 eyes and each eye was like the Great Light. . . . After all this . . . the Holy One, blessed be he, made for me a throne like the throne of glory. . . . Out of the love which he had for me, more than for all the denizens of the heights, the Holy One, blessed be he, . . . fashioned for me a kingly crown in which 49 refulgent stones were placed, each like the sun's orb. . . . He set it upon my head and he called me, "The lesser Yahweh" in the presence of his whole household in the height, as it is written, "My name is in him." (3 Enoch 9:1–4; 10:1; 12:1–5, fifth to sixth century CE)[42]

Jacob reveals his own angelic nature:

> Thus Jacob says: "I, Jacob, who speak to you, and Israel, I am an angel of God, a ruling spirit, and Abraham and Isaac were created before every work of God; and I am Jacob, called Jacob by men, but my name is Israel, called Israel by God, a man seeing God, because I am the first-born of every creature which God caused to live." And he adds: "When I was coming from Mesopotamia of Syria, Uriel, the angel of God, came forth, and said, 'I have

41. Barker, *Great Angel*, pp. 77, 121; Jarl E. Fossum, *The Name of God and the Angel of the Lord: Samaritan and Jewish Concepts of Intermediation and the Origin of Gnosticism*. Wissenschaftliche Untersuchungen zum Neuen Testament 36 (Tübingen: J.C.B. Mohr (Paul Siebeck), 1987), pp. 289, 318–321; Charles A. Gieschen, *Angelomorphic Christology: Antecedents and Early Evidence*. Arbeiten zur Geschichte des Antiken Judentums und des Urchristentums XLII (Leiden: Brill, 1998), pp. 142–144.

42. "3 (Hebrew Apocalypse of) Enoch." Trans. P. Alexander. In James H. Charlesworth, ed., *The Old Testament Pseudepigrapha*. Vol 1, pp. 263–265.

come down to the earth and made my dwelling among men, and I am called Jacob by name.' He was angry with me and fought with me and wrestled against me, saying that his name and the name of Him who is before every angel should be before my name. And I told him his name and how great he was among the sons of God; 'Are you not Uriel my eighth, and I am Israel and archangel of the power of the Lord and a chief captain among the sons of God? Am not I Israel, the first minister in the sight of God, and I invoked my God by the inextinguishable name?'" (Prayer of Joseph, first–fourth century CE)[43]

Asenath,[44] about to become the bride of Joseph, receives a surprise visit from Joseph's angelic counterpart.

And lo, the heaven was torn open near the morning star and an indescribable light appeared. And Aseneth fell on her face upon the ashes; and there came to her a man from heaven and stood at her head; and he called to her, "Aseneth". And she said, "Who called me? For the door of my room is shut and the tower is high: how then did anyone get into my room?" And the man called her a second time and said, "Aseneth, Aseneth;" and she said, "Here am I, my lord, tell me who you are." And the man said, "I am the commander of the Lord's house and chief captain of all the host of the Most High: stand up, and I will speak to you." And she looked up and saw a man like Joseph in every respect, with a robe and a crown and a royal staff. But his face was like lightning, and his eyes were like the light of the sun, and the hairs of his head like flames of fire, and his hands and feet like iron from the fire. And Aseneth looked *at him*, and she fell on her face at his feet in great fear and trembling. And the man said to her, "Take heart, Aseneth, and do not be afraid; but stand up, and I will speak to you."[45] (Joseph and Asenath XIV: 3–23, 100–110 CE)

Jewish and Samaritan tradition elevated the law-giver Moses to supramundane heights, frequently assimilating his ascent of Sinai to receive the Law to his final assumption into heaven (the latter inferred, correctly, I think, from the coy statement of Deuteronomy 34:5–6 that no one knows his burial place), understanding his elevation as to a divine deputy of Yahweh. Moses'

---

43. Quoted in Origen, *Commentary on the Gospel of John - Book II*, 25 Allan Menzies translation (1896), https://en.wikipedia.org/wiki/Prayer_of_Joseph.

44. Also spelled "Aseneth" as in the ensuing passage.

45. Trans. David Cook. http://www.markgoodacre.org/aseneth/translat.htm#XIV.

father-in-law Jethro interprets Moses' dream-vision of his divine coronation.

> "Methought upon Mount Sinai's brow I saw
> A mighty throne that reached to heaven's high vault,
> Whereon there sat a man of noblest mien
> Wearing a royal crown; whose left hand held
> A mighty sceptre; and his right to me
> Made sign, and I stood forth before the throne.
> He gave me then the sceptre and the crown,
> And bade me sit upon the royal throne,
> From which himself removed. Thence I looked forth
> Upon the earth's wide circle, and beneath
> The earth itself, and high above the heaven.
> Then at my feet, behold! a thousand stars
> Began to fall, and I their number told,
> As they passed by me like an armed host:
> And I in terror started up from sleep."
> 'Then his father-in-law thus interprets the dream:
> "This sign from God bodes good to thee, my friend.
> Would I might live to see thy lot fulfilled!
> A mighty throne shalt thou set up, and be
> Thyself the leader and the judge of men!
> And as o'er all the peopled earth thine eye
> Looked forth, and underneath the earth, and high
> Above God's heaven; so shall thy mind survey
> All things in time, past, present, and to come."
> (Ezekiel the Tragedian, second century BCE)[46]

Exalted is the great prophet Moses whom his Lord vested with His name. He dwelt in the mysteries and was crowned with the light. The True One was revealed to him and gave him His handwriting; He made him drink from ten glorious fountains, seven on high and three below. (*Memar Markah* ii:12, fourteenth century CE)[47]

---

46. Tr. E.H. Gifford http://jewishchristianlit.com/Texts/OT/EzekielTheTragedian.html.

47. Trans. John Macdonald in Macdonald, *The Theology of the Samaritans*. New Testament Library (London: SCM Press, 1964), p. 80.

I am not sure the two categories Bart delineates are hermetically sealed. I think that what first looks like adoptionism or exaltation "Christology" of these patriarchs turns out to be more of an incarnational "Christology" since many of the figures are also understood by the ancients to have been pre-existent entities. Enoch was already a heavenly figure before he came to earth. He had forgotten it till informed that he himself was the ancient Son of Man seated at the right hand of the Ancient of Days:

> And that Head of Days came with Michael and Gabriel, Raphael and Phanuel, and thousands and ten thousands of angels without numbers. And that angel came to me, and greeted me with his voice, and said to me, 'You are the Son of Man who was born to righteousness.' (1 Enoch LXXI:13–14, first century BCE–CE).[48]

Ebionites,[49] Philo,[50] Mandaeans,[51] and subsequent Kabbalists[52] believed Adam had been a heavenly being, even the creative Logos of God. Abel ("Hibil-Ziwa"), Seth ("Sitil"), and Enosh ("Enosh-Uthra") were venerated as divine beings by the Mandaeans. Samaritans (whose ancient traditions are enshrined in later texts) identified Moses as a pre-existent being of divine light who had assisted in creation.[53] Enoch/Metatron, too, was instrumental in the creation. These figures were or had been turned into versions of "the Angel of Yahweh" endowed with the Tetragrammaton ("YHWH") which in turn was widely believed to be the Word whereby God created all things. It seems hard to deny that New Testament Christology finds its proper history-of-religions context here. Jesus was exalted to divine dignity, playing Yahweh to his Father

---

48. Trans. M.A. Knibb. In H.F.D. Sparks, ed., *The Apocryphal Old Testament* (Oxford: Clarendon Press, 1984), p. 256.

49. Hans-Joachim Schoeps, *Jewish Christianity: Factional Disputes in the Early Church.* Trans. Douglas R.A. Hare (Philadelphia: Fortress Press, 1964), pp. 68–71.

50. Stefan Nordgaard, "Paul's Appropriation of Philo's Theory of 'Two Men' in 1 Corinthians 15.45–49." *New Testament Studies* Vol. 57, no. 3, July 2011, pp. 348–365.

51. Drower, *Secret Adam*, Ibid.

52. Gershom Scholem, *Major Trends in Jewish Mysticism.* Hilda Strook Lectures, Jewish Institute of Religion. Trans. George Lichtheim (New York: Schocken Books, 1961), Seventh Lecture: "Isaac Luria and his School," pp. 244–286.

53. Macdonald, *Theology of the Samaritans*, pp. 164–165, 179.

El Elyon. Yet as such he became identified with/as the Word, the demiurge of creation. The old puzzle pieces get reshuffled to form a clearer picture.[54]

Bart Ehrman, like Larry Hurtado, Wayne A. Meeks, and others, maintains that this model was applied to a historical figure, Jesus of Nazareth. It's possible, but let's not forget that all the others without exception were mythical, i.e., fictive characters. There never was any Adam, Eve, Abel, Seth, Enosh, Enoch, Jacob, Joseph, or Moses. In fact, it is evident that Enoch and Moses, like Samson, Esau, Isaac, Elijah, and Hercules,[55] were at first sun gods pure and simple, the sun personified. As is the rule with mythological gods, they were eventually reframed as legendary demigods who moved among men though possessing divine parentage and powers.[56] So Enoch, for example, was at first a sun god, period. His lifespan of 365 years, as we now read it, was originally the 365 days of the solar year. He rose to the zenith of the heavens as the noonday sun. He walked with God across the circuit of the heavens—as the sun. But he was then retooled as an earthly man exalted (or a god incarnated)—just like the Mythicist understanding of Jesus, a celestial entity (not incarnated but) historicized. And here we have the exaltation pattern seen in Jesus: what was originally a (sun) god, a mythic being, gets demoted to a demigod human (a legendary being), but then his original character as a divinity returns (the return of the repressed) as this human figure ascends to heaven and becomes a second god, the lesser Yahweh (who is actually, a la Barker, Yahweh himself, left over from the unification of Yahweh and El Elyon).

---

54. If one shrugs off the seeming connection between the exaltation of Jesus and those of Enoch, Moses, etc., is it not like the attempts of Creationist ax-grinders who discount evolution, "arguing" that the similarity between life-forms is pretty much coincidence? See Robert M. Price, "The Return of the Navel: The 'Omphalos' Argument in Contemporary Creationism." In *Creation/Evolution* II (Fall 1980), pp. 26–33.

55. Ignaz Goldziher, *Mythology Among the Hebrews and its Historical Development.* Trans. Russell Martineau (New York: Cooper Square, 1967), Chapter V, "The Most Prominent Figures in Hebrew Mythology," pp. 90–197; Appendix 2 by H. Steinthal, "The Legend of Samson," pp. 392–446; Robert M. Price, *Moses and Minimalism: Form Criticism vs. Fiction in the Pentateuch* (Valley, WA: Tellectual Press, 2015), pp. 118–120.

56. Jaan Puhvel, *Comparative Mythology* (Baltimore: Johns Hopkins University Press, 1987), p. 39.

TWO FOR THE PRICE OF ONE

Bart raises a very astute question: Did early Christians mean what modern ones do when they said Jesus was "God"?[57] First, can we really know what God-concept Jesus or Paul might have held? The conservative apologist takes for granted that Jesus was an Athanasian before Athanasius. He must have held the same opinions on the Hypostatic Union and the Trinity that the apologist does! Fundamentalists, even fairly sophisticated ones, tend to have an anachronistic and essentialist view of the history of dogma that envisions no real evolution of theology. No, the eternal verities were once and for all delivered unto the saints, and so Jesus must have believed them, too. Again, this is the thinking of a party-line spin doctor.

Second, it does not occur to the apologist that if a man did think himself to be God on earth, it would no longer be so clear that he was in fact a monotheist! Jews and Muslims certainly do not deem incarnationism compatible with monotheism. Again, the apologist implicitly assumes a whole intricate conglomeration of theological constructions, in this case blithely equating Trinitarianism with biblical monotheism, something that, while it might be true, is not obvious enough to be taken for granted at a controversial point.

Bart depicts the development of Christology as an effort to reconcile Christians worship of Jesus with monotheism,[58] but what if Christians were at first not monotheists? Margaret Barker explains how the Great Angel was really what was left of Yahweh after the Deuteronomists officially fused him with El Elyon. This would explain the failure to accommodate monotheism with a second hypostasis.

Insofar as Jews were worshipping angels as proper subordinates of the exalted God of Israel, and other Jews condemned the practice, we have, I think, a perfect parallel to the Catholic-Protestant debate over saint worship. Also the Jewish and Islamic critique of Trinitarianism: Christians are merely insisting by fiat that three equals one. Call it monotheism if you want, but it amounts to polytheism: you just can't admit it! I think this is what early binitarian[59] Christians were doing: theological stonewalling. And those who try

---

57. Ehrman, *How Jesus Became God*, pp. 43–44.

58. Ehrman, *How Jesus Became God*, p. 235.

59. Alan F. Segal. *Two Powers in Heaven: Early Rabbinic Reports About Christianity and*

to redefine Jesus-binitarianism as "Christological monotheism,"[60] etc., are just doing more of the same.

Whence this theological funny business? I think it started with the strategic retreat of philosophically inclined Jews to the gimmick of "hypostases." Did God get his hands dirty modeling Adam from fistfuls of clay on the ground? No, he's far too transcendent for menial labor like that. Did he use his finger to chisel the commandments in stone? Ah, no: *what* finger? Did God actually live in the Temple, sitting between the cherubs atop the Ark of the Covenant? Heh-heh, uh, guess not. But was it somebody *else* who did these things? Of course not! Well, *what*, then? Doesn't matter; we just need a buffer, a stop-gap. It was a demiurge who did these things, a semi-autonomous extension of God, the *Name* of Yahweh, i.e., the Angel of Yahweh in whom his mighty Name dwells (Exod. 23:21). Scholars like Charles A. Gieschen[61] try to work out the theology underlying mentions of hypostases, etc, trying to figure out what sort of (modified) monotheism is implied.[62] But I suggest it is a matter of intentional obfuscation and equivocation to make possible the maintenance of two contradictory bits of theology or mythology (exactly like the Trinity, which is the final product of the same trend). We cannot expect and should give up seeking some coherent underlying rationale behind all this. The actual

---

Gnosticism. Studies in Judaism and Late Antiquity 25 (Leiden: E.J. Brill, 1977).

60. Michael F. Bird, "Of Gods, Angels, and Men." In Bird, ed., *How God Became Jesus*, pp. 39–40.

61. Gieschen, *Angelomorphic Christology*, p. 69.

62. Raymond Panikkar, in *The Unknown Christ of Hinduism* (London: Darton, Longman & Todd, 1964), proposes a modern Christology incorporating conceptuality from Advaita Vedanta. Panikkar views the Father in terms of the Nirguna Brahman, "Brahman without qualities," the Absolute Godhead beyond personality This is the ultimate level of Reality in which all is one. The Son is the extension (or perception) of the Brahman on our lower plane of Samsara. This makes him the Christian version of Isvara ("the Lord") or Brahma, a personalized counterpart of the Godhead. This would seem awfully close to the (pre-incarnate) Logos of Christianity. Jesus of Nazareth, then, would be a divine avatar of Isvara. This notion would seem similar to Paul Tillich's characterization of God as "a person and the negation of himself as a person" (*Biblical Religion and the Search for Ultimate Reality*. James W. Richards Lectures in the Christian Religion, University of Virginia 1951–52 [Chicago: University of Chicago Press, 1955], p. 85). The big sticking point, I think, would be that Panikkar's schema might be construed as a form of Modalism as it implies that the Son is placed on a lower ontological level from the Father, hence not a co-equal Person within the Godhead.

rationale would seem to be "We're polytheists but want to be considered monotheists."

CHAPTER SIX

THE WAY, THE TRUTH, AND THE LIE

APOLOGISTS IN SHEEP'S CLOTHING

One of the last and most blatant forms of the mainstream academic apologetics for the Bible that Hector Avalos[1] has bemoaned is the contrived defense of pseudepigraphy as other than a species of fraud. Clark H. Pinnock, the late, great Evangelical theologian, used to speak of "deceitful" literary genres[2] which he could not imagine God using as he inspired mortals to write scripture. Here is one of those places where the opposite ends meet in the middle, for hostile critics like Joseph Wheless[3] were quick to stress the incompatibility of forgery with divine inspiration, too. Of course the difference was that Pinnock would argue that all canonical authorship claims were accurate (because they pretty much *had* to be), while Wheless (an ex-Methodist, hence an ex-Evangelical) admitted the false character of the biblical pseudepigraphs and denied their inspiration. By contrast, it was left to Liberal and Neo-Orthodox theologians, really apologists, to argue sophistically that pseudonymity was a recognized

---

1. Hector Avalos, *The End of Biblical Studies* (Amherst: Prometheus Books, 2007).

2. Clark H. Pinnock, *Biblical Revelation: The Foundation of Christian Theology* (Chicago: Moody Press, 1971), p.p. 187, 190–191.

3. Joseph Wheless, *Is It God's Word? An Exposition of the Fables and Mythology of the Bible and the Impostures of Theology* (New York: Alfred A. Knopf, 1926).

and venerable literary convention that neither intended to nor succeeded in deceiving anyone. Ancient readers would, they urged, see a copy of 2 Peter or the Book of Enoch and immediately know what was going on, as if an Op-Ed piece in *The New York Times* was signed "Abraham Lincoln," as if to offer what the writer believed Honest Abe would say could he apply his wisdom to today's problems.

Bart Ehrman[4] has clarified and exploded these tortuous claims, showing how there is no ancient evidence for such attitudes and that there is plenty of evidence that the ancients took a dim view of forgeries, whatever the motivation for them. I for one cannot help viewing the claims for benign and non-deceptive forgery as akin to the old-time religious Rationalism, still alive and well today, whereby we are told (e.g., by John Dominic Crossan and Barbara Thiering) that the gospel writers did not believe in the miracles they narrated but instead intended them as symbolic: let him who has ears hear.

What Bart has done in his book *Forged* is to apply the "trajectories" approach of Helmut Koester and James M. Robinson[5] to the question of pious fraud. We know how widespread and flagrant such bamboozlement was in the early Christian centuries with their Reports of Pilate, Gospels of Nicodemus, Letters of Paul and Seneca, and Apocalypses of Peter. Does this fact not set a pretty clear precedent and point us in a definite direction back into the New Testament canon? Indeed it does, at least if one refuses to privilege the official canon list. And that is the lesson Hector Avalos and Bart Ehrman would have us learn: The attempt to exonerate New Testament forgers is a case of canon apologetics pure and simple. Otherwise we should recognize that New Testament writers, presumably neither more nor less sincere and zealous in their faith than their extra-canonical successors, must have been just as likely, on average, to tell white lies for a greater good as they perceived it. "If through my falsehood God's truthfulness abounds to his glory, why am I still being condemned as a sinner?" (Rom. 3:7).

---

4. Bart D. Ehrman, *Forged: Writing in the Name of God—Why the Bible's Authors Are not who We Think They Are* (New York: HarperOne, 2011); Ehrman, *Forgery and Counterforgery: The Use of Literary Deceit in Early Christian Polemics* (New York: Oxford University Press, 2013).

5. James M. Robinson and Helmut Koester, *Trajectories through Early Christianity* (Philadelphia: Fortress Press, 1971).

Now Accepting Implications

What does surprise me, though, is how Bart seems to stop short of accepting certain implications for the Pauline epistles he still considers authentic. As so often, he appeals to consensus instead of supplying evidence when he assures us that virtually all scholars accept as authentic the lucky seven, namely, Romans, 1 and 2 Corinthians, Galatians, Philippians, 1 Thessalonians, and Philemon. F.C. Baur[6] argued in some detail that the reasons for rejecting Philippians, both Thessalonians, and Philemon were as serious as the objections lodged against the Pastorals, Colossians, and Ephesians. But Bultmann was already back to the magnificent seven. And it seems to have become an untouchable ark ever since. Why? I think Baur's arguments were quite compelling. At least one ought to reckon with them. And I suspect that the canon of just seven Pauline epistles is another unnoticed vestige of mainstream scholarly apologetics, stemming from an inherited Protestant understanding of religious authority. From the beginning of my participation in the Jesus and Paul Seminars of the Westar Institute, I could not help noticing how Jesus could be thrown to the wolves, most of his ascribed teachings receiving the dreaded black and gray ratings, while the sacred seven epistles of Paul could not be questioned. But "why should it be considered incredible among you" that, if the truckload of ostensibly Petrine writings outside and inside the canon can be dismissed as spurious, all of the Paulines at least *might* be just as questionable?

> Various followers of Paul took contrary lines on such fundamental issues as the unity of the godhead, the nature of Christ, the viability of marriage and sexual relations, and so on. Some among these followers produced writings in Paul's name, all claiming that Paul himself authorized their views. The reality is that he authored none of them.[7]

These apt words from Bart would serve quite well as a summary of W.C. van Manen's understanding of every one of the canonical thirteen "Pauline" epistles, even of most of them individually, which he views as redactional patchworks, each sewn together from warring Paulinist tractates and dueling

---

6. F.C. Baur, *Paul: The Apostle of Jesus Christ: His Life and Works, his Epistles and Teachings*. Trans. A. Menzies (1873–1875; rpt. Peabody: Hendrickson, 2003).

7. Ehrman, *Forgery and Counterforgery*, p. 87.

interpolations.[8] Mainstream critics are quite willing to cut loose about half of the Pauline canon anyway; that already implies an ancient open season on Paulinist pseudepigraphy. It's not much of a step to go the whole way if the same sort of evidence should seem to warrant it. And some of us think it does. The Dutch Radical Critics were repudiated even by Baur as Martin Luther waved away the irritating buzzing of Caspar Schwenkfeld who wanted to go even farther in Luther's direction than Luther had. The Dutch Radicals denied all the epistles to Paul, using astonishing arguments I have never seen refuted, only given the cold shoulder by everyone but Albert Schweitzer,[9] who still did not do them justice. I am not saying Baur and Van Manen and the rest were right.[10] But why are their suggestions unthinkable? I think it is canon apologetics again, albeit what one might call, drawing on Ernst Käsemann,[11] "canon within the canon" apologetics. Paul is still important to academic liberals if only so they may rehabilitate him in the eyes of ecumenical fellow-travelers and use him to convince the conservative pew-potatoes that it's okay to vote liberal. If Paul was pro-Judaism, a feminist, and not anti-gay, then neither do his latter-day admirers have to be.

I suppose it is yet another case of the Apostle Paul de Man's dialectic of "blindness and insight," whereby we can see some things only because we cannot yet see others that will eventually follow. For instance, Bart[12] effectively points to the author of 2 Thessalonians 2:1–2 "protesting too much" about the damnable currency of spurious "Pauline" letters, hoping to throw readers off the trail so they will not notice this is *one* of them! So true. But in his later discussion of the role of *amanuenses* in Paul's letters he refers to Galatians 6:11,

---

8. Willem Christiaan van Manen, *A Wave of Hyper-Criticism: The English Writings of W.C. van Manen* (Valley, WA: Tellectual Press, 2014); see also Robert M. Price, *The Amazing Colossal Apostle: The Search for the Historical Paul* (Salt Lake City: Signature Books, 2012).

9. Albert Schweitzer, *Paul and his Interpreters: A Critical History*. Trans. W. Montgomery (NY: Schocken Books, 1964), Chapter V, "Critical Questions and Hypotheses," pp. 117–150.

10. Though in fact I do think so.

11. Ernst Käsemann, *Das Neue Testament als Kanon* (Göttingen, 1970), p. 405; cited in James D.G. Dunn, *Unity and Diversity in the New Testament: An Inquiry into the Character of Earliest Christianity* (Philadelphia: Westminster Press, 1977), p. 418.

12. Ehrman, *Forged*, p. 108; Ehrman, *Forgery and Counterforgery*, p. 33.

"See with what large letters I am writing to you with my own hand." His point is that Paul did not personally set pen to paper for the rest of the letter, but dictated it to a scribe. But there is something here he does not notice, I think because of ingrained mainstream apologetics. Second Thessalonians 3:17 has the same element: "I, Paul, write this greeting with my own hand. This is the mark in every letter of mine; it is the way I write." And it serves the same function in both cases: to drive home a spurious authorship claim. "This isn't one of those fakes!"

The case of Galatians is even clearer than that of 2 Thessalonians, since the author actually describes the "scene of writing," as Gerald Prince[13] explains. Prince notes how one character in a novel is writing a letter to a friend, and the novelist lets us read over his shoulder. The character is made to remark on how cheap his stationary is, as his friend will note from the way the ink soaks into it. If we were actually reading such a letter in real life, there would be no need for such a note, would there? Oh, our correspondent might apologize for the bad quality of the paper he is reduced to using, but we could see for ourselves why he is apologizing. In just the same way, if one were a Galatian reading an actual autograph letter from Paul, one would scarcely require to be *told* the size of scrawled letters one could see with one's own eyes. The description is there to maintain the illusion that one, living long after the time of Paul, is reading a copy of that original letter. The "copy" will not feature that precious autograph signature. It will only be written in letters uniform with the rest of the letter, as in our printed Bibles. Galatians, then, is fictive, fraudulent, forged. But it is part of the mainstream academic canon of Paul, so Bart does not see the problem. Galatians 6:11, Bart thinks, may be merely Paul's attempt to "personalize" the letter. What sense would it make, he implies, as a gimmick to falsely claim genuine Pauline authorship in a forged epistle, since the reader must know his text is a copy, not the original?[14] But, as I have said, that is the very cloak behind which the forger attempts to conceal himself: he means to give the impression that the original recipients must have considered the text authentic before they agreed to circulate copies, and this is how they "knew." We find the same logic behind 1 Corinthians 15:6. You doubt that half a thousand brethren shared the sight of the resurrected Jesus?

13. Gerald Prince, *Narratology: The Form and Functioning of Narrative.* Janua Linguarum. Series Maior 108 (New York: Mouton Publishers, 1982), p. 34.

14. Ehrman, *Forgery and Counterforgery,* pp. 170–171.

Well, be my guest! Go ask them! Most of them, *whatever their names are*, are still around—*somewhere*!

I think Bart gives us reasons, without meaning to, for thinking Philippians is another pious forgery. First, he calls attention to the business in the spurious Pastoral Epistles about bishops and deacons, a gross anachronism for Paul (at least the way we usually picture him), who would seem to have presided over rip-roaring, tongue-speaking, store-front charismatic conventicles, not stolid church congregations ruled by harrumphing hierarchies. But what about Philippians 1:1b? "To all the saints in Christ Jesus who are at Philippi, with the bishops and deacons." Yikes! But Bart anticipates the question:

> but there is nothing in that verse or the entire letter . . . of Philippians as a whole to indicate that these are persons selected for an office out of a pool of candidates, or that they were ordained by the laying on of hands. In fact, nothing is said about them at all, giving us no way of knowing whether they are comparable to the figures addressed in the Pastorals or not. If we assume they are it is not because of any evidence, since, in fact, there is no hint of evidence; it is simply a hopeful assumption.[15]

But isn't this special pleading? What possible reason is there for thinking "bishops and deacons" means anything else than in the Pastorals? And what the heck else *could* the terminology refer to? As I read him, Bart is trying here to fend off any appeal to Philippians 1:1b as evidence that churches in Paul's day already had an ordered hierarchy and so to ward off the charge of anachronism. But I am saying that Bart is right about "bishops and deacons" being an anachronism but that it cuts both ways, militating against the authenticity of Philippians as well as the Pastorals.

In fact, I consider Philippians virtually a fourth Pastoral Epistle. Second Timothy shows a retrospective awareness of Paul's impending death and thus qualifies as a member of the "testaments" literature, instances of which are plentiful both inside and outside the canon, as in Deuteronomy 33; John chapters 13–16, and Acts 20:17–38 as well as the Testaments of the Twelve Patriarchs, the Testament of Abraham, the Testament of Isaac, the Testament of Jacob, and the Testament of Job. Second Peter is another. Of it Bart writes,

---

15. Ehrman, *Forgery and Counterforgery* , p. 205.

when the [pseudonymous] author is speaking in character, he feigns a knowledge of his own approaching death . . . , giving his book, as widely recognized, the character of a testamentary fiction. He "knows" of his impending death, and wants to give his readers his final instructions. As with all Testaments, this is a fiction put on the pen of someone already residing comfortably in his tomb.[16]

Bart might as well be talking about Philippians 1:19–26; 2:17; 3:8–15, which is heavy with the ironic awareness that the reader knows full well that Paul has gone on to his well-deserved reward, the crown of perfection via martyrdom. What a guy! And yet he continues on for their welfare—by means of posthumous letters like this one!

Bart detects the forger's pen in Ephesians when the author "insist[s] to his readers that he really is Paul," e.g., in 3:1: "I, Paul, a prisoner of Christ Jesus on behalf of you Gentiles."[17] The trouble is, we find the same sort of thing in many epistles ascribed to Paul: 1 Corinthians 16:1; 2 Corinthians 10:1; Galatians 5:2; Colossians 1:23; 4:18; 1 Thessalonians 2:18; 2 Thessalonians 3:17; Philemon 1:9, 19. If you were writing a letter or a treatise, would you *claim* to be you? Sure, you'd sign it or, in the first century, include your name in your salutation. But there would be no point at all in urging your readers to recognize that it is really you on the other end of the pen.

This becomes obvious when it occurs in flagrantly pseudepigraphical works like Daniel 7:15, 28; 8:1, 15, 27; 9:2; 10:2, 7; 12:5; Tobit 1:3; 4 Ezra 2:33, 42; 3:1; 1 Enoch 25:1; Apocalypse of Zephaniah B:7; 2 Baruch 6:1; 8:3; 10:5; 11:1; 13:1; 35:1; 44:1; 77:1; 3 Baruch 1:3, 7; 4:1 5:1; 7:1; 9:1; 16:5; Apocalypse of Abraham 1:2, 4; 6:1; Testament of Levi 2:1; Testament of Solomon 1:3, 5; 2:1, 5, 9; 5:6, 13; 6:9, 10, 12; 7:1, 7; 8:5, 12; 9:5; 10:10; 12:4; 13:3, 5, 6; 14:8; 15:13; 18:41; 19:1; 20:5, 18; 22:6, 17; 23:4; 25:8; Protevangelium of James 25:1; Infancy Gospel of Thomas 1:1; Apocalypse of Peter 2; Gospel of Peter 60; Apocryphon of John 1:19; Book of Thomas the Contender 1:2.

Revelation 1:9 ("I, John, your brother, who share with you in Jesus the tribulation," etc.) and 22:8 ("I, John, am he who heard and saw these things," etc.) form no exception, since, as Benjamin W. Bacon once remarked, if Revelation is not a pseudepigraph, it has the distinction of being the only

16. Ehrman, *Forgery and Counterforgery*, p. 224.

17. Ehrman, *Forgery and Counterforgery*, p. 187.

apocalypse that isn't.[18] As far back as Eusebius, scholars have agonized over whether the Revelation could be the work of John son of Zebedee, or whether the Revelator must not be another man named John, the "Elder John." It seems more natural to suggest that the Apocalypse is *supposed* to be the work of John son of Zebedee but isn't, whether the Gospel of John is the apostle's work or not.

Another case of pseudepigraphy *within the same book* meets us in Revelation 22:16 ("I, Jesus, have sent my angel to you," etc.). I think it is the use of this device in the undisputed pseudepigrapha that really reveals the nature of the beast, the natural function of it. This is protesting too darn much, asserting and affirming what a non-pseudonymous author would unselfconsciously take for granted. And the use of "I, Paul" in the supposedly unimpeachable 1 and 2 Corinthians, Galatians, 1 Thessalonians, and Philemon means the same fatal thing it does when we spot it in the pages of 2 Thessalonians, Colossians, and Ephesians.[19]

OH WHAT A TANGLED WEB WE WEAVE WHEN FIRST WE PRACTICE TO BELIEVE

So much for authorship qualms. Let's turn our forensic gaze on specific gospel materials. As Bart properly notes, there is no question of forgery in the case of the gospels, since the names/titles are secondary anyway. Matthew, Mark, Luke, and John are just educated(?) guesses, as when the rabbis tagged the Pentateuch as by Moses, the Psalms as by David, etc.

Let me first absolve a couple of types of gospel inauthenticity from charges of forgery and underhandedness. Bart[20] rightly laughs off the desperate

---

18. Benjamin W. Bacon, "The Authoress of Revelation - A Conjecture." *Harvard Theological Review* 23 (July 1930), pp. 235–250.

19. The gimmick still hasn't gone out of style. Lin Carter wrote several pretend chapters of H.P. Lovecraft's fictional grimoire the *Necronomicon* by the Mad Arab Abdul Alhazred. Sure enough, virtually all of them sooner or later get around to "I, Alhazred." See Lin Carter, "The Necronomicon: The Dee Translation." In Robert M. Price, ed., *The Necronomicon: Selected Stories and Essays Concerning the Blasphemous Tome of the Mad Arab* (Oakland: Chaosium, 2002), pp. 200, 207 (2X), 221, 225, 230, 236, 237, 238, 240.

20. Ehrman, *Forged*, pp, 123–125; Ehrman, *Forgery and Counterforgery*, pp. 38–39.

expedient whereby some scholars sought to justify false authorship claims (e.g., in the case of Ephesians or Colossians) as the result of the divine inspiration felt by the writers: they felt, we are told, that what they were writing was not really their own work but that of the Divine Spirit. But how would it follow that they would appropriate the name of a deceased historical character? Was the Holy Ghost named "Paul"? Bart is right: it is ridiculous. I have on my shelf, however, a book[21] accredited to Philip the Deacon which is supposed to be a channeled revelation from him. And another by Elizabeth Claire Prophet (*not* a pseudonym!), guru of the Summit Lighthouse/Church Universal and Triumphant, in which she claims to channel Jesus, the Buddha, and other worthies. And thus she places their holy names on the spines of her paperbacks. Maybe she sincerely believes all this. And maybe some New Testament epistolarians were doing the same thing, but I doubt it. But if it were so, that would constitute pseudepigraphy that was not deception (or only self-deception).

The case is no different when we judge many gospel sayings to have begun as the inspired "words of wisdom" and "words of knowledge" justified in Luke 21:13–15 ("I will give you a mouth and wisdom," etc.), Luke 10:16 ("Whoever hears you hears me."), and John 16:12–15. Mark 10:2–9 on divorce and Luke 10:7 on apostolic compensation began as prophetic oracles from Jesus the ascended master (as in 1 Cor. 7:10–11; 9:14, cf. 14:37).[22] Mark 8:34, the cross-bearing saying, obviously presupposes the hearers know all about Jesus going to the cross of Golgotha, which the pre-Passion crowds could scarcely know about, but the readers do. There is simply no reason to suppose early Christians gave a fig whether a "Jesus" saying came from channeled utterances or from historical memory,[23] any more than modern

---

21. *The Gospel of Philip the Deacon.* Received by Frederick Bligh Bond through the hand of Hester Dowden (New York: Macoy Publishing, 1932).

22. E.g., Alfred Loisy, *The Origins of the New Testament.* Trans. L.P. Jacks (London: George Allen & Unwin, 1950), p. 47.

23. Ernst Käsemann, "The New Testament Canon and the Unity of the Church." In Käsemann, *Essays on New Testament Themes.* Trans. W.J. Montague. Studies in Biblical Theology No. 41 (London: SCM Press, 1964), p. 98: "The primitive Christian community did not distinguish, as we do, between the historic Jesus and the exalted Lord. Palestinian and Hellenistic Christian prophecy alike spoke in the name of the Exalted One, as we can see in the Apocalypse of John. In the development of the tradition, these sayings—couched for the most part in the first person—have become

fundamentalists care whether a particular verse is attributed to Jesus, Paul or someone else, as long as it is located on the page of the Bible. Bultmann was right about the prophetic origin of many gospel sayings. And I think it is all very innocent.

BEHOLD THE TEN AMENDMENTS

There are still other gospel materials which result from purposeful alterations of sayings ascribed to Jesus but cannot reasonably be considered fraudulent or deceptive. I am thinking of instances like Matthew's alteration of Mark's divorce ruling. He adds "except for *porneia*," a purposely vague term intended to restore the judicious ambiguity of Deuteronomy 24:1 ("some indecency"). Matthew must have known Jesus was not on record saying this, but it would be absurd to charge the evangelist with "lying" about what Jesus had said, trying to pull the wool over the eyes of his readers. No, it is simply that Mark has become something of a charter document for Matthew's community, and Matthew believes it is in need of a slight amendment. The thinking I ascribe to him is nothing different from his impulse to enlarge and correct Mark in general. It is a sacred text that requires updating, just as the Torah was amended to allow for daughters to inherit (Num. 27:1–11).

To return to Bart's work on textual criticism,[24] I wonder if the same consideration ought to apply to the redactional emendations made by Christian scribes in order to prevent their "heretical" opponents appealing to the texts. What heretics construed as evidence in the gospels or epistles for docetism, Patripassianism, etc., orthodox copyists yanked out from under them by rewording the verses in question. Were these scribes lying? After all, they were charged with making copies of the old texts, and here they are found not to have been faithful scribes. Or were they? I am inclined to give them the benefit of the doubt. They were not textual critics like Bart Ehrman. They were "stewards of the mysteries of God" seeking to save scripture from itself.

---

confused with the words of the historical Jesus and ascribed to him simply because primitive Christianity was concerned not, as we are, with the exact period of their origin, but with the Spirit of the Lord revealing himself in both groups [of sayings] alike."

24. Bart D. Ehrman, *The Orthodox Corruption of Scripture: The Effect of Early Christological Controversies on the Text of the New Testament* (NY: Oxford University Press, 1993).

As an authoritative text, it required slight emendations, lest its readers come away with the wrong impression.

Suppose many gospel stories originated as imaginative rewrites of stories from the Septuagint, as a number of scholars hold.[25] Here we have to envision creative fiction writing. As Strauss surmised, the assumption was that early Christians shared a Jewish belief that whatever Moses, Elijah, Elisha, Joshua, et al., had done, the messiah should do better. It is possible that they simply deduced that "The Lord Jesus must have done something like this, so let's reconstruct what it was." Or they may have simply decided to spin out stories of Jesus based on the familiar stories of scripture without raising the question of whether they actually took place as narrated. I should think that today's literalists, though they do happen also to believe the stories of the gospels are all factual, primarily experience the stories *as* stories, as witness the fact that many of us long read the various Synoptic periscopes many, many times without ever noticing their contradictions. We used to read each one, just as Reader-Response and narrative critics urge us to do today, putting aside the "too much" that we know so we can approach the texts with a second naiveté. But in our first naiveté it simply never occurred to us that there *were* contradictions implying a lack of historical authenticity. Because we weren't really concerned with authenticity of that kind—that is, until some trouble-making apologist brought the matter up to us. We had been (to use Tillich's[26] term) *natural* literalists, but then we put away childish things to become *reactive* literalists, and then it began to matter whether Jonah could have survived inside a whale, etc. Before the commandment came, I should not have known

---

25. John Dominic Crossan, *The Cross That Spoke: The Origins of the Passion Narrative* (San Francisco: Harper & Row, Publishers, 1988); Randel Helms, *Gospel Fictions*. (Buffalo: Prometheus Books, 1989); Dale Miller and Patricia Miller. *The Gospel of Mark as Midrash on Earlier Jewish and New Testament Literature*. Studies in the Bible and Early Christianity 21 (Lewiston/Queenston/Lampeter: Edwin Mellen Press, 1990); John Bowman, *The Gospel of Mark: The New Christian Jewish Passover Haggadah*. Studia Post-Biblica 8 (Leiden: E.J. Brill, 1965); J. Duncan M. Derrett, *The Making of Mark: The Scriptural Bases of the Earliest Gospel*. Volumes 1 and 2. Shipston-on-Stour (Warwickshire: P. Drinkwater, 1985); Frank Kermode, *The Genesis of Secrecy: On the Interpretation of Narrative*. The Charles Eliot Norton Lectures 1977–1978 (Cambridge: Harvard University Press, 1979); Wolfgang Roth, *Hebrew Gospel: Cracking the Code of Mark* (Oak Park: Meyer-Stone Books, 1988); and Rikki E. Watts, *Isaiah's New Exodus and Mark*. Wissenschaftliche Untersuchungen zum Neuen Testament 2. Reihe 88 (Tübingen: Mohr Siebeck, 1997).

26. Paul Tillich, *Dynamics of Faith* (New York: Harper & Row, 1958), pp. 52–53.

what it was either to insist on historical accuracy or to question it. And if that is the way it was for the ancient tellers and hearers of the Christianized Old Testament stories, we cannot be too quick to call anyone a deceiver.

One last case: suppose that Matthew took literally Mark's episode of Jesus walking on the water. He certainly could not have believed in the kindred miracle only he relates, that Peter walked on the waves to join him. As every preacher sees, the Matthean addition means to encourage the reader not to lose sight of the Savior in distressing times lest one plunge into a pitching sea of troubles. And even if one does, calling upon Jesus will make things right. Matthew has expanded the story for obvious homiletical reasons. Was he trying to hoax us? To deceive anyone? Of course not. I should call it midrash.

CHAPTER AND VERSE

There is another phenomenon related to rewriting Old Testament stories into New Testament stories, believing that one was kabbalistically unlocking some hidden Jesus-prediction in the former. It is the use of scripture proof texts by the New Testament writers. It is obvious that our Christian writers cared little for the original sense intended by the Hebrew authors (insofar as we can reconstruct it). They took those quotes from the Psalms, from Isaiah, etc., out of context. Joseph Wheless[27] attacks them bitterly for this, and he is not alone among the older writers. Ever since the Dead Sea Scrolls biblical commentaries came to light, it has become apparent that there was more involved than a cynical, opportunistic cherry picking of isolated sentences. The Qumran Covenanters knew good and well that Habakkuk hadn't had a thought for Essene monasteries or the Teacher of Righteousness. He was talking about other matters entirely. But if that was the end of it, then scripture had become a dead letter, a museum relic. Couldn't scripture speak again, if only one knew how to listen? They believed they could discern a hitherto-hidden message coded into the text. After all, it was inspired by the Spirit of Truth, so there had to be more to it than there was to some mere human treatise. And so they came to discern the esoteric references to their own vicissitudes. And Matthew was certainly doing the same, as Krister Stendahl[28] made so clear. Matthew

---

27. Wheless, *Is It God's Word?*, pp. 277–304.

28. Krister Stendahl, *The School of St. Matthew and Its Use of the Old Testament*

was no Hal Lindsay, pretending the ancient prophets had his era consciously in mind. Matthew knew he was producing *new* goods from his treasury (13:51–52). Once you know this, the picture looks considerably different.

Wheless didn't and couldn't have known about this. Of course, he wouldn't have recognized any validity in the procedure, but at least he wouldn't have been throwing around accusations of fakery. And again it is interesting to compare his attitude with that of sophisticated literalists, evangelicals, today. Gordon D. Fee and Richard Longenecker[29] both grasped what the Dead Sea Scrolls exegetes and Matthew were doing, but to them it is just as unacceptable as it would have been to the rationalist Wheless. The evangelicals are obliged to say that New Testament writers pursuing this strategy were right to do so, since they were inspired by the Holy Spirit (much like sophisticated Roman Catholics having to swallow hard and try to believe in the Assumption of the Blessed Virgin). But they do not believe today's Bible readers dare emulate this treatment of scripture. They know that every brand of fanatic is waiting in the wings, eager to employ the Bible as a ventriloquist dummy.

Does Paul[30] make fraudulent use of various Old Testament verses to cobble together a doctrine of universal sinfulness? Well, there is no way the writers he quotes in Romans 3 were saying what he says, but again I do not think we can call this deception, as if one of us were caught garnishing a scholarly paper with imaginary or irrelevant footnotes. As I read it, it looks as if he is simply making allusions, peppering his discourse with well-known phrases to make his own point.

HOAX OR HISTORY

Having said all this, I want to turn next to several New Testament narratives that seem to me to suggest pious fraud or, to use a wonderful old term from old-time polemics, *priestcraft*. Alfred Loisy nominated a couple of them. I believe he was correct to propose that the story of Peter's denials was a vicious smear

---

(Philadelphia: Fortress Press, 1968).

29. Richard Longenecker, *Biblical Exegesis in the Apostolic Period* (Grand Rapids: Eerdmans, 1977), pp. 214–220.

30. Please excuse my use, for the sake of convenience, of the traditional authorship ascription.

circulated by Paulinists against the so-called Pillar, to discredit him much in the spirit of Marcion's treatment of the twelve.[31] The cautionary tale of Ananias and Sapphira, struck dead magically for welching on their church pledge, is a transparent bit of priestcraft, too.[32] It is a fiction combining elements from the stories of Achan and of Naboth's vineyard, as Thomas L. Brodie[33] has shown, and Loisy showed its malefic, manipulative purpose. We are talking about something much worse than "errors in the Bible" here. We are talking about fraud and imposture.

What about miracle stories? It appears that the gospel wonder tales first functioned as evangelistic propaganda. First Corinthians 1:22–23 represents a modest stance whereby Christian preachers did not offer miracles to demonstrate the superiority of Jesus Christ to competing saviors. "If you're interested in signs and wonders, I'm afraid I'll have to disappoint you. All I've got, and it's more than enough, is Jesus Christ, and him crucified." Accordingly, no Pauline letter mentions a miracle. Mark 8:11–12 appears to embody the same disdain for parlor tricks. But the saying itself grows in the telling throughout the gospels, so as to accommodate the flood of miracle stories that quickly filled the vacuum. We see the same thing in the Koran, where the Prophet Muhammad rebuffs hecklers who ask why he can show them no authenticating miracle. Subsequent hadith, however, are happy to ascribe many wonders to the Prophet. A thousand years later, Nathan of Gaza warned the followers of messiah Sabbatai Sevi not to expect any miracles, for Israel must believe without them.[34] But it turned out faith did not need a basis in miracles; rather, *it* produced *them* as rumors of wonder-working soon abounded. It is not unreasonable, therefore, to ask if the gospel miracle stories are altogether fictive. They may have stemmed from creative enthusiasm, not by anyone's connivance. Indeed, that would be my first guess.

---

31. Alfred Loisy, *The Birth of the Christian Religion*. Trans. L.P. Jacks (London: George Allen & Unwin, 1948), p. 82.

32. Loisy, *Origins of the New Testament*, p. 173.

33. Thomas L. Brodie, "Luke the Literary Interpreter: Luke-Acts as a Systematic Rewriting and Updating of the Elijah-Elisha Narrative in 1 and 2 Kings." A Dissertation presented to the faculty of the Pontifical University of St. Thomas Aquinas (Ann Arbor: University Microfilms, 1988), pp. 272–281.

34. Gershom Scholem, *Sabbatai Sevi, the Mystical Messiah*. Trans. R.J. Zwi Werblowsky. Bollingen Series XCIII (Princeton: Princeton University Press, 1973), pp. 252.

But then think of the outrageous testimonials inscribed on clay tablets on the walls of the healing shrines of Asclepius with their unintentionally hilarious miracle cures. Asclepius restores sight to a man so blind he had an empty socket. His inept disciples sever a woman's head to try to fish out a tapeworm from her intestines. They have, proverbially, killed the patient in order to save her! But the god appears, evicts the parasite, and sticks the woman's head back on. These were, on the one hand, evangelistic propaganda like the gospel miracle stories. On the other, they may be understood easily as fraudulent commercials aimed at attracting gullible customers, just like today's commercial advertisements. It would be sheer chauvinistic bias to assume the Asclepius priests were unscrupulous, while the early Christian tale-tellers, belonging to the "true" religion, were pure as the driven snow. And it would be equally special pleading to deny that the Christian "ministers of the word" could not have been just as deep into charlatanry as the sneaky pagans.

Remember the story of Sostrata, coming to the Asclepium to have a protracted pregnancy resolved but going home disappointed until the Savior himself, incognito, met her on the road home, asking her why she was so sad, then delivered her of a false pregnancy on the spot before disappearing. Is the point of this tale not to mollify disappointed customers who, attracted by the testimonials, received no healing after all? Don't give up hope! Maybe the god will heal you on the way home! So don't ask for your money back! It might make us take a second look at the Emmaus story, which is so very similar to it.

I hope you will not chalk up my skepticism toward the Epidaurus testimonies to an anti-supernaturalist bias. And before you tell me that Asclepius' cures are much more outlandish than those of the gospels, let me remind you of the Gerasene Demoniac with his superhuman strength, his legion of unclean spirits, and his deviled ham. Or how about that woman with a nonstop hemorrhage for a dozen years?

THAT'S NEWS TO ME

There is a group of gospel materials which utilize a deceptive ploy whereby some innovation is retrojected into the past, the holy time of legitimization, with some excuse as to why no one has heard of so-and-so till now. These stories and sayings seek to disarm the suspicions of those who hear the new item and ask where it has been all this time. (This device is quite similar to that discussed by Bart in connection with bogus "discovery" stories concocted by pious forgers to account for the "seeming" novelty of the texts they are trying to palm off as ancient and venerable.)[35] The most famous case is Mark's story of the empty tomb. First Corinthians 15:3–11, a list of resurrection sightings, knows nothing either of the tomb or of the holy women discovering it. Once Mark added the story, people objected, "Son, I've been a Christian for many years, and this is the first I'm hearing of this! How can that be?" "Oh, well, that's because the women never told anybody about it. I've managed to uncover it now, though." Yeah, that's the ticket.[36]

Very similar is the Transfiguration narrative[37] which very likely began as a resurrection appearance as implied in Jesus' warning to his disciples afterwards to: "tell no one what they had seen, until the son of man should have risen from the dead" (Mark 9:9). Presumably the scene was pushed back to an earlier point in the narrative, and some noticed the change. "Wait a minute! I always thought this happened on Easter!" "I can see how you'd *think* that, brother, but it's because Jesus told them to wait till then to start telling people about it. So when they heard it soon after the resurrection they naturally jumped to the conclusion that it had only just happened! See what I mean?"

Gerd Lüdemann[38] suggests that the evangelist Luke was covering for the late origin of his nativity story, unfamiliar as it was to his readers. Why were they hearing/reading of these astonishing events only now? Because "Mary kept all these things, pondering them in her heart" (Luke 2:19). But years later she must have dropped her secrecy, perhaps when she felt death (or assumption into heaven?) coming on.

Acts portrays the risen Jesus vouchsafing elite gnosis to his disciples just before his ascension (Acts 1:3), just as he had opened the scriptures "and beginning with Moses and all the prophets, he interpreted to them in all the scriptures the things concerning himself" (Luke 24:27). What do you suppose

---

35. Ehrman, *Forgery and Counterforgery*, pp. 123–126. Recent sensational reports of Bible-relevant archaeological discoveries, many of them suspected or discredited as modern fakes, raise the same suspicions since their provenance cannot be traced. The notorious James Ossuary, for example.

36. William Bousset, *Kyrios Christos*. Trans. John E. Steely (New York: Abingdon Press, 1970), p. 38.

37. Ibid.

38. Gerd Lüdemann, *What Jesus Didn't Say* (Salem: Polebridge Press, 2011), p. 3.

he taught them? And why are we not told? Quite simply, these scenes are meant to write a blank check for the bishops of the Church, allowing them to father any doctrines they saw fit onto Jesus after the fact.

A similar blank check is issued in Matthew 10:27, "What I tell you in the dark, utter in the light; and what you hear whispered, proclaim upon the housetops." "Yes, of course Jesus said so-and-so. He just taught it to us in secret and said we were supposed to reveal it to everybody else later!" We recognize the subterfuge readily enough in the Nag Hammadi gospels and apocalypses, but theological blinders stop us from seeing it in the canonical books.

I GUESS YOU HAD TO BE THERE

Some make much of the silence of contemporary historians about Jesus. Would not a man who performed the spectacular feats ascribed to Jesus in the gospels have made the headlines? The cogent response of apologists is that, for all the public ever knew, Jesus was a fairly standard healer and exorcist. One may as well wonder why American history textbooks do not devote space to Oral Roberts. No, the spectacular miracles were, ah, "done in a corner." He changed water into wine at a wedding feast, but who knew it? Not even the steward. Jesus walked on water and stilled a squall on the lake, but who saw it? Only the twelve. He multiplied loaves and fishes for thousands of people, but were they aware of where the food came from? It doesn't say so. Only three witnessed the Transfiguration. These things wouldn't have been known and reported because they were not done in public, only secretly or subtly. But then one starts to notice how *convenient* all that is! Perhaps the stories are told this way precisely to explain away the odd fact that there were no public records of these things.

This difficulty is nowhere more serious than in the case of the resurrection. Jesus has returned from the dead! He is risen indeed! But who saw this? There would have been a lot less room for doubt had he appeared in the midst of the Sanhedrin or to Pilate or to great crowds who had seen his crucifixion. But where *does* he appear? Behind closed doors. In a secluded memorial garden to a handful of women. At dawn on the misty shore of a lake, and to a mere seven men. To a pair of disciples on a lonely road. "Oh, believe me, it was quite impressive! Too bad you weren't there to see it!"

But didn't Jesus appear to more than five hundred of the brethren at once

(1 Cor. 15:6)? This prodigy occurs in no gospel, not in any narrative. And it cannot have been original to 1 Corinthians either. Had such a thing been known, there is no way it would not have been mentioned in any and every gospel. It must be later than the gospels, except that it does appear in one version of the Gospel of Nicodemus/Acts of Pilate, where we are told the 500 were the Roman troops assigned to guard the tomb in Matthew, itself a late embellishment.

So Jesus supposedly appeared to small groups of his friends and followers in remote places and behind closed doors. Not exactly evidence that demands a verdict. It is exactly like the lame answer to the scribal objection that Jesus couldn't have been the messiah since Elijah had not returned to herald him: "Oh but he *did*! Three people saw him, and he was there just for a minute or two. You *do* believe me, don't you?"

THE BEAT GOES ON

Finally, it is important to ask if perhaps we are not talking only about ancient history. There are well known cases of pious forgery pure and simple, such as *The Archko Volume*, and many of us place Morton Smith's Secret Mark,[39] and even the much-vaunted Gospel of Judas,[40] in the same category, not to mention the flash-in-the-pan Gospel of Jesus' Wife.[41] But dare we suggest the practice is carried on today in a more subtle form as Christian apologetics?

CANON FODDER

I have already mentioned canon apologetics as the not-so-hidden agenda behind this and that defense of pseudepigraphy in the Bible. What is the danger apologists fear? There are three. First, they cannot brook the notion that

---

39. Stephen C. Carlson, *The Gospel Hoax: Morton Smith's Invention of Secret Mark* (Waco: Baylor University Press, 2005).

40. Richard J. Arthur, "The Gospel of Judas: Is It a Hoax?" *Journal of Unification Studies* 9 (2008), pp. 35–47. In the published article, Arthur did not name the suspected modern forger, but I got him to admit he thought it was Marvin Meyer.

41. http://www.theatlantic.com/magazine/archive/2016/07/the-unbelievable-tale-of-jesus-wife/485573/

biblical writers could lie, since that would implicate the God who supposedly inspired the scriptural writers. Second, if, e.g., the author of 2 Peter cannot be trusted in the matter of who he really is, there is no more reason to trust anything else he says in the letter. Third, the basis for a writing's inclusion in the canon of scripture is its apostolic authorship, and, between anonymity and pseudonymity, the so-called "apostolic authorship" has gone up in smoke. "Thus, even if there were some theological justification for ascribing canonical status to the New Testament, the conclusions of the historian would put us in a hopeless position."[42]

Even if the "lucky seven" epistles are deemed authentically Pauline, this is a tentative, qualified judgment. Two points here: a considered affirmation of this kind is very different from an exercise of faith accepting a group of writings as a canon of scripture. Can you imagine basing your theology on the teachings of a *probably* authoritative text? If your judgment as to biblical authorship is provisional and probabilistic, you must change hats, from the believer's to the historian's. Pious, finger-wagging writers on biblical authority like to say that we must not presume to criticize scripture but must submit to it criticizing us. I would agree that those are the alternatives, and that, once you recognize the dubiety of the canon and of its "apostolic" authority, you are done being a believer. It is as Collingwood[43] says when defining genuinely critical history: the historian no longer views his documents as "authorities" which he is obliged to believe, but rather merely as "sources" of evidence that it is his job to evaluate. It is the same with the biblical documents: they must be treated as Bart and I treat them, as a fund of evidence for understanding Christian origins, nothing more. Naturally, the critical reader may learn and apply much wisdom from the Bible, but the writings will no longer be understood as prophetic revelations of truth otherwise unavailable to the human mind. Instead they will henceforth be understood like the Old Testament Wisdom Literature, a deposit of aphorisms which pretend no other authority than the ring of truth. "Of *course*! I should have *thought* of that!" Robin Scroggs[44] puts it well:

---

42. Robin Scroggs, p. 89. "Tradition, Freedom, and the Abyss." In Martin E. Marty and Dean G. Peerman, eds., *New Theology no. 8* (New York: Macmillan, 1971, p. 89.

43. R.G. Collingwood, *The Idea of History* (New York: A Galaxy Book/Oxford University Press, 1956), pp. 234–238.

44. Robin Scroggs, "Tradition, Freedom, and the Abyss," pp. 94–95. Similarly, David Tracy, *Blessed Rage for Order: The New Pluralism in Theology* (New York: Seabury Press,

I have not the slightest doubt that the reason we have anything at all to do with Christianity today is not that we have swallowed what Christianity has told us to believe and do, but that out of our own sense of how to live we have come to look seriously at Christianity because it seems in part at least to be saying the same thing we know to be right.

And suppose you do take your stand on what you consider the genuine Pauline writings? It would constitute a "canon within the canon."[45] But please notice the major shift that occurs at this juncture. One is attempting to "discern the spirits" within scripture.[46] And, again, on analogy with Collingwood, this makes *you* the authority, not what you are reading.

And beyond this, why is the Apostle Paul to be considered as a unique authority ("At least we have *one* apostolic authority to fall back on!")? Wouldn't you be presupposing a vestigial belief in "biblical authority"? "The Apostle Paul" is authoritative only if you already accept the larger story of the Bible, whether, in this case, pieced together from the epistles or as set forth continuously in the Book of Acts. Otherwise, why not Apollonius of Tyana or Norman Vincent Peale?

Perhaps it all comes down, as Willi Marxsen[47] said it did, to acquiescence to Church Tradition: the biblical canon was chosen by ancient ecclesiastics. No inspired table of contents floated to earth from heaven. Catholics admit this,

---

1975), p. 26: "The liberal's self-referent is principally to the subject-theologian's own modern consciousness as committed to the basic values of modernity, especially the value of insisting upon a critical investigation of all claims to meaning and truth, religious or otherwise. The object-referent is principally to the Christian tradition (usually the tradition of one's own church) as reformulated in accordance with such modern commitments and critiques."

45. James Barr, *The Bible in the Modern World* (New York: Harper & Row, 1973), pp. 160–161. Neo-evangelical E.J. Carnell provided a classic example: his "rules [that] govern Biblical hermeneutics" include "*first*, the New Testament interprets the Old Testament; *secondly*, the Epistles interpret the Gospels . . . *if the church teaches anything that offends the system of Romans and Galatians, it is cultic*." *The Case for Orthodox Theology* (Philadelphia: Westminster Press, 1959), pp. 53, 59.

46. Käsemann, "New Testament Canon," p. 104.

47. Willi Marxsen, *The New Testament as the Church's Book*. Trans. James E. Mignard (Philadelphia: Fortress Press, 1972), Chapter 1, "The New Testament as the Work of the Church," pp. 12–63, a real theological scorcher!

but Protestants (except Marxsen!) deny it because their Biblicism requires them to believe in *Sola Scriptura*, the Bible as the source of faith and practice: text, not tradition. By ostensibly rejecting the authority of Tradition, Protestants were sawing off the limb they were perched on.

Some[48] have sought to mitigate the (I think fatal) difficulty of the collapse of the canon criterion of "apostolicity" by blurring the lines a bit, suggesting that it is enough that the New Testament canon has normativity because it enshrines the earliest, pristine expressions of Christianity. But this strategy once again rests on the fallacy of positing a single, uniform "early church." No, in fact our twenty-seven book New Testament represents an anti-heretical instrument designed completely and specifically to suppress rival theological voices by excluding their documents. Frank Kermode[49] could see (perhaps because he was not a theologian) that the only reason for framing (i.e., *delimiting*) a canon is not so much to *include* but to *exclude* texts, beliefs, and "heretical" believers. Thus continued adherence to the traditional canon is just that: the acceptance of Tradition, an enshrined institutional party-line, that of one particular brand of "early Christianity," not early Christianity per se.

---

48. Hans Küng, *The Church* (Garden City: Doubleday Image Books, 1976), pp. 36–37, e.g., "The fact that these human words are the original testimony of God's word of revelation is the reason why they are incomparable and unrepeatable, uniquely binding and actively obligatory." But see James Barr: "A moment's thought however should reveal that this kind of priority as a historical source is something different from theological normativeness" (*Bible in the Modern World*, p. 80).

49. Frank Kermode, *The Art of Telling: Essays on Fiction* (Cambridge: Harvard University Press, 1983), Chapter 8, "Institutional Control of Interpretation," pp. 168–184.

ABOUT THE AUTHOR

Robert M. Price is a freethought advocate who has written on many subjects in many venues, and for many years. He has been at various times an agnostic, an exponent of Liberal Protestant theology, a non-theist, a secular humanist, a religious humanist, a Unitarian-Universalist wannabe, an unaffiliated Universalist, and a Fellow of the Jesus Seminar. Any way you cut it, his name is Legion. Not your typical atheist, Price continues to love the various great religions as endlessly fascinating creations/expressions of the human spirit. He loves theology, too. He hosts The Bible Geek podcast, and indeed the Bible is his main focus of interest. He lives in North Carolina.